The Crucible of Carolina

The Crucible
of Carolina

Essays in the Development of
Gullah Language and Culture

Edited by Michael Montgomery

The University of Georgia Press

Athens and London

© 1994 by the University of Georgia Press
Athens, Georgia 30602
All rights reserved
Designed by Louise OFarrell
Set in 10/13 Times by Tseng Information Systems, Inc.
Printed and bound by Thomson-Shore
The paper in this book meets the guidelines for
permanence and durability of the Committee on
Production Guidelines for Book Longevity of the
Council on Library Resources.

Printed in the United States of America
98 97 96 95 94   C   5   4   3   2   1

Library of Congress Cataloging in Publication Data
The Crucible of Carolina : essays in the development
    of Gullah language and culture / edited by
    Michael Montgomery.
          p.   cm.
    Includes bibliographical references and index.
    ISBN 0-8203-1623-7
    1. Sea Islands Creole dialect.   2. Language and
culture—South Carolina.   3. Language and culture—
Caribbean Area.   4. Language and culture—Africa,
West.   I. Montgomery, Michael, 1950–   .
PM7875.G8C78   1994
427′.973′08996—dc20   93-32145

British Library Cataloging in Publication Data available

To the fond memory of

Patricia Jones-Jackson

Contents

Acknowledgments

Six of the ten essays in this collection are based on presentations at the Ninth Annual Language and Culture in South Carolina Symposium, held at the University of South Carolina, Columbia, April 26–27, 1985. The symposium was cosponsored by the Department of Anthropology, the Graduate Program in Linguistics, the Institute for Southern Studies, the Department of English, and the Department of History. It drew scholars from many disciplines to discuss recent research connecting the culture, life, and language of Low Country South Carolina, particularly the Sea Islands, with other regions of the world—the Caribbean, West Africa, and Europe.

Such a multidisciplinary gathering required the assistance of many hands. Special credit and appreciation are due to Morgan Maclachlan, who chaired the Department of Anthropology at the time, and Dorothy O'Dell, staff assistant in the Department of Anthropology, for their tireless work in organizing the symposium, making the local arrangements, and ensuring the smooth running of the conference. Appreciation is due to Walter Edgar, director of the Institute for Southern Studies, and William Nolte, acting chairman of the Department of English, for their financial assistance in bringing participants to the campus. Participants in the conference deserve accolades for making the meeting a memorable success through their spirited and generous discussions. All who attended will recall the scholarly interchange and the camaraderie.

An earlier version of "Names and Naming in the Sea Islands," by Keith E. Baird and Mary A. Twining, appeared in *Sea Island Roots: African Presence in the Carolinas and Georgia,* edited by Mary A. Twining and Keith E. Baird (Trenton, N.J.: Africa World Press, 1991); an earlier version of Dale Rosengarten's "Spirits of Our Ancestors: Basket Traditions in the Carolinas" appeared in *Carolina Folk: The Cradle of a Southern Tradition,* edited by George Terry and Lynn Robertson Myers (Columbia, S.C.: McKissick Museum, 1985).

It is on a truly sad note, however, that the editor dedicates this volume to Patricia Jones-Jackson, whose voice and spirit enlivened and charmed our profession for a decade and whose spirited analysis and re-creation of a Sea Island

ix

sermon at the symposium was a tour de force, sparking the first authentic "Amen corner" anyone could remember at an academic conference in these parts. Surely she had a gift of the spirit herself. Barely a year after the symposium, in June 1986, her life was tragically taken in an automobile accident. She was on assignment on Johns Island, South Carolina, working with a film crew for the *National Geographic* and visiting her second family, her Sea Island informants and friends. Pat, this is for you.

The Crucible of Carolina

Introduction

Michael Montgomery

Americans often seem to be looking backward of late—not so much whimsically to the "good old days" a generation or two back, but seriously to their cultural roots of a century or more ago. Many factors—the Columbus Quincentenary observance and related events of 1992, the increasing desire of many ethnic groups for a more prominent role in published versions of the nation's history, and so on—have spurred both academics and the general public to explore their heritage and to identify the contributions of their forebears to the American experience. In no case is this more often true than for African Americans, as demonstrated by the growing demand for university courses in African studies and the popularity of African cultural festivals and observances such as Kwanzaa. But despite major advances, especially since 1970, in documenting and interpreting the history and cultural experience of Africans and their descendants in this country, many gaps remain in our knowledge. A full perspective on the background of African-American life and culture is far from being achieved.

The Low Country of South Carolina and Georgia comprises a 250-mile stretch of barrier islands, now usually called the Sea Islands, and a coastal basin for as much as thirty to forty miles inland. The Sea Islands in particular are widely acknowledged to have "among the Afro-American groups in North America, the culture . . . most closely related to certain African cultures" (Twining and Baird 1991, vii). The Low Country has long been recognized as a cultural zone of special interest for three reasons: (1) its population has been overwhelmingly African derived since the early eighteenth century, outnumbering whites as many as ten to one in some districts;[1] (2) Africans continued to be imported directly from Africa until the very eve of the Civil War, a half century after the official prohibition of slavery in 1808, and this provided a degree of ongoing cultural continuity with Africa; and (3) residents, particularly Sea Islanders, were long isolated from the mainland—many islands were not easily accessible until well after World War II—and there was consequently only marginal contact with outsiders.

1

From at least as early as the end of the Civil War, outsiders such as Thomas Wentworth Higginson, a New England pastor who served as a Union officer in South Carolina and wrote *Army Life in a Black Regiment* (1870), began to comment on the "African" qualities of Sea Island culture—the language (usually called Gullah or Geechee),[2] religious practices, music, and other forms of cultural expression. This documentation has continued, most recently and fully in two monographs, Patricia Jones-Jackson's *When Roots Die: Endangered Traditions on the Sea Islands* (1987) and Margaret Washington Creel's *"A Peculiar People": Slave Religion and Community Culture among the Gullahs* (1988), and in an edited collection of essays, Mary A. Twining and Keith E. Baird's *Sea Island Roots: African Presence in the Carolinas and Georgia* (1991). The latter two books move well beyond viewing the Sea Islands as no more than a reservoir preserving, more-or-less unchanged, West African patterns to focus on how the adaptive qualities of Sea Island culture have enabled it to meet contemporary needs. Creel articulates this well: "I do not argue for 'survivals,' a somewhat lifeless term implying passive existence. But I do argue for the presence of dynamic, creative, cultural trends of African provenance among the Gullahs" (6).

The ten papers in this volume explore similarities and connections principally between coastal South Carolina language and culture, on the one hand, and West Africa and a third region of the world, the Caribbean, on the other. This introduction provides background by summarizing several of the important historical and methodological issues raised to date and showing how the papers in this volume contribute to the ongoing discussion of these issues, many of which are surrounded by controversy. A number of questions still in need of answers are also identified.

The African Perspective

Research on Africanisms in North America has been extensive since Melville J. Herskovits's *The Myth of the Negro Past* (1941) put it on a sound scholarly, anthropological footing.[3] It was Herskovits who defined the field in its modern sense and outlined the widest range of avenues for investigating degrees and types of African influences in the New World. The most recent interdisciplinary collection of essays on the subject is *Africanisms in American Culture,* edited by Joseph Holloway (1990); the fullest examination of Africanisms in American speech is Margaret Wade-Lewis's "The African Substratum in American English" (1988a).[4] Much of the literature is based on research in the Sea Islands; the most exhaustive study of Africanisms in that area alone is

Mary A. Twining's Ph.D. dissertation, "An Examination of African Retentions in the Folk Culture of the South Carolina and Georgia Sea Islands" (1977), which examines Sea Island folk life, expressive behavior, material culture, and social institutions.

Linguistics has led the effort to identify the African heritage in North America since the days of Lorenzo Dow Turner a half century ago. Herskovits used Turner's research to build his more general case for New World African influence. The tools of linguistic science are particularly suitable for this because they can isolate subtle and often disguised patterns in everyday speech. A landmark in the linguistic study of Africanisms was the 1988 international conference "Africanisms in Afro-American Language Varieties," whose proceedings have been edited by Salikoko Mufwene (Mufwene 1993b). Using primarily language patterns, but also preaching styles and basket-making traditions, the present volume examines how elements of West African cultures have evolved into American ones.

All too often, comparisons between African and African-American cultures have searched solely for African "survivals" or "retentions" and have tended to be anecdotal. Generally, these studies have lacked a rigorous, principled basis and have relied on simple descriptive models that equate superficial resemblances with derivatives from Africa. This volume makes direct contributions to our understanding of African elements in New World cultures in two general ways. First, it focuses on the evidence of deeper, more indirect relationships between Old World and New World phenomena that reflect more complex types of cultural transmission. This is the approach that owes much to Melville Herskovits, who pioneered the research beyond less sophisticated models of "cultural survivals" and persuaded other scholars that "reinterpretations" and "maskings" of African cultural elements are important to identify. Second, this volume carefully disentangles the various strands of these relationships.

It comes as no surprise that Lorenzo Dow Turner's research is the touchstone of several of the linguistic studies of African connections here. Turner's nearly two decades of work culminated in his landmark *Africanisms in the Gullah Dialect* (1949), a source all too rarely mined by scholars. Four of the papers in this volume (those by Baird and Twining, Roberts, Montgomery, and Sengova) use Turner's work as a central focus, while others draw on it to a lesser extent.

It would be difficult to calculate creolists' debt to Turner or to say how much we may yet learn from this scholar who almost single-handedly "convince[d] his academic peers that at least in Gullah, and perhaps also in black English generally, the black American has a genuine and continuous linguistic history leading back to Africa" (DeCamp 1973, xi). His book on Gullah is still the most important in the field, a classic almost equal in stature to Herskovits's *Myth of the Negro Past*. Turner's research forms the point of departure for all later studies of the language and has remained almost beyond replication (a significant exception to this is Baird and Twining's "Names and Naming in the Sea Islands," in this volume). Yet Turner's work was very much a product of his time and was, after all, concerned only with the apparent African component of Gullah. Turner viewed research largely as taxonomic, as the comparison of individual forms (especially personal names) to see how similar they were across languages, and he knew almost nothing about the processes of creolization, which, as later scholars have recognized, can radically transform linguistic elements in multilingual contexts. The essays presented here move beyond Turner in at least three ways. First, they deal with discourse and stylistic aspects of Gullah, as in Patricia Jones-Jackson's "Let the Church Say 'Amen': The Language of Religious Rituals in the Coastal Areas," which concentrates on preaching style.

Second, other essays relate patterns of Gullah to other anglophone creoles and to various processes of creolization. Frederic Cassidy's overview essay, "Gullah and the Caribbean Connection," is an example, as are the papers of Ian Hancock ("Componentiality and the Creole Matrix: The Southwest English Contribution"), Tometro Hopkins ("Variation in the Use of the Auxiliary Verb *da* in Gullah"), and Peter Roberts ("Flexibility and Creativity in Afro-American English"). The last two in particular draw on the work of Derek Bickerton (1975, 1981).

Third, in carefully defining terminology that describes the ways African languages may be related to Gullah and other creoles, as in the essays by Salikoko Mufwene ("Misinterpreting *Linguistic Continuity* Charitably") and Joko Sengova ("Recollections of African Language Patterns in an American Speech Variety: An Assessment of Mende Influences in Lorenzo Dow Turner's Gullah Data"), these papers question the usefulness of retention, survival, and continuity as operational concepts in comparative research.

As was stated above, the importance of the South Carolina Low Country as a field for investigating Africanisms rests on the early numerical dominance of Africans (they formed the majority of the population by 1710, according to Peter Wood [1974a, 36]), their continuing arrival directly from Africa, and their relative isolation for many generations. During the eighteenth century, white Carolinians made clear distinctions between different groups of Africans, in turn preferring Africans from the Gold Coast, the Congo-Angola region, and the Windward Coast–Sierra Leone–Liberia region (Curtin 1969; Creel 1988). It was from the last territory, as Peter Wood (1974a), Daniel Littlefield (1981), and Joseph Opala (1986) have demonstrated, that slave traders systematically sought Africans skilled in rice cultivation.

Colonists' apprehensions about the disproportion of whites to blacks were fueled by the Stono slave rebellion of 1739, but slave importation thrived, especially with the escalation of the rice trade. Elizabeth Donnan documents how the traffic in human cargo from Africa was conducted with such voracity that officials were compelled to impose a stiff, prohibitive duty from 1766 to 1768 to bring it under control. Wood (1974a, xiv) estimates that "well over 40 percent [more than two hundred thousand] of the slaves reaching the British mainland colonies between 1700 and 1775 arrived in South Carolina," most of these being brought to Charleston, the Ellis Island for Africans coming in bondage to North America.

Scholars attempting to assess the scope and directions of trans-Atlantic population movements, to reconstruct the streams of the African diaspora, have employed linguistic evidence from Gullah and other creole languages along with demographic records. After scrutinizing the sources of the African linguistic items he had collected in the Sea Islands, Turner became convinced that the Angola-Congo flow of speakers, by far the largest movement in the first half of the eighteenth century, also had the most prominent linguistic influence. Frederic Cassidy (in two essays published in 1980 and 1983) argues that Turner's data reveal a greater contribution from such Gold Coast languages as Twi and Ewe. P. E. H. Hair (1965), Ian F. Hancock (1969), and other scholars have drawn on Turner's work to claim extensive contributions by Mende and Vai, languages of Sierra Leone. Joko Sengova's essay in this volume, the first by a native speaker of Mende, explores and demonstrates the significance of Mende items in some of the songs and stories Turner collected.

On the other hand, examining Gullah's similarity to its creole kin has led to widely differing views about the identity and existence of a common creole ancestor (whose identity and nature can be only hypothesized since it never had a written form). Hancock postulates (1980a) that a Guinea Coast Creole English (GCCE) predated the slave trade and was a precursor to both Krio, the English creole spoken along much of the West African littoral today, and all New World anglophone creoles. He believes that Gullah derived from GCCE directly, brought from Africa primarily by Windward Coast slaves. Hancock discounts Barbados as only "a temporary entrepôt for persons bound elsewhere from Africa. Its significance as a dispersal point must not be allowed to camouflage the linguistic situation" (1980a, 21). Cassidy (both in his 1980 paper and in the one in this volume) emphasizes the importance of Barbados for the dispersion of Jamaican, Djuka (spoken in Suriname), Gullah, and other creoles. His view is that while linguistic and historical evidence may allow for an earlier West African pidgin or trade language, English was probably creolized initially in the New World, first in Barbados.[5] John Roy has found statistically significant identities between many New World creoles, including Gullah and Barbadian (Bajan) Creole. He takes a more radical view than Cassidy, claiming that Barbadian was the grandparent of all Atlantic English creoles and that Krio was planted in the late eighteenth century by freed slaves returning to Sierra Leone: "The historical evidence clearly indicates that Krio came to West Africa long after English Creole was in use in the colonies" (1977, 36).

There is no doubt about the extreme isolation of much of the South Carolina Low Country and the large proportion of Africans in the population there. Only parts of Tidewater Virginia and Louisiana might have rivaled it in these respects. But does this mean that the Low Country was qualitatively different from the rest of the American South in preserving African cultural and linguistic elements? Exactly how different was it from the rest of the plantation belt? In linguistic terms, the question is whether coastal Carolina forms a relic area, with Gullah a remnant of a once far more widespread "plantation creole," a language variety having many African influences that subsequently eroded (underwent decreolization, in linguistic terminology). Most linguists believe, along with Hancock (1980a, 29), that "Gullah is a linguistic isolate whose speakers differ greatly in social and linguistic history from speakers of Afro-American English dialects elsewhere in the country." But others, particularly J. L. Dillard in *Black English: Its History and Usage in the United States* (1972) and William Stewart in a series of papers (see especially 1967, 1968), argue that eighteenth-century literary portrayals and travelers' accounts of black speech reveal that a creole type of English was spoken by descendants of Africans throughout much of the South. According to David DeCamp, Dillard and Stewart

> believe that all or most of black English was originally a creole, perhaps similar to modern Gullah, but that most of its speakers were so influenced by the white standard English that they more or less decreolized, i.e., lost many of those creole characteristics which make Gullah seem so exotic and incomprehensible to outsiders. Gullah remained a relatively pure creole because its speakers were so geographically and socioeconomically isolated. (DeCamp 1973, ix)

In the final analysis, the distinctiveness of Gullah may not be entirely determinable because other plantation creole cultures in the Deep South, if indeed they existed, were shorter lived and have since disappeared.

This issue remained unexplored in detail until recently, due largely to the paucity of data available to address it. But Michael Montgomery's paper based on lexical evidence from the Linguistic Atlas of the Gulf States (in Mufwene 1993b), the papers of Montgomery and John Holm in *The Emergence of Black English* (ed. G. Bailey et al. 1991), which study grammatical features drawn from recorded interviews with ex-slaves in the 1930s and 1940s, and Edgar Schneider's *American Early Black English* (1989), a comprehensive investigation of grammar based on the WPA Slave Narratives, all find significant discontinuities between Gullah and the speech of blacks elsewhere in the South. All this research argues for the uniqueness of Gullah. A typical statement is John Holm's that "there is still no unambiguous evidence that the English of North American blacks was ever completely creolized . . . outside of a few isolated areas such as coastal South Carolina and Georgia, where Gullah developed" (Holm 1991, 244–45).[6] But there is much still to be understood about historical relationships between Gullah and African-American English elsewhere in the South and about the degree of Low Country distinctiveness from the Deep South in general. Considerable research, including original fieldwork, is still needed. If Gullah is to be used as a baseline for comparison with other varieties of African-American English spoken in the South, the partial accounts of it now available must be complemented by more studies like the detailed descriptions that have appeared in recent years.[7] Two papers in this volume (Hopkins and Roberts) examine specific Gullah auxiliary verbs in a comparative creole framework and thus expand the record on Gullah and broaden the basis for pursuing issues of geographical distinctiveness.

Both public interest and academic research continue, on both sides of the Atlantic; in fact, there is a lively interest in the African heritage of South Carolina. In the mid-1980s the Gullah Research Center was founded at Fourah Bay College in Freetown, Sierra Leone. Shortly thereafter, President Joseph Momoh of that country paid a state visit to the Sea Islands. In 1990 a dozen Americans undertook a two-week pilgrimage to Sierra Leone, visiting sites where slaves were once held and using Gullah to communicate with the Krio speakers there. Their trip was captured in "Family across the Sea," a program produced by South Carolina Educational Television, and the relationships forged by their experiences show much promise of further development.

The Caribbean Perspective

Melville Herskovits demonstrated a half century ago how much of the African basis of African-American culture still needed to be identified. It is not nearly so well known that he showed that the main key to this operation was the investigation and comparison of Caribbean cultures, especially in disparate colonial systems under the rule of different European powers.

The cultural motivations and political appeal of establishing the links between the South Carolina Low Country and Africa are obvious. The reasons for connecting South Carolina to the Caribbean are far less apparent, particularly to anyone living outside the Palmetto State or not familiar with the history of the Carolina colony. But it is instructive to examine the South Carolina Low Country as an analogue (having parallel developments) and an extension (derivative to some extent) of the anglophone Caribbean. In both cases the examination highlights its difference from the rest of the American South, and viewing the Low Country in these two ways provides a deeper understanding of how New World languages and cultures have evolved, as Cassidy's overview essay in this collection, "Gullah and the Caribbean Connection," shows.

While historians have detailed the early economic and social development of South Carolina with respect to its largely Caribbean origins, these origins have yet to be factored into modern-day discussions of the state's cultural heritage or into a larger regional consciousness of the contributors to the history of the American South. For instance, the entry "Caribbean Influence" in the *Encyclopedia of Southern Culture* discusses West Indian contributions to Gulf Coast areas, especially Louisiana and Florida, without even mentioning South Carolina (Wilson 1988).

Yet, unique among the mainland North American colonies, South Carolina was first settled by both whites and blacks from the Caribbean; the other colonies grew more directly from European sources. Charles Town was founded in 1670 as "the colony of a colony," an outpost for younger sons of sugar planters and their households from Barbados and other British Caribbean settlements; it remained dependent on these other settlements for decades. Economic and social historians often point this out (e.g., Thomas 1930; Dunn 1970; Wood 1974a; Littlefield 1987; Greene 1987. Richard Dunn cites the crucial role of these immigrants: "Everyone who has examined the founding of South Carolina agrees that planters from the West Indies played a major role—some would say a decisive role—in shaping the new colony" (1970, 81). Peter Wood identifies the role of African slaves in the process, stating that the "first fully documented Negro arrival reached the colony alongside Europeans," and that this was "a pattern of black and white imports which was to predominate over several decades" (1974a, 21). Jack Greene, another eminent colonial historian, has this to say: "The only mainland English colony that began its existence with a preference for African slave labor and a significant number of African slaves among its original settlers, South Carolina early revealed that strong commercial, materialistic, and exploitative mentality that had found such a ready field for action in the Caribbean" (1987, 198).

Historians have done much to document certain aspects of the early extension of the Caribbean into South Carolina, but progress in studies of cultural phenomena has generally been slow, perhaps because of the lack of quantifiable, tangible evidence, particularly the linguistic evidence from which eighteenth-century patterns must be inferred. Because attestations of speech usually date from much later (most creoles achieved a written form only in the twentieth century, if then), linguistic connections must be determined cautiously.

In its early days South Carolina differed from other colonies on the North American mainland in two important respects. First, at least through the end of the seventeenth century, most of the Africans there came from societies in the Caribbean, particularly Barbados, that may have already been creolized and had many African ingredients. As was mentioned earlier, this idea has enjoyed spirited debate. Ian Hancock (1980a) argues that several factors almost certainly prevented the development of a creole form of English on Barbados: the linguistic background of the Africans there (overwhelmingly from Angola-Congo, they would not have already spoken a pidginized English), the relatively low black-white population ratio, the direct contact between Africans and Europeans, and the short period (forty-six years) between the founding of Barbados and Charles Town. Thus, in line with his case that Guinea Coast Creole English was the ancestor of Gullah and other Atlantic English creoles, Hancock doubts that Barbadian English was ever creolized. After that early period, the overwhelming majority of Africans in South Carolina were imported directly from Africa (Donnan 1927–28). In 1717 a special tax was levied on slaves brought from the Caribbean to discourage such trade. Actually, Africans had begun to arrive directly from Africa even before the turn of the century.

The extent to which South Carolina once shared (and may have continued to share) Caribbean culture and how long it formed a part of the Caribbean orbit are fascinating questions. In a tour of early Charles Town, Lewis P. Jones in *South Carolina: A Synoptic History for Laymen* (1978, 17) presents the town's streets, its principal buildings, and "the Charleston house" as all based on West Indian models. It would not be at all difficult to build a case that the Caribbean connection has given modern-day Charleston much of its uniqueness and charm among North American cities. Indeed, in a little book titled *The Barbados-Carolina Connection* (1988), Warren Alleyne and Henry Fraser argue that the well-known Charleston single house originated in Barbados.

But were the first thirty years of the Carolina colony a *formative* period that set the mold for the future? Was this relatively brief period long enough? How crucial these years may have been for language, as shown by the Cassidy-Roy versus Hancock debate discussed earlier, still needs direct investigation, although most scholars tend to agree with Derek Bickerton (1981, 4) that creole languages arise "in a population where not more than 20 percent were native speakers of the dominant language and where the remaining 80 percent was composed of diverse language groups," which makes it unlikely that a creole could have developed in the early days of either Barbados or Carolina.

If Hancock is correct in stating that "by 1720, blacks in South Carolina had come to outnumber whites, the foreign-born to outnumber the native-born, and those from Africa to outnumber those from the Caribbean" (1980a, 24), the Caribbean connection may not have been so important for language; that is, early eighteenth-century factors overrode late seventeenth-century ones. And if Margaret Creel (1988, 33–34) is correct that the Sea Islands, the core Gullah area, were not settled until the 1720s and 1730s, this makes it even more difficult to argue for significant Caribbean input there.

Even so, there is much to be learned from considering the South Carolina Low Country in a Caribbean light, as an analogue to what developed in the West Indies. After the first few years, patterns of slave importation into the colony and resulting black-white population ratios resembled those of the Caribbean more than those elsewhere on the mainland, meaning that South Carolina's "eighteenth-century development was the closest mainland approximation to the West Indian plantation pattern" (Curtin 1969, 145). This is the second respect in which South Carolina differed from other North American colonies. If a pidgin language had been brought to Charles Town, "it would have become creolized as soon as plantation living conditions came to prevail," even without the influence of Caribbean English Creole, according to Cassidy's essay in this volume.

Thus, once we see the South Carolina colony as similar to Jamaica, Barbados, and other Caribbean settlements, we can study all of these as parallel contexts for creolization—for the merging and transformation of African and European patterns into new patterns appropriate to various New World situations. And we can extend models of creolization formulated by linguists to other cultural domains, to see "creolization as a process not only in the formation of language but of society as well" (Twining and Baird 1991, vii).

This has been demonstrated most thoroughly in Charles W. Joyner's *Down by the Riverside* (1984), which reconstructs the antebellum slave community of All Saints Parish and analyzes (to borrow from the phraseology of David Hackett Fischer's *Albion's Seed* [1989]) the work ways, agriculture ways, food ways, building ways, family ways, religion ways, and other practices of that community.

The recognition that the Low Country and Gullah have affinities to the Caribbean today (whether derivations or parallel developments) is not new. Local writers had noted both African and Caribbean connections for at least a decade before Turner and Herskovits published their data. For example, Samuel Stoney and Gertrude Shelby stated in 1930 that

> Gullah is the strongest linguistic connection between America and the
> Antilles and Africa; it links two hemispheres and two eras. Specifically,
> it stands as a curious survival of the Low Country of South Carolina in
> the high days of its great plantations, when Rice, and Indigo and Cot-
> ton made this one of the preeminent regions of the South. . . . [W]ords
> of African origin are at once in use today in Carolina, in the West
> Indies, and in the older English possessions of the tropical West Coast of
> Africa. . . . The branches of the family tree of Gullah are American, the
> trunk is West Indian and the roots English and African. (1930, ix–x)

For cultural phenomena this lead has rarely been followed by North American scholars other than linguists. And it has been their Caribbean counterparts (e.g., Cassidy and Roberts in this volume) who have seen far more clearly the fundamental similarities throughout African-derived New World cultures (it is relevant to recall that Herskovits's awareness of this drew substantially from his fieldwork in Suriname).

As in studies of African influences on varieties of African-American English, linguists have been in the forefront of comparative Caribbean-versus-mainland research. In recent decades, for example, they have been engaged in stirring debates about the origins of creole languages. Do these languages derive primarily from universal, cognitively based rules that appear to structure creoles everywhere in remarkably similar ways? Or can we understand more about the derivation of creoles by using a modified family-tree model based on a detailed examination of each language's constituent European and African elements? In this book, the focus is the latter. Several papers apply componentiality, a model for analyzing a creole language that identifies various superstratal (European) and substratal (African) elements that went into the blend that became Gullah. Hancock's paper elaborates this approach by showing how African, Creole,

and southwest English elements can be identified in Gullah. Rosengarten's
contribution ("Spirits of Our Ancestors: Basket Traditions in the Carolinas")
shows how componentiality can be applied to a nonlinguistic phenomenon—
basket making—to reveal African, Native American, and European components. The advantage of a componential approach is that it allows antecedents
to be investigated, with precision, from a multicultural perspective. Rosengarten and Hancock are committed to showing how strands and components
of basket making and language, respectively, created the unique expressions
found in the Low Country.

Combining Perspectives

The effort to identify and interpret the antecedents of late twentieth-century
linguistic and cultural patterns benefits from the dual African-Caribbean perspective. The Caribbean angles have been largely neglected over the years,
for several reasons. Investigating African connections has both a greater appeal and a clearer research agenda. Direct contacts between South Carolina
and the Caribbean were confined to the colonial period, while relations with
Africa continued until the Civil War. In seeing the South Carolina Low Country as having Caribbean or Caribbean-like elements we gain a much richer
understanding of the components and diversity of South Carolina's cultural
heritage.

In *An Anthropological Approach to the Afro-American Past* (1976), Sidney
Mintz and Richard Price articulate the limitations and problems of an Africa-
only approach that ignores the Caribbean:

> If Afro-American cultures do in fact share such an integral dynamism,
> and if . . . their social systems have been highly responsive to changing
> social conditions, one must maintain a skeptical attitude toward claims
> that many contemporary social and cultural forms represent direct con-
> tinuities from the African homeland. Over the past several decades,
> historical research has reduced the number of convincing cases of formal
> continuities, but has hinted at new levels of continuity—levels which
> may eventually tell us a great deal more about the actual development of
> Afro-American cultures. (1976, 27)

Research on Africanisms, as fruitful and as necessary as it is, has tended to
examine culture in the Low Country and elsewhere from one angle only—as
a residue for Old World patterns—by concentrating on the sources of African-

American patterns rather than by examining parallels in the New World. While some papers in this collection—Baird and Twining's, for example—discuss African antecedents, they emphasize the New World developments and functions of the relevant cultural feature. There are two general strands in all Caribbean cultures, African and European (each of these is diverse, and in some contexts there are others—South Asian and Native American—that have also played roles). All these strands have been interwoven in different ways to produce fabrics that today are seen as wholes rather than as simply mixtures.

We would be quite mistaken if we viewed the connections and continuities of the South Carolina Low Country to West Africa and those to the Caribbean as mutually exclusive and clearly distinguishable. Neither cultural advocates nor researchers can afford to treat them as independent factors. Our discussion here offers no support to cultural genealogists who would like to trace relationships in a straightforward, one-dimensional fashion. In the seventeenth and eighteenth centuries the West Indies were a cauldron of crisscrossing and competing cultures, nationalities, and influences. The islands were certainly not mere way stations for the mainland; in the 1600s they were the primary British settlements in the New World.

In fact, some similarities between the Caribbean and South Carolina may not represent imports *from* the Caribbean but exports *to* the Caribbean, especially to the Bahamas (Parsons 1923; Holm and Shilling 1982; Holm 1983b).[8] The historically close relations of the Low Country with the Bahamas are well known. Not only did several thousand American Loyalists and their households leave the mainland for the Bahamian islands during and after the Revolutionary War, but relations had been close since 1670, at which time "all the Lords Proprietors of the Bahamas were also Proprietors of Carolina, and that colony became something of a second motherland to our own" (Albury 1975, 90). Elsie Clews Parsons examines this in detail in her two collections of folklore (1918, 1923), although she draws no connections between the mainland materials and those from elsewhere in the Caribbean and treats the Bahamian material as derived from the mainland.

South Carolinians of African descent also migrated to Africa, participating, for example, in the colonization of Liberia in the 1840s. It is less well known that thousands of slaves escaped behind British lines in the 1780s and were settled in Nova Scotia for a few years before being taken to Sierra Leone, where many of them had originated.

Exploring the links between South Carolina and the Caribbean and West Africa, both coming and going, enables us to achieve a broader understanding of the diversity of Low Country culture. If from an American point of view the Low Country has seemed to be something of a cultural island, from a Caribbean view it is a very different matter.

This collection raises no new arguments about the exact cultural affinities of Low Country culture and makes no exclusive claims about these relationships. It takes the balanced view that comparative research is profitable for understanding both historical relationships between individual cultures and the processes that produced these cultures in unique contexts. To stress the Caribbean perspective on the Low Country and to discuss similarities and continuities between the two areas is by no means to deemphasize the African perspective. Rather, this approach is a part of seeking, in complementary ways, to know who we are, where we came from, and how we arrived where we are.

Notes

This essay could not have been attempted without many profitable discussions over the past decade with a number of historians and linguists. I wish especially to thank William Stewart, Salikoko Mufwene, Ian Hancock, Charles Joyner, John Roy, Frederic Cassidy, Patricia Nichols, Glenn Gilbert, John Rickford, and Tometro Hopkins in this regard. Of course, the points of view I represent, my discussion of the work of the foregoing scholars, and the conclusions that I draw are solely my own.

1. For example, Charles Joyner estimates that Lower All Saints Parish had a "ratio of nine blacks to each white" (1984, 2) in the antebellum period. Such a population ratio pertained only to the Low Country of South Carolina. In the middle and later eighteenth century Up Country South Carolina was settled, primarily by second-generation English and Ulster immigrants who migrated from the Valley of Virginia and the North Carolina piedmont. Indeed, by the time of the American Revolution, the numbers of blacks and whites in South Carolina were roughly equal, but only because the Up Country was being settled so rapidly.

2. On the etymology of both *Gullah* and *Geechee* there is no consensus but rather two plausible sources for each. As Wood (1974a, 187) states, there is no reason to believe that each did not have two complementary and reinforcing derivations. Nowadays the language is sometimes called Sea Island Creole, a term originated by Irma Cunningham (1970), but *Gullah* is used in this paper in its most general sense, to refer to distinctive speech patterns of the Sea Islands of South Carolina and Georgia, because this is the prevailing convention in the literature. It is also the term most often employed on the Sea Islands.

3. On the definition of *Africanism,* see the essays in Mufwene (1993b).

4. The fullest bibliography on African-American culture is John F. Szwed and Roger D. Abrahams's two-volume *Afro-American Folk Culture: An Annotated Bibliography of Materials from North, Central, and South America, and the West Indies* (1978).

5. In this view, Krio evolved later, from West African Pidgin English.

6. Dillard and Stewart would argue that these investigations all used data from speakers born in or after the middle of the nineteenth century, after the period of decreolization would have erased the evidence of the plantation creole. According to Stewart, literary

> texts may well have been fairly accurate renditions of pidgin and creole varieties of English once used by Negroes throughout the British colonies of North America, but subsequently decreolized to a considerable extent in the North and the inner and upper South. . . . In those areas of the United States in which the decreolization process operated more thoroughly than it did on the South Atlantic seaboard, the use of markedly creole linguistic structures diminished to the point where, by the outbreak of the Civil War, it was no longer possible to regard most American Negroes as speaking a truly creole form of English for any purpose whatsoever. (1974, 15, 35)

Even if a creole form of English was never used by slaves throughout the plantation belt in the South, this by no means implies that their speech was devoid of Africanisms. In the view of most scholars, varieties of American Black English have at least a partial creole basis (Holm 1984; Labov 1982).

7. The Ph.D. dissertations of Irma Cunningham (recently revised as Cunningham 1992), Patricia Nichols (1976), Patricia Jones-Jackson (1978), Katherine Wyly Mille (1990), and Tometro Hopkins (1992) all make important contributions to knowledge of the grammar of Gullah.

8. As I use it here, the term *Caribbean* includes the Bahamas.

Gullah and the Caribbean Connection

Frederic G. Cassidy

In several papers (Cassidy 1980, 1983, 1986b) I have explored the connections between South Carolina—especially Charleston and the Sea Islands—and the Caribbean for the light such connections may cast on the origin of Gullah. The question of origin must take into account historical, social, and linguistic factors. My past focus has been on the linguistic evidence; this paper focuses on the social and historical evidence.

There can be no question that there *was* a South Carolina–Caribbean connection. As a speaker of Jamaican Creole from childhood, I was immediately struck, when I first discovered Gullah, by the many similarities of the two idioms—similarities too numerous to be purely accidental. In 1924 a poem titled "Buddy Quow" was unearthed in Spain in the Archives of the Indies; it was later published by Donald R. Kloe (1974). Composed around 1800, it bears the subtitle "An Anonymous Poem in Gullah-Jamaican Dialect." This does not mean that a Gullah-Jamaican dialect ever existed, but that the author, or the person who presented the poem to General William Augustus Bowles, knew that Bowles had lived in Charleston, was then living in Jamaica, and would presumably be interested in a poem with that subtitle. It might also indicate that the man who presented it to Bowles, Mr. I. A. Beckles, was himself uncertain which of the creole languages it represented. There is a third possibility, to which I incline: that the poem was composed in a literary version of "creole" that white writers developed during the eighteenth century to represent their conception of how Negro characters spoke. Such a "literary creole" certainly existed; one finds examples in novels and plays of the time. But this is not the place to decide just where "Buddy Quow" fits in; I use the poem only to indicate that around the end of the eighteenth century, Gullah and Jamaican Creole were similar enough to be taken as virtual equivalents. There was good historical reason for this association.

The earliest known use of the word *Gullah* is in an advertisement for a runaway slave named Golla Harry, printed in the *South Carolina Gazette* on May 12, 1739 (p. 2, col. 2). He is described as "a short well set Negro man."

16

Since his name is Harry, *Golla* must refer to his place of origin—his "country name." It is clear that the term was current as a tribal or linguistic designation by the second quarter of the eighteenth century. Conclusive evidence is still lacking as to whether *Gullah* refers to the Ngola people who gave their name in a Portuguese form to Angola, or to the Gola people who inhabited the coastal lands of present-day Liberia (Le Page 1960, 38–39). Either is possible, although the large number of slaves imported—and imported early—from Angola seems to favor that source.

The slave trade had existed in Africa, with established routes toward the northeast (Sudan) and the northwest (the Sahara), before Europeans began exploring the West African coast—and that was before the discovery of America. In the sixteenth century the Portuguese, and a hundred years later the English and French, traded along this coast, not for slaves but for gold and ivory. The slave trade to America did not begin seriously until the plantation system was developed in the second half of the seventeenth century. Then the trickle of slaves exported became a great flow which increased for a century and a half—the era of colonization—as the plantation system developed.

As the first important English colony in the Caribbean, Barbados (first settled in 1624) became a testing ground. White indentured servants from Ireland, Scotland, and (in smaller numbers) England proved unable to adapt to field labor in the tropical climate. Besides, many hoped to become sugar planters themselves after they had worked out their period of indenture, and they were thus unlikely to supply a long-term source of labor. Following the Portuguese, from whom they had learned about sugar production, the English planters turned to slave labor as the solution. But Barbados is a small island, and the good agricultural land was soon taken up. Some would-be planters turned to Guyana-Suriname (1651–67), others went to Jamaica after that island was taken from the Spaniards (1655). Thus Jamaica became an area of overflow for Barbadian planters, and the colony of Charles Town (founded 1670) on the Carolina coast soon became another. An early pattern was formed with connecting lines from Barbados to Jamaica, Barbados to Charles Town, and further lines between other Caribbean colonies. When Suriname became Dutch in 1667, the majority of the English planters there moved—with their slaves—to southwestern Jamaica. And when the Charles Town colonists began importing slaves to work on plantations, they got them from Barbados and Jamaica. I want to emphasize that this was in the early years. By 1690 the Charles Town planters were no longer dependent on Barbados or Jamaica; they obtained their slaves directly from Africa. Though this weakened the pattern of connections, the pattern held to some extent into the eighteenth century. There is a 1697 notice of the sloop *Turtle* bringing slaves (quantity unknown) from Barbados to Charles Town (Donnan 1935, 4:249–50). Also, a 1709 report from the governor and Council of South Carolina to the Board of Trade mentions, "We are also often furnished with negroes from the American Islands, chiefly from Barbados and Jamaica" (Donnan 1935, 4:256). These may, of course, have been transshipped slaves, and not ones who already lived or had been born in Barbados or Jamaica.

Two other factors further weakened this early pattern of importing slaves from other New World colonies. One was the Barbadian and Jamaican planters' preference for Gold Coast slaves (Le Page 1960, 58–59); the other was the Charles Town colony's shift to rice as the chief crop. As to the first, both the English and the Dutch had established trading posts (called "factories") on the Gold Coast as early as 1630, and more actively by 1650. In 1640 the English chartered the company of Royal Adventurers. Its new charter of 1663 mentioned, for the first time, that slavery was one of its objectives (Le Page 1960, 58–59). This company was succeeded in 1672 by the Royal African Company, which traded along the entire West African coast. Figures on importation are no more than fragmentary, but it seems clear that Gold Coast slaves were among the first brought to Jamaica. They never formed as much as half of the total import, but they were always a considerable proportion (Le Page 1960, 58–76).

Of the Royal African Company's trade goods sent out in 1724, more than one-half went to the Gold Coast and Whydah; one-fourth went to Gambia, Sierra Leone, and the Windward Coast; and about one-sixth to the coast from Benin southward (Le Page 1960, 61, 74). Since the trade was largely for slaves, this should give a fair idea of the areas from which they were being brought, and in what proportions. Thus Gold Coast slaves were among the first to be imported, and they were preferred to slaves from Congo and Angola (Le Page 1960, 75–76). In Jamaica the "Coromantee" seem to have dominated the other slaves; certainly the largest number of surviving African-derived words in Jamaican Creole speech today are from Twi, the important Gold Coast language (Cassidy 1961b). The Coromantee showed an uncomfortable tendency to run away to the hills. There they established communities of "Maroons," whence they would raid the lowland plantations. Perhaps the fear of insurrection was what made the Charles Town colonists, in 1717, place a head tax of three pounds on slaves brought from Africa and thirty pounds—ten times as much—on slaves "who had lived over five months in any other colony in America" (Clowse 1971, 190). Nevertheless, it is certain that Gold Coast slaves were among the earliest in Charles Town—during the first ten or twenty years—however much they were outnumbered by later importations from other parts of Africa.

The second factor weakening the Charles Town colony's link with the Caribbean was the shift of emphasis from sugar to rice. This shift powerfully affected the formation and survival of Gullah. Rice cultivation was introduced to the Carolina settlement almost accidentally: about 1680, Captain John Thurber brought some Madagascar gold seed rice to Charles Town and "gave about a peck of it to Dr. Henry Woodward who succeeded in getting a good yield from it. The seed from his crop was then distributed among his friends. By 1690 the production had grown to such proportions that the planters asked that it [rice] be specified as one of the commodities made receivable for quitrents" (Rhett 1940, 23). There was plenty of low, swampy land adaptable to rice growing, on the mainland and on the offshore islands. The trouble was with malarial fever. Whites who remained in swampy areas after dark in summer and fall when (as we now know) the *Anopheles* mosquito was about were almost sure to contract the disease. But blacks seemed to be immune and were therefore the ideal labor force for growing rice. Further, rice was already an important crop in parts of Africa, including the area of present-day Liberia and Sierra Leone. Slaves skillful in this kind of agriculture were therefore sought after. Because of malaria, whites stayed out of the rice plantations as much as possible, leaving the slave communities relatively undisturbed. It was surely this relative isolation of the rice lands that allowed a creole language—what we now call Gullah—to become established and to be preserved on the American mainland when blacks in all other mainland areas generally decreolized their language or, in some cases, acquired English directly without passing through a creole phase.

From which parts of Africa did the slaves come? Considerable scholarly effort has gone into examining this question, and we now have some plausible answers. In this matter Philip D. Curtin's book *The Atlantic Slave Trade* (1969) is "required reading," especially the first chapter, in which Curtin reviews the existing literature and shows to what a great extent authors have guessed, or have repeated previous guesses, instead of investigating and assessing facts without prejudice. After an exacting examination of all the evidence he could find, Curtin concluded that the total number of slaves brought to the Americas was far less than has generally been claimed—not twenty million: probably not much more than half that number.

The plantation system differed greatly from small farm or subsistence farming. Essentially, it was industrialized, mass-crop agriculture. Once it proved successful, the slave trade became big business, and, in familiar big-corporation style, private interests became entangled with national interests. Competition either led to war, or else the interested nations tacitly divided the trade among themselves, seeking the best market wherever it could be found. The Portuguese had the field to themselves for a century before other nations entered it. By 1642 the Dutch had succeeded in capturing the Portuguese forts in the Gold Coast and Angola coast areas and became the chief traders to the Caribbean. The English, beginning in Gambia, extended their activity to the Gold Coast (present-day Ghana). Toward the end of the eighteenth century, the French dominated the more easterly area: Benin and Calabar. One of the chief reasons why it is impossible to be exact about many aspects of the slave trade is that a large part of it was pursued illicitly. The English Royal Adventurers and the Royal African Company, whose monopoly supposedly was guaranteed by the English government, could do little to thwart the swarms of interlopers. In more modern terms, government protectionism could not prevent competition by private enterprise. The trade was so lucrative, for both Africans and Europeans, that it suffered all the illegal activities that any lucrative business produces. (A present-day analogue is the drug traffic, whose huge profits encourage criminal activity, ultimately involving national rivalries.)

Curtin (1969, 122) accepts the figures of Kenneth Davies (1957) as the most authoritative available on the number and origin of the Royal African Company's imports to the Caribbean in the latter seventeenth century (1673–89), just the time the Charleston colony was beginning to grow. These figures show that the area from Senegambia south and eastward through the Windward Coast accounted for almost 40 percent of imported slaves; the area from the Gold Coast (present Ghana) eastward through Whydah (present Dahomey) accounted for 36.6 percent, but slaves from Angola formed only 12 percent of the total. If one broadly assumes that at this early stage the coast lands of Africa rather than the interior furnished the slaves, one may further expect speakers of the Kru languages (including Gola) to have been somewhat more numerous than speakers of the Kwa language group, and a decidedly minor portion would have spoken Bantu languages.

It seems clear that the beginning of the colonial period and the later plantation period were socially quite distinct for Carolina and other English colonies in the Caribbean. During the first years, blacks were few and their contacts with whites were closer than they later became—blacks might have learned a form of real English rather than a creole. It is probable also that if a pidgin language had been brought into Barbados, Jamaica, or Charles Town, it would have become creolized as soon as plantation living conditions came to prevail. Slaves in their own quarters, away from whites in the Great House, had to communicate with each other. If they could not do this in their various African languages, what was more natural than that they should adopt the pidgin English used in the slave trade and carried wherever ships traded on the African coast? Ian Hancock has convinced me that what he calls Guinea Coast Creole English was probably this kind of English-based *lingua franca,* the original form used at slaving posts from Gambia to Ghana—with many local variations but having a core of sameness. I suggest that this kind of pidgin was brought early in the plantation period to Barbados, Jamaica, and Charles Town and creolized somewhere along the line—but here I differ from Hancock (Hancock 1980a; Cassidy 1980). I still hold to Barbados as the most probable place where this process might begin and from which it might spread through the Caribbean and so account for the basic similarities that survive in all these colonies as well as in Guyana and Suriname. It seems more plausible to me that one form of pidgin should be dispersed than that many different types of pidgin should produce creoles so similar. In short, I believe that in the period up to 1660 or 1670 the conditions necessary to formation of a creole had not yet arisen, because the proportion of blacks to whites was much smaller than it was soon to become. Thereafter the change was very rapid, however, and it must have been then that creolization took place—first in Barbados, then elsewhere, using the same English-based pidgin but making local changes both under English dominance and through the accession of new slaves from Africa.

Hancock has found no evidence of an "early, distinctively Barbadian pidgin or creole based on English," and I must admit that I have no direct evidence either. But if by "early" he means before approximately 1670, he has accepted, as I cannot, the common claim that Barbadian English never went through a creole stage. He repeats the often-quoted request of a representative of the Royal African Company in 1673 for "40 or 50 negroes from Barbados that have been bred up their [*sic*] and speake only the English tongue." He takes this to mean that they spoke "good English"—that is, noncreole. I read this request quite differently. What the representative is asking for is blacks who speak *no African language.* But that does not guarantee that their English was not creole. Indeed, by this time, 1673, almost fifty years since the founding of the colony, and with the plantation way of life in existence for more than a generation, it is very hard to believe that a large number of new slaves, many knowing no English at all, could have learned any but a creolized form of English. They would learn it on the plantations under conditions of daily life and work, as best they could, from those who already knew it, their fellow slaves. The question cannot be settled here. New fieldwork done in 1991 by John R. Rickford in Barbados (reported in Rickford 1992) gives clear evidence of creole in present use, which indicates a much longer-standing use.

So, to summarize the social and historical evidence:

1. There was certainly a close historical connection, and continuity, in the founding of the English colonies Barbados, Guyana-Suriname, Jamaica, and Charles Town in the seventeenth century.

2. Striking similarities among the creole languages of the colonies cannot be accidental; the similarities imply some common source.

3. In the colonies' early years, before the plantation system was in full force, conditions for the development of creole language did not yet exist, since there were relatively few blacks and they had relatively more contact with whites. After the plantation system was established and large-scale importation of slaves began, conditions for creolization were both present and compelling.

4. An English-based pidgin had developed along the West African coast by at least the third quarter of the seventeenth century. This pidgin was most likely the common basis of the Caribbean creole languages.

5. Given a community, polyglot but stabilized, as the slave communities were on large plantations, a system of communication must develop. It takes only one generation for a creole language to begin to develop.

6. African influences in the early creoles were from both the Kwa and Kru languages; the Kwa dominated in Jamaica, but the Kru seem to have had more influence on Gullah.

We badly need more descriptive studies of Gullah. Perhaps William Stewart will publish his long-awaited collections, making them available for analysis. Then we may come a little closer to answering more precisely some of the questions about Gullah and the Caribbean connection.

Names and Naming in the Sea Islands

Keith E. Baird and Mary A. Twining

In the South Carolina–Georgia Sea Islands it is not unusual for a person to have two given names. One is an official, generally English (or European) name; the other is a kind of nickname, a "basket" name. The official name (e.g., *Joseph, George, Mary, Jane*) appears on the individual's birth or baptismal certificate, school records, social security card, and other documents relating to dealings with the outside European-American community. The basket name is known and used only in the family circle and within the individual's home community, but there is usually a difference between a basket (or pet) name and a nickname. The basket name is usually given soon after birth, when the infant is still in arms or in a cradle (or "basket"), but a nickname may be acquired later, during adolescence or afterward, because of some physical or temperamental characteristic or some incident in which the person has been involved. In any case, for Sea Islanders the nickname, basket name, or pet name by which an individual is known within the community is the owner's operative personal name.

Questions about the extent and source of basket naming and nicknaming constitute key issues in the "Sea Island Creole controversy," chiefly between Guy Johnson (1930, 1980) and Lorenzo Dow Turner (1949), because naming relates to both the African influences on Sea Island language and culture and the contemporary persistence of African folkways in the region. Turner unequivocally states that the Sea Island nickname is nearly always a word of African origin and declares that

> in many instances both the given-name and surname are African words. Some of my ex-slave informants explain this by saying that during slavery they used for their surname (which they called "trimmin") the surname of their owner. After slavery, many of them refused to use any longer the name of their former enslavers. Likewise many former slave-holders refused to allow the freedmen to use their names. Thereupon, the former slaves chose their nickname for their surname and gave them-

23

selves another surname. This also is frequently an African word. (Turner 1949, 40)

Against Johnson's minimizing of African linguistic continuities in the Sea Islands (a position Johnson adopted in his 1930 book *Folk Culture on St. Helena Island, South Carolina* and continued to maintain), Turner argues that the distinctive speech of Sea Islanders (known as Gullah or Geechee), including personal names, is strongly influenced by the people's African origins.

Sometimes a Sea Island nickname may seem to be simply an English name, so that a person whose official name is *Richard,* for instance, may come to be known as *Joe.* The reason for this might be that the African-originated name *Kojo* (the Ga and Ewe name for a male born on Monday) has either been affectionately apocopated by the bearer's fellow islanders or mistaken by European Americans for the familiar short form of the English name *Joseph,* as Peter Wood (1974a) has demonstrated. J. L. Dillard (1972, 129) shows how the African-originated *Fiba* (from the Ewe name for a girl born on Friday) was incorrectly heard and perpetuated by European Americans as *Phoebe* (an ancient Greek name for the moon goddess).

Traditional attitudes toward names and naming persist in the Sea Islands. Not long ago a man on Johns Island who had been burned so that his skin showed a most atypical pink-and-white mottled complexion was called *Buckra* by his friends. By this appellation they were commenting jokingly on his resemblance to a European man; in Efik, *mbakara* means 'European person.' A remarkable feature of the physiognomy of another man, Joe Bligen, nicknamed *Cunjie,* is his broad cheekbones. The nickname closely approximates the pronunciation of the Hausa word *kunci,* which means 'cheek' or 'the side of the face.' Joe Bligen's sister, Ms. Hunter, worked for a family down the road from her home, and the children there called her *Dada,* which means 'mother' in Ewe. She is also known as *Miss Delia* and Janie Hunter.

Turner (1949) lists over one thousand Sea Island (Gullah) personal names, which he traces back to their origins in some thirty African languages. He conducted the research on which this material is based between 1932 and 1940, and the extent to which African-derived naming practices persist today, a half century later, is a matter of continuing scholarly interest and one of many indexes that might be used to measure change in the culture. Even in the 1930s it was not easy for a researcher from outside the culture to obtain information from Sea Islanders concerning their naming practices. Dillard praises Turner's achievement in the face of the difficulties involved and explains his success in these terms: "It thus took an outstanding act of sympathetic and discreet inquiry by a Black researcher, Turner, to come up with the fact that thousands of naming patterns traceable to West African practices were still in effect among the Gullah speakers" (1972, 132–33).

It should hardly be surprising that African names and African attitudes toward naming were and have been maintained in the Sea Islands. One reason is certainly the importance attached in African societies to the naming of a child, since "in the African tradition, today as yesterday, a name is not [a] mere identification tag; it is a record of family and community history, a distinct personal reference, an indication of present status, and an enunciated promise of future accomplishment" (Baird and Chuks-Orji 1972, 86). The choice of a name for a child might be influenced by a number of considerations, including the day or time of day the child was born, its place in numerical order as regards its siblings, whether it was the elder or younger of twins, and if children preceding it had not survived. Family or community circumstances as well as more cosmic events such as flood or famine or war at the time of birth might determine the child's name. The Yoruba people of Nigeria neatly encapsulate the notions connected with this African attitude in the saying, We consider the state of our affairs before we name a child.

The fondness that Africans have for children means that the arrival of a child into the family is the cause of great rejoicing. This can be seen in the following examples of names from West Africa, whence most of the ancestors of the Sea Islanders came to America.

The Yoruba male and female name *Ayo* means 'joy' and forms part of another name, *Ayodele,* whose meaning, 'joy comes to the house,' is an even more explicit expression of a family's gratification at the long-hoped-for arrival of a child. The Igbo people of eastern Nigeria express a similar sentiment when they bestow on a newborn male child the piously thankful name *Chukwuemeka* 'God has dealt kindly with us.' The day on which a child was born is often celebrated through the bestowal of a dayname. Thus the name *Yaa* among the Ewe people of Ghana indicates that the baby girl who bears it was born on Thursday; a baby boy born on that day would be named *Yao.* The attention given to birth order as well as multiple births is observed in the name *Twia,* given by the Fante ethnic group in Ghana to a boy born after twins.

The basket names and nicknames of Sea Islanders listed by Turner (1949) came from countries of West Africa as far north as Senegal and as far south as Angola. They thus indicate that among the ancestors of the Sea Islanders were speakers of a variety of languages, which Turner identifies as Bambara, Bini, Bobangi, Djerma, Efik, Ewe, Fante, Fon, Fula, Ga, Gbari, Hausa, Ibo, Ibibio, Kikongo, Kimbundu, Kpelle, Mende, Malinke, Nupe, Susu, Songhai,

Twi, Tshiluba, Umbundu, Vai, Wolof, and Yoruba. The linguistic and cultural
patrimony of Sea Islanders thus involves an expanse of territory that includes
Senegal, Gambia, Mali, Guinea, Sierra Leone, Liberia, Ivory Coast, Ghana,
Togo, Benin, Niger, Nigeria, Cameroon, Equatorial Guinea, Gabon, Congo,
Zaire, and Angola.

To this point our discussion has focused on names themselves rather than on
social patterns of naming. We have emphasized the sounds, shapes, meanings,
and provenances of the names rather than the acts and attitudes associated with
the conferring, accepting, or assuming of nicknames in the Sea Islands and the
sociohistorical context in which this behavior takes place. Although Turner,
himself a linguist, was mainly preoccupied with linguistic considerations, he
did not neglect the customary practices of Sea Islanders regarding naming that
reflect their familial attitudes and societal values. He was careful to note personal names that his African informants could identify as well-known African
names as he included them in his list. Noting, however, that various naming
methods were used in West Africa, Turner remarks that African-originated Sea
Island names in his list not known by his informants to be used in Africa might
nonetheless have been used as personal names by the Sea Islanders' African
ancestors. He goes on to make the following significant comment:

> Even though my Gullah informants do not remember the meanings of
> these unmarked personal names (nor the precise meanings of most of
> those that are marked), they continue to use them in naming their chil-
> dren because their older relatives and friends so used them. That they
> would choose many words whose meanings they do not know is not sur-
> prising. As already indicated, even though the Africans attach very great
> importance to the meanings of the words they use as personal names,
> they do not follow this practice exclusively. The meanings of many
> of their names are not known. Like many other peoples, the Africans
> sometimes choose a name because it is that of some ancestor. (Turner
> 1949, 41)

Several other writers on Sea Island culture have commented on attitudes and
customs about naming. Elsie Clews Parsons (1923), for example, reports that
Sea Islanders name a child on the ninth day after birth. Mary Twining (1977,
1:65) records that "the custom of a person's having several names is particularly well developed on the Islands." The latter statement is based on fieldwork
carried out in the area from 1966 to 1975 and is thus fairly recent. Observations to the same effect were made as long ago as 1893 by the schoolteacher
Elizabeth Botume in her *First Days Amongst the Contrabands*.

Pressures toward acculturation have no doubt caused some African personal names to disappear (at least from official use), to be supplanted by the more usual Anglo-American names. Other African names have acquired negative associations and have fallen into disuse or have been changed into a more acceptable form. Dillard (1972, 130) comments on how *Sambo,* a Hausa name for the second son in the family (but meaning 'disgrace' in Mende and Vai), came to have an exclusively pejorative connotation.

In general, Turner's (1949) study of Africanisms in the speech of Sea Islanders merits recognition for its contribution to the African substrate theory of the origin of the Atlantic creole languages. His approach, and consequently his conclusions, have not been unchallenged. Salikoko Mufwene (1985) has identified and responded to some of Turner's critics, particularly Morris Swadesh (1951) and P. E. H. Hair (1965), scholars who, while they do not strongly dispute the African substrate theory, nevertheless question whether the African names in Gullah are sufficiently probative of that view. Mufwene observes that African names in Gullah exhibit some African phonological features and remarks that until other, essentially grammatical, evidence is offered, "it is doubtful that the African proper names prove anything in support of the linguistic Afrogenetic hypothesis" (1985, 160–61). Mufwene does not dispute that the names identified by Turner as African are such in fact, but he concludes regarding their persistence in use that "the best we can now tell is that they certainly represent cultural, non-linguistic, Africanisms since in this regard the custom seems to have continued" (1985, 161).

Irrespective of whether Turner's list of Sea Island names does or does not offer satisfactory proof that Gullah (and by extension Afrish, the so-called Black English) is fundamentally African in its grammatical structure, the African origin of such names is not now substantially in dispute. If these names and the practices and attitudes associated with them are still found in the Sea Island region, it is reasonable to conclude that they are functional within the society and that their persistence may therefore properly be regarded as expressive of African cultural continuity.

We have been interested in discovering the extent to which distinctive basket names and nicknames are still encountered in the Sea Islands, forty years after the publication of Turner's *Africanisms in the Gullah Dialect.* The informants in our study were between forty and fifty years old in 1985. The names in the list below, most of which they have supplied, are of individuals personally known to them, mainly from their native Johns Island region, which includes Charleston. The youngest of the bearers of the names are around twenty years old, but these are conspicuously few. The majority of the names are of persons thirty-five years of age or older.

Our informants called these names nicknames because they are not the official names of the bearers. A large number of names (e.g., *Chance, Monkey, Nuttin, Plum*) are recognizable English or near-English words. What makes them distinctive in the Sea Island context is that (1) they relate specifically to physical, mental, or moral characteristics of their bearers as perceived by fellow Sea Islanders; or (2) they refer to some incident or situation in which the nicknamed individual was involved. There are other nicknames that are neither Euro-American names nor English words; neither are they Sea Island creolisms such as *Chance-um, Lickey-too,* and *Do-um Bubba,* but, like *Buckra* and *Minna,* can be documented as having African origins. Also listed, finally, are some names for which there is no explanation except in terms of conjectural African origins. For these entries we have had recourse to Turner (1949) when the name in question appeared to bear some relationship or resemblance to an item listed in that work. References to the Turner study in this connection are indicated in the comment on the particular entry by the letter *T* followed by the relevant page number (thus, T 141 = Turner 1949, 141). We use conventional English spelling for the names, since the majority of them are either English words or are based on English words. The sex (m. or f.) of the person to whom the name was given is also indicated. Following this list of names is a discussion of their significance in modern-day Sea Island culture. In many entries African language sources and parallels are cited in their phonemic forms (this includes those from Turner's *Africanisms*). Many of these include subscripts representing the tonal pitch levels in the African forms.

Beep-Beep (m.)   The individual so nicknamed was saved from possibly fatal injury by the timely sounding of an automobile horn, which warned him to leap to safety.

Betsy Ben (m.)   A matronymic, indicating that Ben is the son of Betsy.

Big (m.)   Descriptive of the individual named.

Blue (m.)   The individual is so named because his complexion is so dark as to appear blue.

Old Bo (m.)   The world *old* distinguishes the bearer from his son, *Young Bo.* Ewe *bo* means 'far away,' 'high up' (T 66). Fon *gbo* means 'charm' (T 67).

Boda (f.)   Daughter of *Old Bo,* preceding. Fon *gboda* 'to play' (T 67).

Bodick (m.)   Cousin to *Old Bo,* above. Ewe *bo* 'far away,' 'high up' (T 66); Fon *gbo* 'charm' (T 67), *diga* 'long,' 'be long' (T 74).

Bo Jibba (m.)   For *Bo,* see *Old Bo* above. Fula *dʒiba* 'pocket' (T 100).

Boody (m.)   The individual so named has remarkably long arms and is fond of gambling. Kongo *budi* 'cat' (T 68).

Boogah (m., f.)   Vai *b'u₂gi₂kai₁* 'something frightful' (T 68). The individuals bearing this name share no specific characteristic such as attractiveness or unattractiveness. Africans traditionally name a child on the basis of a positive physical, mental, or moral characteristic; they may also give an uncomplimentary name to a child to deceive the ancestors, who might otherwise, it is thought, wish to take back to themselves a very desirable infant. (See Baird and Chuks-Orji 1972, 76.)

Boot (m.)   The individual so named has a very dark complexion.

Bubba (m.)   As a family term, this name corresponds to the English *brother*, of which it is a childish pronunciation (Botume 1893). It is possible, however, that there is also a convergence with Vai *bɔ₁bɔ₁*, the name given to a boy when his real name is not known (T 65), which extends its use into the community at large.

Buck (m.)   The individual bearing this nickname is robust, very masculine.

Buckaroo (m.)   The bearer of this name worked on a farm where he developed a reputation for his skill in handling animals. The name is an Anglo-American rendering of the Spanish *vaquero* 'cowboy.'

Buckra (m.)   From Efik *mbakara* 'he who surrounds or governs,' hence in the slavery and early postslavery period a European (especially English) person. This term was applied as a nickname to a man who suffered facial burns that removed his dark-pigmented epidermis, leaving the pink underskin visible.

Butcher (m.)   The bearer of this nickname is a big, tall (6′ 6″) man noted for his aggressiveness, his "readiness to slaughter" anyone who offends him.

Cat (m.)   The individual bearing this name is reputed (it is not established whether justly or unjustly) to be a clever and agile burglar.

Chance (m.)   This name is borne by an individual known for his willingness to take a risk.

Chance-um (m.)   That is, 'risk it,' whether in the area of business or romantic relations. There are several persons with this nickname.

Cheetah (m.)   The face of the bearer of this name is spotted by scars.

Coodle (m.)   The individual so named has a particular attraction to funerals and attends the ceremonies whether he is acquainted with the deceased or not. These facts point firmly to the origin of this name in the Ewe *ku₃du₁* 'announcement of a death' (T 117).

Country (m.)   Nickname given to the bearer because of his very pronounced rusticity in speech, dress, and general comportment.

Croak (m.)   The individual has a physical condition that gives his skin
an unusual roughness, seen by his associates as comparable to that of a
croc; that is, a crocodile.

Cunjie (m.)   The bearer of this name has very broad cheekbones. Hausa
kun₃tʃi₃ 'the side of the face, the cheek.'

Cuteness (f.)   This nickname is accurately descriptive of the young lady
who bears it, according to our informant.

Dada (f.)   This is the term of address used by children and young adults
to an older woman, especially when she has responsibility for their care.
Ewe *da₁da₃* 'mother' (T 70).

Dahlin (f.)   The Sea Island form of English *darling.* This term of en-
dearment is the name by which the bearer is known not only within the
intimate circle of family and close associates but also within the wider
community.

Dan (f.)   This is the nickname of a very beautiful young woman who is
a professional model. *Dan* may be the abbreviation of either one of two
names listed by Turner, considering a certain degree of correspondence
between the description of the bearer of the name and the connotations
of the suggested etyma. The full entry for each of the two Sea Island
names as given by Turner is here cited (slightly edited for the purpose of
simplicity):

Dana (f.)   Yoruba *da₃na₂* (personal name) 'to pay a dowry,' *da₃na₃* 'to
make a fire,' *da₃na₁* 'to commit robbery on the highway'; Bambara *dana*
'faith, confidence,' *ndana* 'a bell' (T 71).

Dane (m.)   Mende *ndane* (personal name), literally 'mouth sweet' (T 72).

Delia (f.)   It would be easy to assume that we have here the English form
of the epithet of the Greek goddess Artemis (Diana to the Romans) as
worshipped at Delos (see Partridge 1959, 38). *Miss Delia,* however, is
the nickname of a matron and folk artist on Johns Island whose official
first name is *Janie.* The explanation of this name, admittedly conjectural, seems to relate not to the distant isles of Greece but to the much
nearer Sea Islands. Turner records the name *dilɛlɪ* (f.), stressed on the
first syllable, and supplies the following information: Mende *ndilɛlɪ* (personal name) 'peace, contentment' (T 74). The name is fully in accord
with the calm and gentle nature of its bearer.

Dink, Dinky (m.)   Mandinka *diŋke* (personal name) 'male child' (T 75).

Dog (m.)   The individual bearing this name is not considered handsome.
It should be noted, however, that the Yoruba people of Nigeria give

the name *Ajayi* 'this dog' to a child born face-down (Abraham 1958).
Turner includes this name in his list (T 47) as well as the name *imbuwa,*
which he shows to originate in the Kimbundu word *imbua* 'dog' (T 96).
Thus there exist African precedents for naming a person *Dog,* and such
an appellation would not necessarily be pejorative any more than is the
English surname *Hogg.*

Do-um (m.)   That is, 'do it'; an injunction to assiduous application to an
endeavor, or an incitement to audacity in sexual adventure. The bearer
of this sobriquet is reputed to have earned it by reason of conduct that
embraced both definitions of the name. He was in his twenties at the
time he acquired the name.

Do-um Bubba (m.)   (Younger) brother of *Do-um,* preceding.

Dreg (m.)   The individual so named is regarded as lazy and therefore
worthless.

Dukey (m.)   The bearer of this name is a great admirer of the actor John
Wayne, "the Duke," and he affects many of Wayne's mannerisms. His
fantasy identification with the actor is aided by the fact that he is so light
complexioned that he could "pass" for a European American.

Essie (f.)   Bini $\varepsilon_1 se_{3-1}$ 'goodness, favor' (T 84).

Fair (m.)   This nickname was bestowed on a young man of particularly
respectable character and engaging disposition, "a really nice person."

Fat (m.)   Nickname of a man who returned home to the Sea Islands after
having become rather affluent in New York City.

Foxy (m.)   Name of a clever gambler.

Gal (f.)   That is, 'girl.' It is not unusual for African peoples to give a
child a name that is simply the gender designation *boy* or *girl. Boysie* is
a common nickname for a boy in the English-speaking Caribbean. (Cf.
Dinky, above.)

Gotta Love Me with a Feeling (m.)   This name was taken from the favor-
ite song of the bearer, for whom it seems to serve as an admonition to
potential female admirers.

Gussie (m.)   The bearer's official name is nothing like *Augustus* or *Gus-
tavus,* of which it might be presumed to be an abbreviation. Turner,
however, lists the Bambara-derived female personal name *gasi* 'misfor-
tune' (T 90). Since some names both in Africa and in the Sea Islands are
not absolutely restricted either to males or females, the Bambara name
might conceivably have been the original.

Handful (f.)   The woman bearing this nickname is around ninety years of age. It was not possible to establish whether it was due to her diminutive size, forceful disposition, or a combination of the two characteristics that she received this name in her youth.

Head (m.)   This name was conferred on its bearer because of his rather sizable head.

Hog (m.)   The bearer of this name received it because he is aggressively acquisitive; he "hogs everything."

Jackie (m., f.)   Not an official name of any of the bearers. Turner lists the male personal name *Jake* and relates it to Vai *dʒaʒke₁* 'to prophesy' (T 98). A Sea Island woman bearing the name *Jackie* is reputed to have the gift of precognition.

Kyah (m.)   This is not the abbreviation of another name (such as *Hezekiah,* for instance). Turner lists the Sea Island name *koiya* from the Vai *kai₃a₃* (*kai₃a₃*) "a fish trap made by placing sticks across a creek so that only a small opening is left into which a long cone-shaped basket, made of bamboo sticks from three to six feet long, is inserted in such a way that the fish are forced into it by the strong current of the water" (T 113).

Lab (m.)   Many people whose official name is *Arthur* bear this nickname. Our Sea Island informants could offer no explanation of the connection between the two names. A possible explanation that we venture is that the first Arthur to bear the name had the initials L. A. B., which became the nickname *Lab.* Other individuals having the official name Arthur subsequently either had it conferred on them or assumed the nickname.

Lady (f.)   This name indicates the attractive appearance, dignified bearing, and exemplary personal reputation of its holder.

Licky-to (m.)   The bearer of this name defeated an antagonist not only in a verbal confrontation but in physical combat as well.

Lilah (f.)   Turner lists *laila,* giving its origin as *la ila!* 'Oh God!' an exclamation used by the Mandinka and other people of the "Gambia, whether Muslim or not, to express great astonishment" (T 120).

Lizard (m.)   The individual so nicknamed is an excellent dancer noted for the nimbleness of his feet.

Louse (m.)   This name was conferred on its bearer because he was perceived as conspicuously lacking in amiable personal qualities.

Lovey (f.)   There are at least three persons so called on Johns Island. The origin of the name most readily appears to be the English word *love* and would thus express affection felt for the bearer by those who bestowed the name on her. Another possibility is that *Lovey* is an Anglo-American-oriented acculturative adaptation of the Sea Island name *lafiya* listed by Turner as derived from Fon *lafiya* 'to be in good health'; also, Hausa *la₃fi₃ya₁* 'health, outward prosperity' (T 120).

Lula (f.)   This fairly common name is not the official name of any one of its bearers. Kimbundu *mululu* 'great-grandchild' (T 134).

Mattus Momma (f.)   Mattus is a place on Johns Island. The bearer of this name is the respected matriarch of that locality.

Minna (f.)   Turner lists the name *mina* (m. and f.) and relates it to the Vai personal name *mi₁na₃* and the Fon *mina*, denoting an African from Elmina or Accra in the former Gold Coast (present-day Ghana) and refugee to Popo in the present-day Republic of Benin (T 131).

Minna Bill (m.)   That is, 'Minna's Bill,' nickname of Minna's grandson, Bill.

Monkey (f.)   The nickname of a very attractive young woman whose charming antics as a child amused and delighted her elders.

Neen (f.)   Turner lists the Sea Island name *nina* from the Bambara *nina* 'a gift' (T 137).

Neeny (f.)   Diminutive of *Neen,* above.

Nubber (m.)   The bearer of this name butts people. Butting as a form of physical assault consists of one person's use of the head to deliver a blow to the head of another person, often with stunning effect. The *Oxford English Dictionary* (compact edition, 1971) lists as boxing slang the word *nob,* meaning 'to strike one on the head' (attested for 1812). *Nobber,* meaning 'a blow on the head,' is attested for 1818, and the same word is attested for 1821 as meaning 'a pugilist skilled in nobbing.' It seems, therefore, that there is some justification for assuming that the unusual word *nubber* is a variant of *nobber.*

Numprel (f.)   The French *nombril* 'navel' has been proposed as the original form of this nickname (Frederic Cassidy, pers. comm., 1985). In many African populations, both continental and diasporic, it is not uncommon to see infants and small children with notably protuberant navels. In our research, however, we have identified only one individual with the name *Numprel.* One of us (Baird) sees the name as possibly related to *pela* (f.), cited by Turner as originating in Kimbundu *mpela* 'the season when the grass is burned (from July to October),' 'the ground which has been cleared by fire'; also Mende *kpela* 'to mature, to reach puberty,' used of females (T 148).

Nuttin (m.)   That is, 'nothing.' This appears to be a basket name, as distinct from a nickname. The bestowing of a somewhat derogatory name is in accord with the practice among some African peoples of giving an

uncomplimentary name to an infant. (See Boogah, above; and Baird and
Chuks-Orji 1972, 76.)

Peewee (m., f.)   Turner lists *piwi* as a female name, but males also have
this name. Its origin is Kimbundu *mpivi* 'an orphan' (T 149).

Pig (m.)   The individual so nicknamed has a reputation for overindul-
gence.

Plum (m., f.)   Persons with this nickname have a light, smooth complexion.

Plummy (m., f.)   Diminutive of *Plum,* above.

Pompey (m., f.)   The similarity of this name to that of the ill-fated rival of
Julius Caesar is accidental and potentially misleading. Turner lists a Sea
Island name *pambi* from Mende *kpambi* 'line, course' or 'a red handkerchief' (T 147). The misperception of African names and their alteration
into forms more familiar to speakers of English has been remarked by
such scholars as Dillard (1972, 129) and Wood (1974a, 183).

Pook (m.)   The pronunciation of this name requires the rounding and pro-
trusion of the lips, thus reproducing the salient physiognomical feature
of the bearer of this sobriquet.

Poor-Man (m.)   This nickname was given to the bearer because he is
regarded as jealous, tough, and stingy.

Pop (m.)   Not a reference to its bearer's name as a father, but to his
paunch, or *pop-belly;* that is, *pot-belly.*

Prosper (m.)   The bearer of this nickname is a distinguished Sea Islander.
The very auspicious meaning of the name calls to mind the *oriki,* or
'praise-name,' which is a feature of Yoruba naming practices.

Puddin (m.)   That is, 'pudding.' The nickname reflects the fact that the
bearer likes to eat, and also that he is "a lovable character."

Queen (f.)   Name of a young lady much admired for her beauty and
meticulous good grooming. The name *Queen* or *Queenie* is found quite
widely not only among African Americans but also among English-
speaking Caribbean people. Both of these groups appear to have a
greater consciousness of the complimentary character of the name than
exists generally in the United States and the Caribbean regarding its
Latinate equivalent, *Regina.*

Rabbit (m.)   The bearer of this name is perceived as being tricky, like
Br'er Rabbit of African-American (and originally African) folklore.

Reb (m.)   That is 'rev(erend).' The bearer of this nickname carries a pack
of cards, even in Sunday school, with a constancy and pride similar to
that with which a clergyman carries the Holy Book.

Sambo (m.)   Turner lists this name, relating it to Hausa *sam₃bo₁* 'name given to the second son in a family,' 'name given to anyone called *Muhammadu*,' 'name of a spirit'; Mende *sambo* 'to disgrace,' 'to be shameful'; Vai *sam₃bo₁* (personal name) 'to disgrace' (T 155).

Shadda (m.)   That is, 'shadow.' The individual so nicknamed is very dark-complexioned.

Shine-eye (m.)   Nickname of an individual whose eyes have an extraordinary glitter.

Shug (m., f.)   Diminutive of *Sugar,* a widely current sobriquet indicating the affection in which the bearer is held.

Sip (m.)   The personal feature that characterizes the individual so nicknamed is alluded to by its opposite in this case. The bearer of the name is in fact a very tall person, such as is humorously described as "a long drink of water."

Sister (f.)   Persons called by this kinship designation used as a nickname are not necessarily related to those who know and address them as such, even though the name may have first been given within the family. The institutional (e.g., church) use of the title *sister* is different and is not relevant here.

Skinny (m.)   The bearer of this name is in fact presently rather corpulent; "he has a gut on him." He was, however, quite slender at the time the nickname was first conferred. In this case, the name has outlasted the circumstances that gave it origin and justification.

Slim (m.)   A number of persons so nicknamed are, as a matter of fact, slim. Some persons called *Slim,* however, are, as in the case preceding, now fat.

South (m.)   The bearer of this name is left-handed.

Spike (m.)   The person so nicknamed is very tall, very thin, and has a long head.

Step (m.)   The bearer of this nickname is a very short person.

Stretch (m.)   Persons called by this name are very tall and slim. The head is not necessarily long, as with *Spike.*

Sugarnun (f.)   The first element of this name, *Sugar,* is readily recognizable. The element *nun* (or 'none') requires some explanation. There is no cultural basis for presuming any convential connection, and the ungenerous prohibition suggested by the concept "none" negates the pleasant indulgence associated with sugar. A review of terms related to *sugar* that have or have had currency within the African-American community reveals the word *sugar-tit*. The item thus designated is a piece

of cloth folded or rolled into a cone so that a kind of nipple is formed
at the end. This end part is dipped into sweetened water and inserted
between the lips of a fretful infant, who sucks on it and is calmed into a
more complacent mood by the artificial but nonetheless gratifying *sugar-
tit,* or *sugar-teat.* Turner (137) lists the name *nono* from Hausa no_3no_1
'the mammary gland of the female, and the corresponding structure
in the male,' 'the fins below the head of fish,' 'a cluster of fruit' (T 137).
The name *Sugarnun,* accordingly, is apparently synonymous with *sugar-
tit* or *sugar-teat* and connotes oral pleasure and sensory satisfaction.

Swag (m.)   The individual so nicknamed wears pants that are too big and
as a result 'sag,' or 'swag.'

Sweet (f.)   A complimentary description of the person so named.

Toady (m.)   The bearer of this name is considered to resemble a frog.

Tuhmee (f.)   Turner lists the name *toma* (f.) and relates it to Kongo *toma*
'to be good, to be pleasant,' 'to taste sweet'; Kimbundu *toma* 'to stick';
Vai $to:_3ma_3$, personal name (m. and f.) (T 171).

Trader (m.)   The individual bearing this nickname "likes to swap stuff."

Ucker (m.)   Turner records the name *okra* (m.) and relates it to Twi *ɔkra*
(personal name, m.) 'soul' (T 141). The bearer is an elderly man.

Wah-Wah (f.)   The bearer of this name, an older woman, is very religious.
Turner records the name *wawa* (m.) and relates it to Hausa $wa:_3wa_3$ 'a
fool,' 'a cloth of native make worn round the body and thrown over the
shoulder'; $wa:_3wa_1$ 'scrambling to obtain possession of a portion of an
animal which has been killed'; Kimbundu *vava* 'to wish for,' 'necessity';
Ewe $\beta a_1v\bar{a}_{1\text{-}3}$ 'a wasp' (T 178).

Yacky (m.)   This name may be a variant pronunciation of *Jackie.* A possible alternative source might be the name *yako* (m.), which Turner
records and relates to Yoruba ya_2ko_2 (personal name, m.) 'to be a male,'
'to be odd' (T 184). The individual so named is an elderly man.

The foregoing list, by no means exhaustive, indicates the shapes, sounds,
semantic associations, and origins (actual and conjectural) of extant Sea Island
personal names. The names included were selected on the basis of the following
criteria:

a. They are the basket names or nicknames of the bearers, as distinct from
their official given names.

b. They are known and used by Sea Islanders within the family and the
community to which the bearers belong. The family is to be understood in

this context not as conforming to the European and European-American nuclear model but as the African (so-called extended) family which through its ramifying interconnections becomes, at its maximal extension, the community.

c. Their family and community connections, and the circumstances under which they were conferred or assumed, could be accounted for by our informants.

d. Their origins could be traced to African or other etyma to explain their occurrence and use.

The bearers of the basket names or nicknames listed were all at least twenty years old. The list has no names of young or adolescent individuals. It appears that, due to acculturative influences, fewer parents have been bestowing basket names on their children in recent years. Moreover, the greater mobility of Sea Islanders today, together with their rising socioeconomic expectations and achievements, move the younger element into a wider sphere of activities in which the more formal, official, European-American name is more appropriate. Thus, even if a child is given a basket name or nickname, the period during which the recipient lives in an undiluted folk society may not be long enough to ensure the lifetime attachment of the name.

The evidence indicates that some basket names and nicknames are still in use in the Sea Islands today, even though their number is gradually being reduced. To the extent that they continue in use, these names form a part of the intimate family and community relationships between people in the culture. The attitudes and values expressed in these names seem to constitute an inner core of cultural integrity and thus have been remarkably resistant to outside influences. The extant names continue to express familial affection and friendly regard, to compliment praiseworthy characteristics, sometimes to point out less laudable features, and to commemorate personal incidents and communal events. In view of these considerations, it is fair to conclude that some elements of traditional Sea Island naming practices persist to the present day, even though in attenuated form and with declining vigor.

Note

The authors acknowledge with gratitude the invaluable assistance rendered them in the preparation of this essay by Mr. William Saunders and his brother Mr. Alphonso Saunders, both lifelong residents of the Sea Islands.

Misinterpreting *Linguistic Continuity* Charitably

Salikoko S. Mufwene

The title of this paper was prompted by the original formulation of the theme of the symposium at which it was presented, namely, "South Carolina and the Caribbean: Linguistic and Cultural Continuities." Seeing it for the first time in a context that was not exclusively diachronic, I was struck by the ambiguity of the term *linguistic continuity* and wondered which of the following three interpretations may have been intended. The first is diachronic and applies most often when discussing particular languages without necessarily relating them to others. In this interpretation, structures of language varieties of people of African descent in the New World are allegedly continuations of structures of some African languages; their predominantly European vocabularies would simply mask this state of affairs. This position, associated today with the relexification hypothesis (e.g., Lefebvre 1986), follows Suzanne Sylvain's (1936) claim that Haitian Creole is Ewe spoken with a French vocabulary.

The second interpretation is synchronic and spatial, referring to features shared by several varieties. Given the historical connection between the Caribbean and South Carolina, it is certainly justified to speak of continuities in this sense. The anglophone colonization of South Carolina started in 1670, when the first colony of British subjects and African slaves (a minority in the overall population) landed in Charles Town from Barbados. It has been argued by, for example, Frederic Cassidy (1980) that Gullah must be the continuation of a creole spoken at that time on the Caribbean island. This particular migration and similar ones from one colony to another in the Caribbean, as well as the fact that early Carolinian planters imported a great proportion of their slaves from the Caribbean, would account for similarities in the language varieties spoken by the descendants of Africans in the Caribbean and North America.[1]

The third interpretation is both diachronic and synchronic, claiming that the language varieties spoken by descendants of Africans in the Caribbean and North America are similar both because they have retained similar features from more or less the same, or related, African languages and because they have influenced each other through mutual contacts.

To be sure, the term *linguistic continuity* has been used for some time, particularly by William Stewart (1968, 1974), J. L. Dillard (1972), and Mervyn Alleyne (1980, n.d.). Stewart (1968) and Alleyne (n.d.) use it along with the term *change* in their titles. Both authors seem to have used *linguistic continuity* in free alternation with the terms *retention* and *survival,* the latter being a term first used by Melville Herskovits (1941). Like the latter, Stewart, Dillard, and Alleyne capitalize on the fact that blacks in the New World share many cultural and linguistic features. These scholars appear to subordinate the spatial interpretation to the diachronic interpretation, assuming that the different African-American language varieties share these linguistic features essentially because of their common African linguistic substratum (Herskovits, Alleyne) or because of their common West African Pidgin origin (Stewart).[2] So, given the right circumstances, the observations below about the interpretation of *linguistic continuity* could have been made at least since soon after the publication of Stewart (1968).

In connection with the ambiguity of the term, the following question also arises as long as African-American English (AAE, traditionally called Black English), Gullah, and Caribbean English creoles (CEC) in particular are assumed to be related both historically and typologically: Does either historical or typological relatedness entail the other? Do AAE, on the one hand, and Gullah and CECs, on the other, share linguistic features necessarily because the former must have evolved from a Gullah-like or Guyanese-like creole once spoken by all African slaves in the Caribbean and North America, as proponents of the decreolization hypothesis assume? (See, e.g., W. Stewart 1968, 1974; Dillard 1972, 1985; Labov 1972; Rickford 1977; and M. Alleyne 1980.) In other words, are the features that AAE shares with Gullah and CECs diachronic continuities of features of a (seventeenth-century?) proto-creole of which Gullah must putatively be the lone survivor in North America? This question too is addressed below.

In order to answer the question of which of the above interpretations of *linguistic continuity* best describes the relationships between AAE and Gullah, on the one hand, and between both of them and CECs, on the other, I start by impartially assuming both of the basic perspectives suggested above: the diachronic and the spatial. While I focus more on AAE and Gullah than on CECs, I discuss all of them indirectly, alternating between the diachronic perspective, considering them as individual languages, and the spatial perspective, considering them as a group.

Also, although I am concerned primarily with language varieties of descendants of Africans, I refer occasionally to white American speech. After all, the times of European and African settlements coincided, especially in South

Carolina and, in a sense, the Caribbean. Any adequate analysis of the linguistic characteristics of descendants of Africans in these areas that does not consider the possibility of both African and European contributions, aside from innovations, is question begging (Mufwene 1986c, 1990b, 1992a, 1993a).[3] Although the circumstances of slavery in the New World led Africans to discontinue using African languages as vernaculars (i.e., the primary means of intragroup communication), the only forms of the lexifier language they could learn were the nonstandard varieties that they were in contact with.[4] Kindred of such English varieties still survive (e.g., Appalachian English), and these share features with AAE in particular (Wolfram and Christian 1976; Christian et al. 1988). To the extent that they are related to some conservative varieties in the British Isles, these English varieties tell us a lot about the native varieties of English brought to the New World, and they present relevant material for a comparison that may shed light on the origin of some African-American speech features as well.

Lastly, I use the term *charitable misinterpretation* in my title to describe modified interpretations of *linguistic continuity* which, though in conflict with what some authors have claimed, seem to make more sense on account of the sociolinguistic contacts that have resulted in AAE, Gullah, and CECs. These modified interpretations, intended to make the best sense of what Mervyn Alleyne, J. L. Dillard, Melville Herskovits, and William Stewart, among others, could have meant by *linguistic continuity,* are discussed in the following section.

Interpreting *Linguistic Continuity*

Continuity *versus* Survival *versus* Retention

The terms *survival* and *retention* (with which *linguistic continuity* alternates freely in the literature) are diachronically oriented and presuppose that a widespread change, which could have affected the elements so identified, has taken place. In the linguistic context of the New World, the terms allude to the fact that Africans there shifted languages in favor of the colonial varieties now called African-American English, Gullah, or Caribbean English creoles. In the process they retained very little of the vocabulary of the African languages but preserved at least some of their grammatical features, which now supposedly underlie the new language varieties. Note that although *continuity* may be interpreted diachronically in this case, it does not presuppose a widespread, across-the-board process among all Africans at the time of language shift. It simply indicates that some features of a linguistic system have been preserved in spite of changes that have affected others. In the context of AAE, Gullah, and CECs, *continuity* may be a more neutral and more adequate term because it has the advantage of not being restricted to one particular system that has practically disappeared. Unlike *retention* and *survival,* the term *continuity* may well apply to substrate influence in a newly learned system to which the foreign speaker need not have contributed much, or even anything.

The primary explanations for why *continuity, survival,* and *retention* have been used interchangeably seem to lie de facto in the assumption that features of African languages persisted even after a colonial language was adopted and restructured (M. Alleyne 1971, 1980), as well as in the belief of some users of the terms in the monogenetic origin of African-American language varieties. In order to understand why *linguistic continuity* in the context of South Carolina and the Caribbean may be interpreted more adequately, we must avoid the terms *survival* and *retention,* because they require more convincing evidence than the literature provides. We may assume that while Africans shifted to new vernaculars in the New World (although probably not abruptly), and they may have influenced the structures of these language varieties with features of their substrate languages, they did not necessarily lay European vocabularies over African substrate grammars.

Continuity and the Genesis of African-American Speech

Since the term *substratum* has also been brought into the picture, a brief review of major hypotheses on the genesis of African-American language varieties is certainly in order here because it may shed light on some of the issues arising from the above diachronic interpretation of *linguistic continuity.*[5] At the same time it is imperative to highlight an important difference between the ways Stewart and Alleyne in particular use the term *continuity.* Even though Stewart (1968, 247; 1974, 14) leaves room for African substrate influence (which presumably took place before the development of AAE itself), his main reference is to a West African Pidgin of the early seventeenth century from which AAE can allegedly be derived through processes of creolization and decreolization (see also W. Stewart 1967, 1969a). On the other hand, Alleyne (1980, 140) uses the term primarily to refer to a putative common West African substratum— predominantly Kwa—that would have survived the processes of creolization and decreolization. In restructuring their lexifier into AAE, Gullah, and CECs, the Africans would have retained features of their substrate languages in various ways and to various extents. This variation in the nature and extent of continuities would account for differences between what Alleyne (1980) calls Afro-American dialects.

Regarding AAE and to some extent Gullah, however, many dialectologists have argued that some of the linguistic features now assumed to be characteristic of pidgins and creoles are relics of speech features of the seventeenth- and eighteenth-century colonists from the British Isles (e.g., Krapp 1924; McDavid and McDavid 1951; D'Eloia 1973; Schneider 1982, 1983, 1989; and Hancock 1988). Such features include the preverbal use of *done* for perfect, lack of subject-verb agreement in the present tense, invariant or distributive *be*, confusion of past tense and past perfect forms, prenominal usage of *dem* as a plural distal demonstrative, and usage of *aks* (also spelled *axe*) for the standard English verb *ask*. The dialectologists' claims appear to be supported by documents published by Norman Eliason (1956) and Peter Wood (1974a), as well as by attestations of the features in some rather conservative rural dialects spoken today in the British Isles and in some isolated communities in the United States such as the Appalachians, the Ozarks, and in Delaware among the Old Order Amish.[6] Recognizing such probable models in the lexifier, however, does not rule out possible innovations in the sense explained above (see also note 3), so that, for instance, the function of *dem* as a determiner has been extended to that of plural marker in the basilects of Gullah and CECs. Recognizing such innovations does not rule out diachronic continuities in the sense that features of some substrate languages have continued in the new vernaculars, influencing ways new usage has been innovated, compared with the lexifier.

Without attempting to resolve the debate here, note that the substrate and the dialectologist hypotheses regarding the development of AAE, Gullah, and CECs are not necessarily mutually exclusive (Mufwene 1993a, 1992a). Models in the European lexifier languages and some of the African substrate languages must have converged in a number of ways in forming the new vernaculars. Many options that may now be interpreted as less marked were selected into these language varieties either because they were shared structurally by some varieties of both the lexifier and the substrate languages (the primary sense of *convergence*) or because they were more compatible with other developing patterns, an extended interpretation of *convergence*. For instance, *done* was selected to mark the perfect aspect not only because it has had such usage in some varieties of British and white colonial English but also because a similar construction with a verb meaning 'finish' is used with a verb in Kwa and some other African languages. Why *done* rather than *finish* (as in Tok Pisin) was selected is a question that future research on colonial speech should help to answer. Owing to sociohistorical factors such as the significant majority of Africans on rice and sugar cane plantations, the importance of serial verb constructions in Gullah and CECs may be attributed not only to models such as *go get* in white English but also to the importance of the construction in

(West) African languages. The general loss of verbal inflections, including the *-ing* ending and the finite/nonfinite distinction (Mufwene 1991b; Mufwene and Dijkhoff 1989), must have contributed to the increase of serial verb constructions.[7]

Arguments against substrate influence have often been as unconvincing as most of the justifications for predominant substrate influence in the sense of "survival" or "retention." Against the extreme dialectologist position, note that it would be rather surprising for a language that has been adopted by a foreign group as a vernacular to survive in its original form without being affected by that group's native language(s). By the same token, since the new language varieties have not been created ex nihilo and the English spoken by the Europeans in the colony played a role in defining the lexifier—assumed here to be the second-language variety spoken by slaves during the first thirty to fifty years of the colony—it is hardly surprising that the vernaculars spoken today by descendants of Africans and by some whites share certain features. The point here is to avoid extreme interpretations that claim as exclusive substrate or superstrate influence many features that could be analyzed in different ways, including convergence.

What Counts as Continuity?

Coming back to the question of the diachronic interpretation of *linguistic continuity,* we encounter a long overlooked question. Should the nonstandard features of English in the British Isles that are attested in CECs and Gullah (as well as in, say, Appalachian and Old Order Amish English) but not in educated varieties of English also count as continuities? In a slightly different vein, the fact that the first colonial settlement in South Carolina came from the Caribbean (Wood 1974a) is also noteworthy. It would thus not be out of place to ask whether speech varieties in South Carolina originated in the Caribbean. At least for Gullah, the question would not be hypothetical. Cassidy (1980, 1986b) has proposed this development for Gullah—a view disputed by Ian Hancock (1980a)—and continues to do so (see Cassidy's essay in this volume).

Focusing on Gullah and AAE, much of the discussion on what *continuity* means depends on which position is assumed about their genesis. For instance, according to George Philip Krapp (1924), Hans Kurath (1928), and many of today's scholars who subscribe to the English dialect origin hypothesis, these African-American varieties of English in North America are preservations of the earlier colonial English spoken by whites of comparable socioeconomic status. To those like Edgar Schneider (1993) who admit limited African substrate contributions to the structures of these languages, continuity—a term they do not actually use—might mean no more than the influence that the Africans may have exerted on the structures of the new colonial vernacular to which they were shifting. This is indeed the interpretation suggested by Schneider's (1993) recognition of such a possibility in accounting for features of AAE that he could not trace back to British or colonial nonstandard varieties of English.

Against the extreme dialectologist position of the 1920s, Lorenzo Dow Turner (1941)—deriving partial support from Herskovits (1941) on African cultural continuities in the New World—argued that an important African element is identifiable in Gullah's system and vocabulary. This thesis has been extrapolated by extreme substratists to mean that Gullah and its Caribbean kin owe their grammatical systems primarily to the African languages spoken by the slaves when the varieties were formed. Applied to works in this tradition, the term *continuity* may then assume the diachronic sense of "continuations of structures of some African languages" with the predominant European vocabulary putatively masking the underlying African system.

The differences between the substratist and dialectologist positions are significant enough to justify my attempt in this paper to highlight the common ground between them. Let us note first that both the dialectologist and the substratist positions have very few adherents today in their extreme versions, although there are still disputes over which linguistic features are innovations and which are African or European influences. More and more scholars assume that the structures of AAE, Gullah, and CECs have been determined to varying extents by both the African languages of the slaves who produced them and the colonial nonstandard English varieties of the Europeans the slaves interacted with on the plantations (see most of the papers in Mufwene 1993b). The main problem remains to sort out the extent of these influences.

Given this development with regard to the genesis of AAE, Gullah, and CECs, one of the most charitable ways of making sense of Stewart's use of *continuity* mentioned above is to refer to the West African Pidgin English (WAPE) stage, when European and African elements were being selected into the pidgin system. Since a pidgin is from one point of view a restructuring of its lexifier, the African elements would be the most obvious candidates to be continuities. It is from the African languages that the Africans were presumably switching in developing the pidgin.

Stewart's versus Alleyne's Uses of Continuity

An important factor in interpreting Stewart's position is the question of whether or not WAPE played a determinative role in the formation of AAE, Gullah, and CECs, and hence in the selection of structural features now associated with these vernaculars. Even if the answer is affirmative, it must be recalled that many Africans were imported to the New World from areas in central Africa (Wood 1974a) where WAPE was unknown, and not everybody brought from West Africa was familiar with the pidgin. Thus, continuities from WAPE make sense mostly as continuities from *some* African languages, to the extent that some of its features, reinforced by their sources in *some* African languages, were favored by the ethnolinguistic ecology of the critical formative stage and were selected into the new systems. By the same token, some WAPE features of British origin could have been favored. As we focus on language varieties of African descendants in the New World, this situation provides one more reason for preferring Alleyne's diachronic interpretation, because we are concerned with the fact that the Africans shifted vernaculars in favor of one lexified by a European language and may have reorganized part of its system according to some African models.

The fact that some WAPE features may have no connection with African languages of the region is significant. As indicated most recently in Schneider (1982, 1983, 1989, and 1993), based to a large extent on Eliason (1956), D'Eloia (1973), and other sources, many of the features used to support the alleged pidgin and creole ancestry of AAE can also be related directly to regional dialects of the British Isles, which contributed significantly to colonial nonstandard English in the New World. Phonetically, this is particularly true of pronunciations such as [g(w)ain] for *going* (spelled *gwine* or *gine* in the literature); of random omission and insertion of word-initial [h], as in *im* for him or *hit* for *it;* and of the omission of postvocalic /r/ in preconsonantal and word-final positions, as in *heart* and *water*. Morphosyntactically, Schneider's argument is also strongly supported by the cases of nominal pluralization with *them,* verb delimitation with perfect *done* (as in *he done gone*), possessive delimitation by word order (involving mere preposing of the noun without a possessive marker to the head noun, as in *my brother date*), and the use of an invariant relativizer *what/weh* (as in *everything what he said*). Also, according to Schneider (1982, 37), based on the Slave Narratives of the Federal Writers' Project, today's AAE "does not differ greatly" from "Early AAE" (see also Schneider 1993, 274). More and more it seems that AAE was never restructured to the same extent that Gullah and CECs were (Mufwene 1987; Schneider 1990; Holm 1991). Thus similarities that obtain today between AAE, Gullah, CECs, and English creole varieties in West Africa need not be attributed to the WAPE ancestry suggested by Stewart (1968) and Dillard (1972) via an unsubstantiated route of creolization and decreolization. By the same token, today's cross-system variation may date from the inceptive stages of the varieties, owing primarily to differences in the ethnolinguistic and demographic ecologies of their development.

That is, while the fact that the same features are attested in CECs certainly lends support to the spatial interpretation of *linguistic continuity,* it is not necessary to assume prior creolization of AAE to account for them. Nor is it necessary to invoke decreolization to account for features found only in CECs and Gullah that are not attested in AAE. Even the creoles themselves started with some colonial (ultimately British and Irish) English inputs, to which several features associated with them may be traced, although not, of course, without invoking the kind of selection principles discussed in Mufwene (1990b, 1991c).

Let us focus now on Alleyne's conception of continuity. As things stand, there may at first seem to be no reason why his position should exclude a parallel conception of European linguistic continuity if, as he acknowledges himself (M. Alleyne n.d., 29), we are dealing here with new languages that have left room for old habits to continue. As I noted above while discussing Stewart's use of *continuity,* however, this extrapolation is ruled out by the fact that we are dealing here with Africans in the New World. They are the ones who shifted vernaculars and restructured the lexifier into a new variety. Plantation owners, overseers, and bond servants from the British Isles were not under the same pressure, even though their language varieties may have been affected by the emergence of AAE, Gullah, and CECs. Also, the lexifiers of these new vernaculars were akin to the colonial nonstandard varieties spoken by the Europeans, except that these lexifiers were spoken by the Africans who had arrived earlier (during roughly the first fifty years) and had interacted more intimately with the Europeans. This was the case before racial segregation was legally instituted around 1720 in the Carolinas (Wood 1974a). So, the claim of European continuities parallel to African continuities does not seem justified, at least in these particular European-African contact situations.

Continuities from Which African Groups?

The above clarification does not resolve the question of the diachronic interpretation of *linguistic continuity* for AAE, Gullah, and CECs. In general, New World Africans came from various linguistic groups. While many of the semantic and morphosyntactic structures identified as non-European *do* have parallels in *some* African languages, the question remains whether they are continuities for all, or most, African languages (which would then justify generic reference to them). Do they correspond to what Alleyne claims is a "common African substratum"? Note, for instance, that not all African languages are isolating. The Bantu languages (claimed since Turner 1949 to have influenced African-American language varieties in some ways) are agglutinative. If the fact that Kwa languages are isolating played a role in determining the isolating morphosyntax of Gullah and CECs, would it be adequate to describe this characteristic as an African rather than a Kwa continuity?

Unfortunately, even this supposition is open to debate. Assuming for discussion's sake (like Stewart 1962; and Dillard 1972) some sort of African monogenesis for Atlantic creoles, and AAE in particular, note that the Kwa area lies outside the "Upper Guinea coast" (from Senegambia to Liberia) identified by Hancock (1980a, 1986b) as the cradle of Guinea Coast Creole English, which, he claims, has contributed significantly to Atlantic English creoles.[8]

Even if Mande languages are isolating to some extent, Kru and West-Atlantic languages (all spoken in the Senegambia-Liberia area) differ somewhat from Kwa languages (spoken from the southeast of Ivory Coast to the southwest of Nigeria). For instance, Kru languages still have a derivational morphology, and the morphology of their verbs varies according to aspect and tense. West-Atlantic languages are still reminiscent of the Bantu nominal class system, for instance when nouns are modified by other nouns. In these cases they trigger class affixes (attached to the delimiters or modifiers) reminiscent of the Bantu concordial system. Further, they have a pronominal system that varies according to mood, aspect, and syntactic function (see Sauvageot 1981). These are features that Kwa languages either do not have or carry only to a limited extent.

Even the Kwa languages vary among themselves. As noted in Mufwene (1986c), the Eastern Kwa subgroup, to which Yoruba belongs, differs from the Western Kwa subgroup, most often cited in the literature as representative of the Kwa family, in having an infinitive and a gerund, as well as deverbal nouns, that are clearly marked morphologically (Bamgbose 1971; Awoyale 1983). Thus they are not absolutely isolating. Western and Central Kwa languages also differ from their Eastern Kwa counterparts in the way they position the possessive noun phrase (Heine 1976). In the former group (which includes Ewe and Twi), the possessive NP precedes the head noun (as in English genitive constructions), whereas in the latter group it follows the head noun, as in Bantu languages, though it seems to need no particular marker.[9]

If continuity explains the resemblance of some features of AAE, Gullah, and CECs to (Western) Kwa languages, then some other explanation is obviously needed for the selection of these (Western) Kwa features over those of, for example, Mande and West-Atlantic languages. The very principle of selection is tantamount to denying the assumption of simple continuity for Africans

other than the Kwas (Mufwene 1985), which is a denial of the common African
substratum assumed by Alleyne (1980; see Mufwene 1991d, 1992a).

Continuities and Selection

Many other examples could be invoked, but they would make basically the
same point. We may thus focus on the question of whether the fact that it is
rather inadequate to speak of African continuities unrestrictively invalidates
the substratist position of Alleyne (1980) and others. To counter the above observations, it could be argued, for instance, that language diversity on the West
African coast is not in itself a serious problem. Under the African monogenetic
hypothesis, it could well be assumed that as the original (Portuguese) pidgin
or maybe Lingua Franca spread along the West African coast and relexified
(e.g., in being converted to WAPE), some linguistic groups may have been
more influential and some features of their speech may have been adopted later
on by speakers of other languages, particularly by slaves in the New World.
The kinds of factors associated with markedness in Mufwene (1991c)—for example, salience, semantic transparency, and typological kinship—are relevant
here, as are other factors to which the literature has traditionally paid more
attention, such as the demographic significance of a group (also considered in
Mufwene 1991c, 1992a) and its prestige. Worth keeping in mind here is an analogue of population geneticists' notion of the "founder principle" (Mufwene
1990b, 1991d, 1993a), according to which much of what is shared by a population may have been predetermined by the makeup of the original "founder"
population. That is, in many ways it might have been more cost-effective to
maintain original features of the new vernacular than to modify them, even for
simplicity's sake.

Incidentally, although Alleyne questions the validity of this monogenetic hypothesis (1971, 169–70; 1980, 144), he points to the particular influence of
the Senegambia area, locus of the original European-African contacts, where
mostly West-Atlantic and Mande languages are spoken, as well as to the influence of the Gold Coast area, where Western and Central Kwa languages are
spoken and where a number of trade posts were created by the British, the
Dutch, and the Portuguese (1980, 146–47). He emphasizes the role of Mande
languages such as Bambara and Mandinka (which share some features with
Kwa languages—in contrast with the Bantu family—e.g., plural marking with
a third-person plural pronoun), the Akan languages (Twi, Ashanti, and Fanti),
and Ga, Ewe, and Yoruba among the other Kwa languages (1980, 147). The

importance of these groups varied from colony to colony in the New World, depending on the proportion of the slave population they represented.

Ignoring the conflict between this picture (with emphasis on West Africa) and the one that follows from the lexical statistics of Africanisms in Gullah (Turner 1949, in which Kongo contributions appear to be significant), it is worthwhile noting again that what Alleyne presents leads ultimately to the kind of position assumed in Mufwene (1985, 1986c). That is, where it did occur, substrate influence must have operated selectively, regulated by the linguistic and nonlinguistic factors mentioned above.

For the vast majority of the settings in which pidgins and creoles developed, substrate influence must have applied selectively from alternatives available in the multitude of languages spoken by the slaves. This observation applies chiefly to the critical stages of the formation of these languages. Since there must have been determinative substrate influence (Mufwene 1992a), the preference of, for instance, Kwa-like features over West-Atlantic-like alternatives can be attributed to the hypothesis that the former features may be less marked and less taxing on the language faculty or, simply, on the population in the contact situation.

Thus, the absence of Bantu morphosyntactic features in Atlantic creoles is a function not only of the chronology of European-African contacts but also of perhaps some sort of degree of markedness in the kinds of distinctions and constructions involved (Mufwene 1992a). As noted in Mufwene (1986c, 1988a, 1990a, 1991c), even Bantu-based creoles such as Kikongo-Kituba and urban Lingala selected a simpler morphosyntax when there was variation either in the lexifier or among the languages in contact. This is more obvious in the case of Kikongo-Kituba, since the verb conjugation pattern of Kikongo-Kimanyanga, its lexifier, contains inconsistencies and some of the Bantu languages in contact with it do not seem to have a (complete) subject-agreement system. These aspects of its structure were changed on the model of other, simpler or more regular, alternatives, which are sometimes available also in the lexifier itself.

Coming back to Atlantic creoles, even though the Yorubas in the New World are said to have been as influential as the Akans,[10] generally CECs seem to have selected the Akan-like system over the Eastern Kwa–like system, especially where inflections and derivational morphology are concerned. The features that may be related to Yoruba are generally those that may also be related to Akan languages. Where the Akan languages and Yoruba differ, the Akan features seem to have prevailed, although this observation is not without exceptions. Thus, like the Akan languages, Gullah and CECs generally prepose the possessive NP to the head noun (instead of postposing it) and have no (morphological) finite/nonfinite distinction (Bickerton 1984; Mufwene 1991b; Mufwene and Dijkhoff 1989).

On the other hand, as Mufwene shows (1991c, 1992a), the fact that many of the selections have analogues, if not models, in some of the nonstandard varieties of the lexifier itself bears significantly on the substrate hypothesis.[11] Thus, double modals in AAE and Gullah, as well as combinations such as *bin kyan* 'could' and *bin mos* 'had to' in CECs, are as much a consequence of the loss of the infinitive in these varieties (under the determinative influence of Kwa languages) as of the existence of double modal structures (e.g., *might could*) in nonstandard varieties of the lexifier. This state of affairs affects how we may speak of continuities, since it seems that some African continuities would not have prevailed without the complicity of the lexifier itself.

Even at the phonological level—at which, according to Alleyne, African continuities seem to have been best preserved—the same principle of selection must have applied. Not all African languages lack closed syllables. According to Bernd Heine (1976), Kwa languages split into two groups in this regard: the Western and Central Kwa languages do not seem to have closed syllables, and the Eastern Kwa languages do. Even some Bantu languages have closed syllables, though the final consonant is normally a nasal or liquid consonant, contrary to the common assumption that their canonical syllabic structure is (C)V. I can cite among these Kiteke, Kisakata, and my own native Kiyansi, all of which belong in the Bantu subgroup B. Hence the often claimed predilection for open syllables in Atlantic creoles cannot be a general African, nor a general Kwa, continuity. If anything, its common occurrence in Atlantic creoles may be explained by some principles of phonological markedness, owing to the fact that many languages whose features were in competition while these new vernaculars were developing had either only open syllables or a predominant proportion of open syllables. The dominance of this pattern would have increased the frequency of word pronunciations with open syllables and helped these variants prevail over alternative pronunciations. As a matter of fact, words claimed to have lost their closed syllables, compared with their etyma, often have alternative pronunciations that are like their etyma,[12] just as there are several words with only the closed-syllable pronunciation (e.g., *dead* 'die, dead'; *sik* 'sick'; *taak/talk* 'talk'; *back* 'back'; and *lef* 'leave'). I will not elaborate on the principle of markedness here, since it is not central to the main concern of this paper.

To be sure, some of the sounds that have been attributed to the African substratum, such as the sporadic labiovelar stops and bilabial fricatives in Gullah, are marked segments even among African languages, in that they are attested in only a few languages. The fact that they are rather sporadic in Gullah and CECs (see Mufwene 1985 for Gullah), however, is equally significant. While they could have been continuities for speakers of some African languages (such as Mende, Yoruba, Hausa, Efik, and Twi), for many Africans these sounds were just as novel as the new words they had to acquire. *African continuity* could not make sense except under the more restricted and selective interpretation of *continuity* from *some* African languages and for speakers of these particular languages. Note that labiovelar stops, for example, exist only as variants of other pronunciations (e.g., *very well* pronounced as either [vɛɪ wɛl] or [βɛɪ βɛl], or half-and-half in Gullah). This indicates that substrate linguistic features marked either because they were unusual or difficult or used by a tiny minority did not stand a good chance of being selected by the entire community of speakers.

Implications for the Substrate Hypothesis

I must emphasize that the above charitable, qualified interpretation of *African continuity* is not in itself a denial of the hypothesis that AAE, Gullah, and CECs have been influenced by some African languages. Elsewhere (Mufwene 1992a, 1993a) I discuss how such influence must be interpreted. Basically, African languages influenced AAE, Gullah, and CECs in determining those features that distinguish them from other English creoles that bear no African linguistic influence, more or less in the same way that Melanesian languages converged to create English creoles (more commonly referred to as pidgins) that differ from Atlantic creoles (Mufwene 1990b).

Such differentiating features need not originate in African languages. They may simply be variants in the lexifier that happened to converge with features of some substrate languages; for instance, the selection of *doz* in Guyanese and *duhz* in Gullah (pronounced with a schwa) as a habitual marker, the extension of the continuative/durative marker *a* as a habitual marker in Guyanese, the postnominal use of *dem* as a plural marker in Jamaican and Guyanese, or the introduction of relative clauses with a complementizer-like *what* or *weh* in AAE, Gullah, and CECs. The habitual markers have a partial model in the English emphatic *does* + verb construction, which has a habitual interpretation with nonstative verbs, and in the extension of the progressive verb + *-ing* for habits. Why exactly the same features were not selected into all Atlantic creoles is a question that future research will have to address, taking into account ecological ethnolinguistic conditions that have influenced the genesis of each creole.

On the other hand, some differentiating features may reflect exclusively African substrate influence. As Charles Gilman notes (1986), some of these features are quite widespread among African languages, such as the use of a verb meaning "to surpass" to indicate the comparative or superlative for adjectives and the expression of the notions "very much" and "too much" with the same term, usually one meaning "excessive." [13] These are indeed the kinds of features that can indisputably be called general African continuities. The reality remains, however, that they are only a small proportion (Mufwene 1993a) of the features that can be claimed to be African continuities only in the qualified sense stated above.

Spatial Continuities

The spatial interpretation of *linguistic continuity* as the primary, rather than secondary, one is my second charitable misinterpretation. I call it a misinterpretation only because, as I noted earlier, the term *continuity* has been used since Herskovits primarily in the diachronic sense. Strictly speaking, all I am doing is selecting a particularly adequate reading of the term. Misinterpretation or not, this view of continuities among AAE, Gullah, and CECs raises questions only when the notion of decreolization is appended to it.

Even if some of the features formerly used by William Stewart (1967, 1968, 1969a) and Dillard (1972) to argue for the putative pidgin/creole origin of AAE can now also be used to suggest a direct ancestry from nonstandard dialects of English in the British Isles (see D'Eloia 1973; and Schneider 1982, 1983, 1989, in particular), there is little evidence yet that disputes the fact that some aspects of AAE grammar are indeed very similar to those of Gullah and CECs. The following features (among others) attested as variable ones in AAE have correlates in Gullah and CECs:

1. Nominal plurality is sometimes formed with *them* (e.g., *them chickens, them boys*) almost as in Gullah, although in the basilect of Gullah the suffix *-s* is typically missing. There is also similarity with CECs, even though plurality and definiteness are dissociated in their *di* + N + *dem* construction: for example, *di bway dem* 'the boys.' All three varieties also have an associative plural in which, typically, *an' dem* or simply *dem* follows a proper name, as in *Larry (an') dem* 'Larry and his associates/friends/family.'

2. The possessive NP is often simply preposed without a possessive inflection to the head noun, as in *Da' Jean sister* 'That's Jean's sister.'[14]
3. In some idiolects of both Gullah and AAE the relativizer *what* is invariant (e.g., *The man what own the land* and *everything what he say*); and in some relative clauses there is often a gap in the position of the subject relative NP (e.g., *this here is one family eat anything,* or *this da young man come here last week* [Smith 1973; Mufwene 1986b]). Compare the following Jamaican Creole sentences from B. L. Bailey (1966):
   a. *Di dentis we a go pul mi tuut kom.*
      'The dentist who will pull my tooth has come.'
   b. *Jan fain di mango we Kieti ena haid.*
      'John [has] found the mango which/that Katie was hiding.'
   c. *Enibadi nuo mi wi help yu.*
      'Anybody that knows me will help you.'
4. The marker *done* is preposed to the verb (unmarked or in past tense or past participle inflection) for perfect (e.g., *I done ate when John come; I done tell/told you the joke; I done done/did it.*
5. The marker *bin* is preposed to the verb, sometimes in combination with *done* (as in *I bin done read that book*), for anterior tense in AAE, Gullah, and CECs or for remote past in AAE.[15]
6. The copula is most absent in AAE just in those environments where Gullah and CECs do not need one (especially before predicative adjectives and in durative and prepositional constructions (Mufwene 1983c, 1992a; Holm 1976, 1984; Baugh 1980; Winford 1992). From a slightly different perspective, the copula occurs (in full or contracted form) mostly where an equative verb is needed in creole grammar—that is, before a predicative NP. In this paper I treat the AAE and Gullah progressive suffix *in'* as the counterpart of the durative markers *de* and *a* in CECs, with the difference that it is a verbal suffix and the others are preverbal free morphemes. I assume that no copula is missing in constructions such as *he workin'* 'he is working,' because, at least for part of the AAE, Gullah, and CEC systems, the sentence may be simply expanded into NP + predicate phrase, with no requirement that the predicate phrase be headed by a verb (Mufwene 1990a, 1992c), as long as the form *workin'* is not considered fully verbal. The same is also true of *gon* + verb constructions, where, based on Labov 1972 (86), the averaged rate of "copula deletion" before *gon* for the Jets and Thunderbirds (inner-city gangs) is 90 percent. Here, I treat *gon,* itself a further grammaticized form of the verbal marker *goin'/gonna,* as the counterpart of Gullah

go + verb or Jamaican *a go* + verb constructions, in which no copula is expected. The *a* that occurs in *a go* in Jamaican is the locative preposition *a* (Mufwene 1984), which has been grammaticized for the durative function. By the same token, *a go* is basically a durative motion construction that has been grammaticized for future in preverbal position.

7. The preferred interpretations (or potential ambiguities) of morphosyntactically undelimited predicates vary depending on whether they are stative or nonstative. Thus, *John sick* has a preferred concomitant interpretation, but *John run home* has a preferred past interpretation, unless the discourse context suggests otherwise in both cases, as in *John always sick/run home*, which warrants a habitual interpretation.

8. The tense system seems in many respects to be a relative system (Mufwene 1983a), though not consistently (Mufwene 1992b). As in the case of *John sick* cited above, the interpretation of a construction such as *John workin'* varies depending on whether the reference time of the discourse is past, as in *John workin' yesterday* or *John workin' when Mary come/came in,* or concomitant, as in *John workin' every time I see him* (which is ambiguous between timeless habit and past habit) or *John workin' now* (Mufwene 1983c, 1992b).

9. AAE, Gullah, and CECs all use *say,* typically pronounced [sɛ], as a complementizer, mostly for (quotative) reported speech (see Mufwene 1989 for Gullah).

There are, of course, several significant differences between AAE (Gullah) and CECs, some of which are noted in Mufwene (1983c). Such differences exist between any related languages, however, and can be overlooked here. More relevant for this paper is the fact that the similarities enumerated above do not in themselves prove that AAE developed from an erstwhile pidgin or creole. Schneider's (1989) view that AAE has changed little from Earlier AAE, as evidenced by the WPA Slave Narratives, highlights another aspect of the sociolinguistic makeup of AAE, Gullah, and CECs that has generally received little attention (even though it is acknowledged by Alleyne 1971, 180; 1980, 184–85), namely, that several lects of these language varieties may have always existed from their beginnings as vernaculars in the New World.

Along the same line, Mufwene (1991a, 1991e) shows that Gullah's basilect has not changed over the past fifty years, a period during which factors typically associated with decreolization (e.g., mass education, mass media, and greater socioeconomic mobility) should have converged to yield the greatest effect. Katherine Mille's comparison (1990; written after Mufwene 1991a) of strategies for time reference in today's Gullah and in Ambrose Gonzales's literary representation of the variety at the turn of the century suggests more stability in Gullah than might have been expected from a decreolizing language.

In any case AAE, Gullah, and CECs often differ from Standard English and other varieties of American English in the very respects in which they differ from one another, such as in their pronominal systems, negators, pluralization of proper names, and durative constructions. It is one thing to argue that AAE did not develop from an erstwhile pidgin and/or creole or that Gullah is not more decreolized than CECs; it is another to claim that these language varieties are not related or that no spatial continuities exist between them. For all we know, virtually the same kinds of Europeans and Africans were involved in the contacts that led to these new vernaculars in various New World communities. The contacts occurred essentially in similar socioeconomic conditions, generally bringing European and colonial nonstandard varieties of English into contact with African languages. We can correlate regional differences primarily with differences in the superstrate-substrate numerical ratios, the substrate ethnolinguistic makeups, and, among other factors, the demographic significance of speakers of individual substrate languages (as discussed in Mufwene 1993a, 1992a for Gullah). But this variation has little, if anything, to do with whether or not these language varieties are related historically and typologically. The history of settlements in the New World and the identity of the languages that came into contact with one another in the seventeenth and eighteenth centuries are crucial to determining the historical connections among them and to assuming spatial continuities as Alleyne does.

Likewise, whether the features that AAE, Gullah, and CECs share—or in which they differ—have been selected from British or colonial English or from any other source is irrelevant to establishing, based on other factors, that there are similarities among all these varieties, just as there are differences. The history of colonial settlements in and economic exploitation of the New World in itself suggests a plausible spatial interpretation of *linguistic continuity* for the new vernaculars spoken primarily by people of African descent. Perhaps this interpretation may be extended to include white American nonstandard varieties of English too, at least regarding some features, since it was with speakers of nonstandard varieties of the lexifier that the Africans interacted (Krapp 1924). Such a generalization presupposes a more comprehensive study than that on which this paper is based, however, and must thus be left an open question.

This paper is about the interpretation of the term *linguistic continuity* with regard to AAE, Gullah, and CECs considered both individually and as a group. Two interpretations were proposed, one diachronic, equated with survival or retention, and the other synchronic-spatial, equated with common features that need not have followed from mother-daughter relationships among the language varieties.

In regard to the first interpretation, it appears that if there are some continuities from African languages, the most charitable interpretation of *linguistic continuity* must in most cases be "continuity from *some* (groups of) African languages" rather than "from African languages in general." The second, spatial, interpretation seems to be the least disputable one. AAE, Gullah, and CECs are typologically related in the Wittgensteinian family resemblance way. They share several features, which may have come independently from British and colonial nonstandard varieties of English or from some African languages. As suggested generally by Pieter Muysken (1983) and Sarah Gray Thomason (1983), many of the features may well be due to convergence of English and African linguistic features (see Mufwene 1992a for a more elaborate discussion), aside from, I must add, the way features normally are selected in a language contact situation. More detailed and sophisticated analyses with more extensive data from British and colonial nonstandard English and from African languages will help us assume more informed positions on the probable sources of many features.

Though the primacy accorded to the spatial interpretation of *linguistic continuity* represents a reversal of the traditional perspective since Herskovits (1941), I am not in any way suggesting that we should discard the diachronic interpretation as absolutely unwarranted in this context. Rather, my purpose here is to show that, given similarities in population contact scenarios in the different parts of the New World since the first European settlements and the increasing evidence that British and colonial English contributed to the structures of the new languages, we cannot rush into the diachronic interpretation until things have been better sorted out. The more fully we understand the role of Universal Grammar in the formation of new languages (Mufwene 1990a, 1991c), the more accurate a picture we can develop of the complementary contributions of the lexifier and the substrate languages to the structures of AAE, Gullah, and CECs. The position of this paper is thus a caution against hasty conclusions rather than outright condemnation.

Notes

An earlier version of this paper was presented at the Ninth Annual Language and Culture in South Carolina Symposium, held at the University of South Carolina, Columbia, April 26–27, 1985. Because several years elapsed between that presentation and this publication, I have tried to relate the original paper's contents to my later work. On the other hand, I could not entirely rewrite the paper without driving Michael Montgomery crazy. I thank Michael heartily for allowing me to make adjustments, and I apologize to readers for any apparent incoherences the updating may have created.

1. Mufwene (1992a) argues that even if some of the slaves in the original colony may have spoken a creole, the demographic and social conditions of the first fifty years, characterized by a lower proportion of Africans and intimate living conditions between Europeans and Africans (at least according to Wood 1974a), were not conducive to the preservation or development of a creole. Actual creolization must have started around 1720 with the passage to a predominant plantation economy, the massive importation of new slaves (to sustain the industrial growth and replace and increase the rapidly dying labor force), and the institutionalization of segregation. In these conditions, speakers of basically the same African languages and dialects of English settled under comparable conditions of plantation industry in various parts of the New World in the seventeenth and eighteenth centuries. It is plausible that contacts of more or less the same language varieties in similar conditions then led to similar results. Thus, similar linguistic features were "selected" (Gilman 1981; Goodman 1985; Mufwene 1986) because the similar conditions of the emergence of the new language varieties were conducive to similar outcomes. In connection with this assumption, the spatial interpretation of *linguistic continuity* is still conceivable. I return to this below.

2. Dillard (1972, 123) appears to be rather uncommitted to either position, but he claims that "a language 'belongs' to the group which speaks it, and African Pidgin English is in a real sense as African as ivory carvings." West African Pidgin English is assumed by him to be the ultimate ancestor of African-American English (British English dialects, Maritime Pidgin English, and African languages set aside).

3. In the most extreme position assumed by Derek Bickerton (1981, 1984), *innovation* denotes creation of grammatical features that supposedly do not exist in the languages in contact; for instance, in Gullah, the preverbal use of *duh* (pronounced with a schwa; apparently a reinterpretation of the English locative adverb *there*) as a durative/progressive marker, the preverbal use of *done* as a marker of perfect (in the sense of a past event that bears on the current state of affairs), or the preverbal use of *bin* (from English *been*) as a marker of anteriority. In light of Boretzky (1993), which is more consistent with the tradition in historical linguistics, innovation is not mutually exclusive with a model usage in the lexifier (English in the case of AAE, Gullah, and CECs) or some substrate languages then spoken by some Africans. Thus, *innovation* means novel usage even if it is partly patterned on a previous usage.

4. To be sure, as noted by Robert Chaudenson (1986, 1989, 1992) and Philip Baker (1990) for French creoles—and sociohistorical information on the British

New World suggests the situation must have been the same (Mufwene 1992a)—
the immediate lexifiers of creoles appear to have been the second-language varieties of the European languages spoken by the slaves during the first fifty years
or so of the (sub)tropical colonies. I am referring to slaves imported before the
industrialization of the plantation economy, which called for an enormous slave
labor force greatly disproportionate with the European population. Regardless of
this fact, most of the Europeans with whom the Africans communicated then and
during the plantation industry period (including overseers and indentured laborers)
spoke nonstandard English (Krapp 1924). Adding complexity to the scenario is the
fact that the English dialects imported to the New World varied among themselves.
Some were actually still emerging then—for example Irish English, which is itself
the result of language contact (Harris 1991). These varieties are largely responsible
for the specific features of the lexifiers selected in the ensuing creoles.

   5. I use the term *substratum* consistently with the literature discussed in this
paper, with reference to the languages of the subordinate group. For convenience,
I am ignoring both Morris Goodman's (1993) survey, which shows that the present
usage of the term in the anglophone creolist literature has diverged from its original usage in Romance philology, and Chaudenson's (1990) objection to the same
practice.

   6. See, for example, Wolfram (1980), Brunt et al. (1983), Wolfram and Christian (1976), Christian et al. (1988), and Montgomery (1989) for attestations in
white speech of features typically associated with the speech of descendants of
Africans in the New World. Various chapters in Cheshire (1991) also contain information relevant to the connection between, on the one hand, AAE, Gullah,
and CECs, and, on the other, British and colonial white nonstandard varieties of
English.

   7. I overlook Universal Grammar or the Bickertonian "language bioprogram"
because, as regards the genesis of AAE, Gullah, and CECs, I do not consider it
an alternative in competition with influences from the lexifier and the substrate
languages; rather, it is a body of constraints on the outcome of the selections made
by the inventors of the new language varieties (Mufwene 1990b, 1991c).

   8. This is the same area where WAPE allegedly started.

   9. According to at least one recent classification of Kwa languages, Ijo, which
is invoked in Mufwene (1986b) against sweeping generalizations about the Kwa
family, is no longer classified as Kwa (Jenewari 1989). This follows in part from
its divergence from the canonical Kwa family regarding several features. For instance, aside from being partly SOV—it is SVO when serial verb constructions
are involved (Kouwenberg 1991)—Ijo also has postpositions and gender markers.

   10. For instance, Cassidy traces some of the Gullah function words back to
Yoruba.

   11. This explains in part why the possessive NP follows the head noun in Hai-

tian Creole and other French creoles, a question addressed by, for instance, Guy Hazaël-Massieux (1982, 1984).

12. Interestingly, one might note a correlation here between the duration of exposure to the lexifier and the phonological restructuring of words. Most examples of (C)VCV restructuring have been cited from CECs of Suriname, particularly Saramaccan. These varieties developed in almost complete isolation from their English lexifier, due to the change in the superstrate population from English to Dutch, after only a brief exposure to English. This linguistic state of affairs is also consistent with claims that creoles have often selected features on which a significant proportion of the languages in contact converged (e.g., Muysken 1983; Thomason 1983).

13. "Quite widespread" is used here not in the sense that they are attested in almost every single language from Senegal to Angola but rather in the sense that they are attested across language family boundaries; perhaps more languages have them than do not. Such a situation is likely to offset other factors determining markedness.

14. Witness also the pronouns *you* and *they,* instead of *your* and *their* in Gullah, in this type of construction; for example, *Da' you sister* 'That['s] your sister' (Mufwene 1993c).

15. I am considering here particularly those constructions in which *bin* may not be claimed to be the past allomorph of the copula, as in *I bin sick.* Although it is often claimed that predicative adjectives have a verbal status, the fact that they are usually modified in the predicative function just like attributive adjectives—as in *Alvin (bin) sicker/more sick than Larry*—suggests that they are not used as verbs, only that AAE, Gullah, and CECs allow predicate phrases not headed by a verb (Mufwene 1990a, 1992b). See also Seuren (1986, 1987) for elaborate evidence on Sranan, though my position does not endorse the possibility of an underlying null copula (Mufwene 1988b).

Variation in the Use of the Auxiliary
Verb *da* in Contemporary Gullah

Tometro Hopkins

A major problem creolists faced in the 1960s and 1970s was how to explain the nature of the variation taking place in many creole languages presumed to be in the flux of developmental change (commonly called *decreolization*). It had become clear that existing theories accounting for change in creole languages were designed for static, homogeneous language systems and were incapable of handling the heterogeneous systems characteristic of creole languages. Out of their efforts there emerged the concept of the *creole continuum,* a continuum of speech varieties ranging from the system of the creole itself, referred to as the *basilect* variety, and extending to a targeted superstrate language system, called the *acrolect,* with intermediate varieties, *mesolects,* between the two.

The creole continuum has typically been viewed as a unilinear model (see, e.g., DeCamp 1971b; Todd 1974; Bickerton 1980a), according to which linguistic variation and its resultant change proceed only up the continuum, that is, away from the grammar of the creole and toward a well-specified linguistic target—the associated superstrate language such as English or French. In the last decade or so, however, some creolists have questioned this view of variation and change. For instance, William Washabaugh (1977) reports that linguistic variation in Providencia Island Creole is tridimensional. In one dimension change is directed toward the acrolect, the "typical" change in the creole continuum. In another dimension change is directed toward the mesolect. And in the third dimension change is directed toward an undetermined source and may result in the acquisition of a near-acrolectal form, a basilectal form, or a zero form.

The tridimensional variation and change in Providencia Island Creole, according to Washabaugh, is motivated by three types of social pressures: to acquire the acrolect, to vary the mesolect, and to avoid the basilect. Washabaugh considers avoidance of the basilect to be the primary reason for decreolization in Providencia Island Creole rather than social pressure to acquire the acrolect, which has traditionally been considered responsible for variation and change in decreolizing communities.

This paper describes another linguistic situation that may bring into question the directionality of variation and change in the creole continuum. The situation involves the use of the aspect auxiliary verb *da* in Gullah.[1] My research on the Gullah tense-aspect system reveals that some Gullah speakers use *da,* which is found in Gullah and other English-related creoles, in ways not previously reported for this auxiliary. The auxiliary has generally been viewed as a durative or continuative marker positioned before the main verb in finite rather than nonfinite clauses (see Thompson 1961; Bickerton 1975, 1980a; and Muysken 1981, among others).

Some Gullah speakers have been observed using the auxiliary *da* in finite and nonfinite clauses, however, as well as in semantic functions not limited to durative or continuative meaning but including perfective as well. I explain these various uses of the auxiliary *da* in Gullah by arguing that they represent a change that does not seem to be converging with English, the superstrate language and presumed linguistic target, but rather is proceeding toward an as-yet-undetermined target. My argument against the claim that the creole continuum is unilinear in nature begins by illustrating the functions of *da* in the prototypical creole.

The Creole Tense, Mood, and Aspect System

Among the most striking features of the creole grammar are the tense, modality, and aspect (henceforth TMA) auxiliaries (commonly called *markers* or *particles*). According to Derek Bickerton, "No matter if the phonological form of the markers varies—and it does—from one language to another, *the semantic area covered by the marker is either identical or close to identical,* even when you're dealing with creoles which have quite different linguistic affiliations, or when these creoles are separated by 6,000 miles of ocean" (1979a, 3; emphasis mine). This semantic similarity in the tense/aspect auxiliaries is also supported by Pieter Muysken, who notes that "we find in the Creole languages, which are only partially related to each other historically, and spoken in places widely distant from each other such as the Caribbean, the Gulf of Guinea, the Indian Ocean, South East Asia, and the South Pacific, pre-verbal particle systems that resemble each other closely" (1981, 181).

The creole TMA system consists of three types of auxiliaries (markers or particles), defined by Muysken as tense, mood, and aspect (1981, 182). According to R. W. Thompson (1961) the auxiliaries indicate durative (aspect), perfective (tense), and contingent or future (mood). Bickerton, on the other hand, describes them in his prototypical creole TMA system as anterior (tense), irrealis (mood), and nonpunctual (aspect).

The auxiliaries precede the main (uninflected) verb in finite clauses (e.g., main clauses or tensed subordinate clauses), and their order, should more than one occur, is fixed (see Bickerton 1979a; Muysken 1981). The anterior (tense) auxiliary will precede either an irrealis (mood) auxiliary or nonpunctual (aspect) auxiliary; likewise, an irrealis auxiliary will precede a nonpunctual auxiliary if both occur in the same verb phrase (Bickerton 1979a, 3).

The surface phonetic forms of the three types of auxiliaries are considered to share their cognate with the associated superstrate language to which the creole is lexically related. The aspect auxiliary in most English-related creoles is represented as *(d)e/(d)a/də* or any of its variants.[2] For instance, in Jamaican it is *a/da;* in Krio it is *dè;* in Sranan it is *(d)e;* in Guyanese Creole English it is *a;* and in Gullah it is spelled *də* or *da* (see Voorhoeve 1973; Alleyne 1980; Bickerton 1980a).

There has been some disagreement about the linguistic source of the aspect auxiliary *d(a)* and its variants in English-related creoles. Two opposing views have been proposed. One view argues for Afrogenesis as the linguistic source of this auxiliary verb in the creole grammar (see Turner 1949; Cassidy 1961a; Alleyne 1980). For instance, Lorenzo Dow Turner argues that the verb *da* in Gullah may have its origin in the Ibo verb *de,* and his data illustrate the structural and semantic similarities of the two verbs (1949, 214). A second view suggests an English origin. Salikoko Mufwene, for instance, argues that the durative markers *d(a)* in Jamaican and Guyanese creoles may have an English etyma, with *da* coming possibly from the Dorsetshire dialect in England and from the early English construction $a + V_{ing}$ (1986, 171–75). Whatever its phonetic shape or origin, it is generally held that the semantics of this aspect auxiliary are expressed the same way across creoles having both the same and different lexical stocks.

The aspect auxiliary is generally viewed by linguists as a durative or continuative marker. Bickerton describes it more distinctly as a nonpunctual marker. The semantics of this linguistic category include "habitual, iterative, and also continuative and progressive. Any action that is not a point action, a single action at a particular instant of time would be marked by a non-punctual marker" (1979a, 4). John Singler (1990b) points out that what Bickerton and others regard as nonpunctual in terms of the study of aspect is what Bernard Comrie (1976) classifies as imperfective (see also M. Alleyne 1980, in which the term *imperfective* is used for this auxiliary verb in the Afro-Creoles).

The semantic functions of the aspect auxiliary will be illustrated with data from Guyanese Creole English. As I pointed out above, the aspect auxiliary in Guyanese Creole English is *a* (phonetically [ə]). Bickerton states that "*a* marks both continuative and iterative verb phrases, and (for truly basilectal speakers at least) it does this irrespective of whether temporal reference is past or nonpast" (1975, 34). His examples illustrating these functions of *a* in Guyanese Creole English are given below (Bickerton 1975, 34).

Continuative nonpast:

1. *i se we yu a go wid bondl.*
   'He said, "Where are you going with that bundle?" '
2. *mi a kom back haptanuun.*
   'I'm coming back in the afternoon.'

Continuative past:

3. *di kuliman bin prapa fraikn di blakman—evribadi a wach aut de an nait fu si wa go hapn.*
   'The Indians were really afraid of the Negroes—everybody was watching out to see what would happen.'
4. *a beg me a beg dis bai nau se le i ker aut wan baks fu mi bka mi son na de hoom.*
   'I was literally begging this boy to carry out a box for me because my son isn't home.'

Iterative nonpast:

5. *dem na laan awi notn gud* [Interviewer: *wai?*] *dem a gyaf a an na laan awi notn.*
   'They don't teach us anything properly. [Why?] They gossip and don't teach us anything.'
6. *evri de mi a ron a raisfiil.*
   'Every day I hurry to the ricefield.'

Iterative past:

7. *dis a hapn an dat a hapn aal abaut a wizma, makenzi an so, bot awi—awi na bin gat no distoobans a bushlat nat ataal.*
   'This happened and that happened all around at Wismar, Mackenzie and so on, but we—we hadn't any disturbance in Bushlot at all.'
8. *evribadi bin gatu wach aut an evribadi a de aal abaut a rood, striit, dam.*
   'Everyone had to be on the watch and everyone used to be all over the place, on roads, streets, dams.'

In its semantic function as a nonpunctual marker, the aspect auxiliary is incompatible with stative (main) verbs. As Bickerton puts it, "One of the strongest rules in basilectal Guyanese Creole is that which restricts the use of *a* to non-stative verbs. . . . One seldom if ever encounters sentences such as **mi a no, *dem a waan,* 'I am knowing,' 'They are wanting' " (1975, 34).

Bickerton recognizes that there are examples that run counter to his claim. One he cites is the use of *a* with what most speakers would treat as a stative verb, the locative verb *de* (e.g., *a+de*) in sentence 8 above. But since *de* in his view indicates a temporary rather than a permanent state, "it may be that some speakers interpret its marker [-durative] as being fully equivalent to [-stative]" (Bickerton 1975, 35).

I view the use of *a* in sentence 8 as just another function of the auxiliary—as a habitual. Bickerton has pointed out that nonpunctual meaning encompasses habitual, iterative, continuative, and progressive situations. The problem that seems to arise in Bickerton's analysis is whether these meanings can apply only to nonstative verb senses. That is, in order for *a* to function as a nonpunctual marker with these meanings it must occur with nonstative propositions or somehow be interpreted as [-stative]. This view suggests that the aspect auxiliary is unacceptable with stative propositions. This paper argues that the aspect auxiliary in Gullah, and possibly other similarly related English creoles, can convey these meanings with nonstative as well as stative verb phrases. The aspect auxiliary *be* in English occurs with progressive, habitual, and iterative meanings with stative and nonstative verbs (Quirk et al. 1985; Mufwene 1984).

Before proceeding, let me point out that a problem of translation exists when one creolist examines data analyzed by other creolists. That is, not only must one try to provide an adequate description of the syntactic functions of grammatical features, one must do this by adhering as closely as possible to the meaning intended by the speaker involved. In some cases, there may not be an exact morpheme-by-morpheme equivalent in the superstrate language; in other cases, what may be considered characteristic of a particular grammatical feature in terms of its meaning may not be the case in another utterance of syntactic equivalence if this is not the meaning intended by the speaker. Bickerton warns against glossing creole structures with a morpheme-by-morpheme equivalent in the superstrate language. It may be that not all creole (basilectal) structures are necessarily distinct in function and meanings from equivalent structures in the superstrate language.

In his analysis, Turner (1949) shows how the aspect auxiliary *da* in Gullah may acquire any number of meanings, depending on the context.[3]

The Aspect Auxiliary *da* in Gullah

Turner describes the verb *da,* phonetically [də], as having "incomplete predication" and translates it as equivalent to English "to be." The verb *da* in Gullah functions as an aspect auxiliary and also as a copula. Turner gives the following account (1949, 213): "In Gullah the verb *də* 'to be' is used in a present, past, or even future sense, dependent upon the context. Most often it can be rendered in English by a present or past tense, and the action to which it refers may or may not be continuous. When *də* is used in a future sense, it is often followed by the progressive form of some other verb."

Turner illustrates the various functions and meanings of the verb *da* in Gullah with the following examples (1949, 213):[4]

9. *wɛn də delait, ai mek mi lo kači.*
   'When it is daylight, I make my low curtsy.'
10. *də gad wak.*
   'It is God's work.'
11. *dat də dɛbl we de da gi yu nau.*
   'That is the devil's way they are giving you now.'
12. *dɛm dɛ də kəmplen.*
   'Those there are complaining.'
13. *wat dɛm də gi yu?*
   'What are they giving you?'
14. *ai də ste dɛ.*
   'I am staying there.'
15. *nau di čilən də frɛt.*
   'Now the children are fretting.'
16. *sʌpm də kamin.*
   'Something is coming.'
17. *di katn də drap blasm.*
   'The cotton was dropping its blossom.'
18. *him bai də fiks fa di solǰa.*
   'His boy was fixing for the soldiers.'
19. *ən də him sew mi.*
   'And it was he who saved me.'
20. *di wʌl də gwain ʌpsaid daun.*
   'The world is going upside down.'
21. *ai no də agəs.*
   'I know it was August.'

22. *de se də gwain fal in an əs.*
    'They said it was going to fall in on us.'
23. *ɛwitiŋ də krai.*
    'Everything was crying.'
24. *mi də gwain gan.*
    'I am going to go.'
25. *dɛn yu də brag.*
    'Then you will brag.'

Turner argues in favor of a West African origin of Gullah *da,* contending that it resembles the Ibo *de,* a verb of incomplete predication meaning 'to be,' in function and meaning. He observes that Gullah *da* resembles the Ibo verb in phonetic shape, that both verbs function both as an auxiliary and as a copula, and that both share the meaning 'to be' (1949, 214).

Like the auxiliary in the prototypical creole TMA system, Gullah *da* is usually positioned before the main (uninflected) verb (e.g., *da* + V). In this function it typically expresses continuative or durative meaning, referring to a situation in progress or having duration. This is illustrated in sentences 11–15, 17–18, and 23 above.

While expressing duration may be its typical function as an aspect auxiliary, *da* in Gullah also expresses other meanings. Turner (1949, 225) states that the expression *ai də go* "may mean any of the following: 'I go,' 'I went,' 'I am going,' 'I was going,' 'I shall go,' or even 'I had gone.' " This means that *da* can mark durativity, futurity, perfectivity, and past temporal reference.

While the main verb typically occurs in its base (e.g., uninflected) form in both the prototypical creole TMA system and in Gullah, the auxiliary verb *da* sometimes precedes an inflected main verb, as illustrated in sentences 16 and 20, in which it occurs with a main verb inflected in *-ing* (i.e., *da* + V + *-ing*). This construction is similar to the English pattern of *be* + V + *-ing* to convey a progressive reality. Since the construction deviates from the prototypical creole construction, its presence in Gullah would normally be explained as a mesolectal pattern, representing a shift away from the Gullah basilectal system up the creole continuum toward its structural equivalent in English (i.e., *is coming, is going*).

Turner cites only a few instances of this pattern in Gullah, which suggests that it was a fairly recent development from the main construction, the use of *da* with uninflected verbs (i.e., *da* + V). More interesting is the fact that apparently only the action verbs *come* and *go* were inflected in *-ing* and took the auxiliary *da*. Another example from Turner showing *da* with an inflected main verb is the following (1949, 213):

26. *ɛnti də kʌmin bak?*
   'Is it not coming back?'

The Gullah use of *da* with the verb *go* + *-ing* is reflected in the verb *gwain* in examples 20, 22, and 24 above, in which *gwain* is presumably derived from *go* + *-ing*. This differs from the use of *da* with other lexical verbs in two ways. First, with other verbs, *da* functions as the primary auxiliary verb. With *gwain* it does this also (example 20), but it also combines with *gwain* to constitute an auxiliary verb phrase (examples 22, 24). Turner considers *da* + *gwain* to be equivalent to English *be going to,* a phrase Quirk et al. (1985) identifies as a semiauxiliary. Second, the construction *da* + V conveys progressive aspect, while the combination *da* + *gwain* in Gullah—as in 22 and 24—like *be going to* in English, indicates futurity, which is also reflected in the pattern *da* + V in sentence 25 above. In the latter example, *da* is equivalent to English *will*.

In its function as a copula, however, *da* in Gullah appears to be less expansive than *de,* its presumed substratal source in Ibo, or than *be* in English. Sentences 9–11, 19, and 21 show that as a copula *da* takes only noun complements. Ibo *de* can take noun, adjective, and adverb complements (Turner 1949, 214), as can the copula *be* in English.

Turner's observations of the auxiliary verb *da* in Gullah show a number of different semantic functions not previously reported for the aspect auxiliary verb in the creole prototypical TMA system. Other studies on the Gullah TMA system have followed Turner's, and some of their observations with respect to the aspect auxiliary will be discussed here.

Two decades after Turner, Irma Cunningham published her study of Gullah, a language she calls Sea Island Creole (1970, revised in 1992). Her observations on the verb *da* parallel Turner in some ways but not in others. Like Turner, she transcribes the auxiliary verb as [də] and defines it as a marker of progressive aspect. Unlike Turner, she restricts the use of *da* in this semantic function to present time reference. Cunningham's examples showing this function of *da* are given below (1992, 49–50).

27. *You də yent.*
   'You are kidding.'
28. *My head də hurt me.*
   'My head is hurting me.'

According to Cunningham, Gullah conveys present progressive aspect in either of two ways: the construction *da* + V or a verb by itself inflected in *-ing* (i.e., V_{ing}), but not the combination of the two (*da* + V + *-ing*). She explains her view as follows: "The present-progressive aspect markers are *da* and *-ing*.

These markers occur with transitives and non-transitives. *da* always precedes the verb; *-ing* always follows, thus resulting in the form, V_{ing}. The two aspect markers do not co-occur" (1992, 49). Thus, while Turner says that *da* + V_{ing} can occur in Gullah, Cunningham considers such structures ungrammatical. She illustrates the complementarity of the two patterns as follows (1992, 49):

29. a. *I still də look.*
       'I am still looking.'
    b. *I still looking.*
       'I am still looking.'

Cunningham considers these constructions synonymous but does not suggest on what basis a Gullah speaker would choose one over the other, whether a Gullah speaker uses both structures in free variation, or anything else about the nature of this variation in the Gullah verbal system—that is, whether it depends on linguistic or extralinguistic factors, or both, or whether the variation indicates some kind of (unidirectional) developmental change.

According to Cunningham, both *da* and *-ing* not only make a verb progressive, they also convey present time reference. Progressive aspect with past time reference is formed by the auxiliary *been* plus a verb inflected with *-ing* (e.g., *been* + V_{ing}) or the auxiliary *been* combined with an auxiliary *a* (presumably a reduced form of auxiliary *da*) plus the lexical verb (e.g., *been* + *a* + V). Cunningham's examples showing past progressive aspect are given below (1992, 50–51).

30. *When you call me, I beenə cook my dinner.*
    'When you called me, I was cooking my dinner.'
31. *I been driving one day.*
    'I was driving one day.'
32. *When we been living over yonder . . .*
    'When we were living over there . . .'

Cunningham illustrates present and past progressive aspect in Gullah with the following schema (1992, 51):

Present	Past
də + verb	*been* + *ə* + verb
verb + *-ing*	*been* + verb + *-ing*

There seems to be a discrepancy in Cunningham's description of present/past progressive aspect in Gullah, though. In one of her examples she glosses *da* as a past time rather than a present progressive, contrary to her claim about how *da* marks the verb only for present progressive aspect (1992, 50).

33. *[I] come back in see what he də do.*
    'I would come back in, to see what he was doing.'

Hence, Cunningham's observations of *da* in Gullah differ from Turner's in two ways. First, Cunningham considers *da* to be a marker of present time reference, while Turner considers it to be omnitemporal, capable of referring to situations either past or not, with the context of use being the determining factor. Second, Cunningham restricts the occurrence of auxiliary *da* to uninflected lexical verbs. In this case, she does not acknowledge that *da* occurs with inflected verbs in a pattern such as $^*da$ + V_{ing}. Turner, on the other hand, considers such structures (e.g., *da* + V_{ing}) permissible.

Other researchers have also examined the verb *da* in Gullah. In her dissertation, published thirty years after Turner's work and eight years after Cunningham's, Patricia Jones-Jackson (1978) describes the Gullah verb *da* in a variety of functions. Like Turner and Cunningham, she describes it as an auxiliary verb, or, as she terms it, a preverbal marker. To describe how it functions, Jones-Jackson uses the term *continuative* in the same way that Turner and Cunningham use *progressive*. Her examples of continuative *da* are as follows (1978, 50):[5]

34. *i də šek tetə.*
    'She is shaking potatoes.'
35. *də mʌŋki də hol.*
    'The monkey is holding on.'

Jones-Jackson states that *da* in its continuative function conveys present time reference only. She found no cases in which *da* as a continuative conveyed past time reference but observes that *da* also expresses iterativity. In illustrating this she shows that it can convey either present time or past time reference. Her examples of this are as follows (1978, 51):

36. *də fai də blez ndi tšimi.*
    'The fire is/was blazing in the chimney.'
37. *mi ɛn də dɔg də ries fə git də mit fə it.*
    'Me and the dog raced to get the meat to eat.'

Jones-Jackson also observes that auxiliary *da* sometimes conveys future time reference (1978, 51).

38. *i də go.*
    'He will go.'
39. *ai go dʌk n tro mʌŋgi dɔŋ.*
    'I will duck and throw the monkey down.'

She admits, however, that this use of *də* is atypical and that *go* generally conveys futurity in Gullah, even though—depending on the speaker's frame of reference, context, and intonation—*da* can do so as well. She also notes that *da* can be used as a copula, as illustrated in the following sentences (1978, 52):

40. *i də ske.*
    'She's scared.'
41. *i də hom.*
    'He is home.'

According to Jones-Jackson, these sentences show that *da* as a copula (i.e., main) verb can be followed by an adjective or a noun complement. In my view, however, the complement in sentence 41 appears to be an adverb rather than a noun. Jones-Jackson also recognizes this function of *da* (1978, 52).

42. *i də dɛ.* (*də* stressed here)
    'It is there.'

Let us sum up the foregoing observations on *da* in Gullah. The verb *da* can function as either an auxiliary verb or a main verb. As an auxiliary verb, *da* typically conveys continuative or progressive aspect, with either nonpast (e.g., present and future) or past time reference. As a main verb, *da* functions as a copula and can be followed by noun, adjective, and adverb complements. The functions and meanings of the Gullah verb *da*—as an aspect auxiliary—are unlike *da* in the creole prototypical TMA system in many respects, but not unlike those of the English verb *be*. According to Turner's observations, the Gullah verb *da* is not unlike the Ibo verb *de* in function and meaning.

New Observations on the Verb *da*

During the course of my research I observed that the Gullah verb *da* functions much as earlier researchers found—as both an auxiliary and a main verb. On the other hand, I found that some aspects of these functions differ markedly from those noted previously. The auxiliary verb *da* exhibits several additional semantic functions, as this section describes.

The Speakers and the Data

The contemporary Gullah data used in this essay come from six individuals from the South Carolina Sea Islands, identified according to their geographical region as follows: E. R., from Yonges Island; G. B., from Hilton Head Island;

S. B., Hilton Head Island, E. H., Daufuskie Island; D. G., Wassaw Island; and R. B., St. Helena Island.

The speakers, all female, ranged from 69 to 109 years in age. Their average education was three years of primary school. Essentially, all were homemakers. On a few occasions the speaker from Yonges Island had worked on a farm as a day laborer. All the individuals were native to and permanent residents of their respective islands, and none had spent significant time elsewhere.

My data are part of a larger corpus collected during field research in the late 1970s and early 1980s in the South Carolina and Georgia Sea Islands and adjacent mainland areas. The data consist of 45 minutes of spontaneous conversations and narratives that I recorded from each speaker while living with them and participating in their everyday activities. As a participant, I observed the speakers and listened to their speech in natural settings. I was thus able to record many uses of masculine gender for individuals of feminine gender and the variable use of TMA particles.

The Verb da *as an Auxiliary*

As an auxiliary verb, *da* (phonetically [də]) occurs before the uninflected form of the verb as a preverbal marker, or particle, to use terms often employed in creole studies to identify the tense and aspect functions of this auxiliary in the creole grammar. The auxiliary verb *da* is considered by both Turner and myself to have only aspectual functions. It is semantically empty for tense reference (this view differs from those of Cunningham and, to some extent, Jones-Jackson, who see it as occurring only in the present tense and thus as having de facto tense reference).

Turner and Cunningham call the auxiliary *da* in Gullah a (preverbal) progressive marker, and Jones-Jackson says it is a "preverbal marker" used as a "continuative." These terms seem to reflect the different ways this verb has been interpreted in the Gullah verbal system. Before I go on to discuss these terms, let me provide some observations on the various ways the verb *da* is used as an auxiliary.

The auxiliary verb *da* sometimes is used to denote an event in progress, as shown in sentences 43–47 below.

43. *sɛ brata də pen de. sɛ, yea, sɛ hi də pen de nau.* (EH)
    '[She] said brother [nickname] is painting. [She] said, yeah, [she] said he is painting there [in the house] now.'
44. *ai də tɛl yu nau yu də tɛl mi. ai də tɛl yu æn yu də tɛl mi.* (GB)

'I am telling you, now you are telling me. I am telling you and you are telling me.'

45. *ši sɛ wɛl sista ši de in yir æn ai də han yu al abaut.* (SB)
    'She said, "Sister is in here [the bedroom] and I am hunting you all about [looking all around for you]." '

46. *ɛvri gaad de də git hol a dɛm fuud stæmp ples æn al.* (ER)
    'Every god [person] there [at the place where one obtains food stamps] was getting a hold of those food stamps and all [other food items that were given out at the food stamp place].'

47. *wat dæt man də han mi fa? æn no di man də han fə ɛm fə diil in diz ruuts hir.* (GB)
    'What is that man hunting me for [Why is that man looking for me]? And [he] knew [that] the man was hunting [looking] for him to deal in these roots here [in order to do some root work for him].'

These examples show that the auxiliary verb *da* conveys progressive action in Gullah similar to the English verb *be,* is used in verb phrases with uninflected verbs (e.g., without the *-ing*), and reflects either past time or present time reference. In these examples, the Gullah auxiliary *da* is not unlike a continuative or durative marker in the creole basilectal system, its typical function.

Most studies of the Gullah verb *da* have dealt essentially with its auxiliary function as a progressive marker (equivalent to English *-ing* in *walking, coming,* etc.). The patterning of *da* with inflected and uninflected main verbs has generally been attributed to Gullah speakers' attempt to acquire the English progressive construction, which is formed by the auxiliary verb *be* plus a main verb with the *-ing* suffix. The occurrence of the English verb form inflected with the *-ing* without the auxiliary verb *be* (cited by Turner and Cunningham and found in my data as well) suggests that the development of the English suffix *-ing* precedes the auxiliary verb *be* when Gullah speakers acquire English progressive constructions. This would thus represent the linguistic development in which *da* + V constructions converge toward English and assume the structure *be* + V + *-ing* in its final output.

As I said earlier, Cunningham argues that two patterns (the auxiliary *da* with an uninflected main verb, and a main verb inflected with *-ing* without *da*) are equivalent and that either can be used to express progressive aspect in Gullah. Because she provides no examples in which the auxiliary verb *da* plus the inflected form of the verb combine to convey a situation in progress, her data seem to suggest that this is not possible in Gullah. Turner observed that auxiliary *da* was sometimes combined with an inflected verb form, a construction that occurred only with the action verbs *come* and *go*. My observations resemble Turner's. Some examples of this use are the following:

48. *æn den di flu də goin raun tu, yu no.* (ER)
    'And then the flu is going around too, you know.'
49. *æn ši də goin.* (EH)
    'And she was going [attending school].'

Like Turner, I found this pattern to be associated with verbs of action like *go*. This might give reason to suspect that the English inflection *-ing* is not productive in Gullah. The lack of examples of it on other action verbs in previous studies suggests that *going* and *coming* may have been acquired in their inflected forms and thus represent special cases. While there may be some justification for believing this, there is evidence to warrant another explanation. I will return to this later.

Although he derives the verb from Ibo, Turner equates auxiliary *da* with the English verb *be* in both function and meaning. Just as *be* occurs in English with a verb inflected in *-ing* to convey progressive aspect, Gullah *da* also occurs with verbs that are identically inflected to convey the same thing.

The use of the *-ing* form of the verb combined with the auxiliary *be* to express the progressive is characteristic of English; but in Gullah, as illustrated above, the progressive is usually conveyed by the auxiliary *da* combined with the base form of the verb. If the Gullah verbal system is changing and the inflected form of the main verb is being acquired to convey progressive aspect, then is the auxiliary verb *da* also changing, being replaced with auxiliary *be?*

In the corpus examined for this paper, only two examples show the construction *be* + V + *-ing,* but some of my data show what might be a transitional phase in the use of *be* with *da*. Consider, for example, the following:

50. *æn ai taat hi wa də fan.* (EH)
    'And I thought he was funning [joking].'

This example shows auxiliary *da* used with the English verb *was*, a form of *be*, along with the uninflected main verb. This construction suggests that Gullah speakers may be acquiring the English auxiliary *be*. Note that this is not accompanied by the inflected form of the verb; a form of *be* seems to have been acquired on an already existing *da* + verb structure.

I found no instances in which *be* (or an inflected form of it—*is, are,* or *am*) occurred with the auxiliary verb *da* and the inflected form of the main verb. The patterns used to convey the progressive in Gullah included *da* + V, *da* + V + *-ing,* V + *-ing,* and *be* + *da* + V; but not *be* + *da* + V + *-ing.* The nonoccurrence of the last one may be due to the fact that the same semantic function is not usually expressed using two, possibly opposing, patterns. That is, the Gullah *da* + V structure plus thc English *be* + V + *-ing* are both used for progressive aspect. The remaining patterns (*da* + V + *-ing*, V + *-ing*, and *be* + *da* + V) may represent a possible developmental sequence showing the gradual acquisition of the English progressive pattern *be* + V + *-ing*, a development that is generally described as unidirectional in which the creole structure *da* + V converges with the construction *be* + V + *-ing*, its presumed model in the associated superstrate language.

There are other situations, however, in which a form of the English auxiliary verb *be* (*ain't*) is used with the Gullah auxiliary *da*.[6]

51. *hi en də han fə mi; šo en də han fə mi.* (GB)
    'He isn't hunting for me; [he] sure isn't hunting for me.'
52. *ai no dæt æn ai en də taak wat ai hir kaz ai bin wit dɛm.* (GB)
    'I know that, and I am not talking [about] what I heard because I was with them.' (The speaker was letting me know here that she witnessed the information she gave me and that it was not based on hearsay.)

Gullah speakers use *ain't* to negate *da* + V patterns, although never when *da* co-occurs with an inflected form of the verb, such as **en* + *da* + V + *-ing;* nor were structures observed in which *ain't* occurred as a negator along with a nonnegated form of *be*, such as **en* + *be* + *da* + V + *-ing*.

We have observed some of the ways Gullah speakers use auxiliary *da* for progressive aspect, but this is not the only way *da* functions as an auxiliary verb in Gullah. Consider the following examples:

53. *ɛvribadi də wek.* (SB)
    'Everybody [on the island] works/is working.' (In uttering this statement the speaker was informing me that everybody on the island now works outside the home, whereas in the past this was not the case.)
54. *dis taim a yiə wi də ho . . . wi də pik piiz.* (RB)
    '[During] this time of the year, we used to hoe . . . we used to pick peas.'

Sentences 53–54 show that *da* can convey habitual aspect. Note that this use of *da*, like the progressive, denotes situations in the present or in the past. The auxiliary *da* can also express an iterative situation.

55. *ai gaan on dæt tiin, yu no, fə go . . . stida go ap, ai gaan raun di wan wat kam daun æn ai sii dæt tiŋ də šʌb, də šʌb; wail ai waz trai fə go di tiŋ jis šʌb, də šʌb.* (SB)

'I went on that thing [the escalator in Kresge Department Store], you
know, for going up . . . [in]stead [of] going up, I went around [to] the
one that came down and I saw that thing [the escalator] shoving, shoving;
while I was trying to go [up] the thing [was] just shoving, shoving.'

In this example, the speaker, in commenting on the movement of the escalator, refers to a series of actions. Because the incident took place in the past,
da has past time reference. Other data from my study also suggest that *da* as
an iterative auxiliary can have nonpast temporal reference. The example above
also shows the use of *da* in a nonfinite verb phrase (*da shob*), although some
creolists argue against the presence of nonfinite structures in the creole grammar (see Bickerton 1980a; Mufwene 1991b). Another example showing the use
of *da* in a nonfinite structure is the following:

56. *its tʌf gʌl wit dɛm šʌbəl æn tiŋz də dig dɛm ol, put dɛm triiz daun in di
pain tri so de plan pain tri . . .* (ER)
'It's tough, girl, with those shovels and things digging [to dig] those old,
[to] put [putting] those trees down in the pine tree so they could plant
pine trees . . .'

These observations on the Gullah auxiliary *da* show that it can express an
event in progress and also events that are habitual and iterative. But how do
we classify these different functions of *da?* By what term(s) do we define the
semantic functions of this auxiliary verb in the Gullah verbal system?

Clearly, *da* cannot be defined as a progressive auxiliary verb alone, as Turner
and Cunningham describe it, since we have seen *da* used in habitual and iterative contexts. My data confirm and supplement the findings of Jones-Jackson,
who shows *da* functioning as a continuative and iterative marker.

In his observations on Guyanese Creole English, Bickerton describes the
functions of the auxiliary verb *a*—which is presumed to be similar in form,
function, and meaning to the Gullah auxiliary verb *da*—as continuative and
iterative (and possibly habitual). He says that "*a* marks both continuative and
iterative verb phrases" (1975, 34) and classifies this auxiliary verb, which he
considers to express a universal property of creoles, as a nonpunctual marker.

Comrie (1976) employs the term *imperfective,* which he uses to embrace the
semantic concepts habitual and progressive, as well as the combinations habitual with progressive and habitual with perfective. Alleyne uses *imperfective*
in his description of the aspect auxiliary in Afro-creoles. Before determining which term is appropriate to describe the functions of the auxiliary *da* in
Gullah, let us consider another of its functions.

In his analysis of the creole verb system, Bickerton distinguishes between stative and nonstative verb phrases. The auxiliary verb *a* is restricted to nonstative verbs because it functions as a continuative and iterative marker. The same semantic restrictions appear to hold for the Gullah auxiliary verb *da,* which also functions as a continuative and iterative marker. Thus, under these circumstances, one would not expect to find any examples in which *da* co-occurs with stative verbs, such as *ai də no* 'I am knowing,' *ai də sii* 'I am seeing,' and *ai də yir* 'I am hearing.'

My data provide linguistic evidence to the contrary, however. Consider the following examples:

57. *ai sɛ B——, yu də sii B——?* (GB)
    'I said, "B——, have you seen B——?" '
58. *æn dæt gal də tɛk dæt ples æn sɛl em ta a kræka den.* (GB)
    'and that girl took that place [the home and property she had inherited from her parents] and sold it to a cracker [a name used to identify a southern white person].'
59. *ai fiil laik dæt tiŋ də kræk den. . . . it jæɛs də kræk den.* (SB)
    'I felt like that thing [the speaker is referring to her leg] cracked/had cracked then. . . . It had just cracked then.'
60. *kaz ai də yir somin hir ai en no.* (EH)
    '[Be]cause I heard/have heard something [some news] here I didn't know [before].'
61. *dæt stoom də staat an sætde nait æn . . .* (DG)
    'That storm started on [a] Saturday night and . . .'

These examples show that *da,* or at least a form that is [də] phonetically, can be used to denote perfective situations with stative verbs, something not observed in earlier studies of Gullah. Whether this form represents the aspect auxiliary *da,* however, has been called into question. Ian Hancock (pers. comm., 1991) claims that the auxiliary in examples 57–61 is not *da,* though it appears to be that phonetically, but rather is actually a reduced form of the English morpheme *did* in its auxiliary function (i.e., *did → di → da*) (cf. also Mufwene 1988b).

Hancock (1987, 301) maintains that the construction *a da go* in Gullah could correspond either to *a de go* 'I'm going' or *a did go* 'I went'; however, his only example of the latter construction is from another source. He writes: "SIC [Gullah] also alternates *bin* with *did: dem did come* 'they came' (Jones 1888, 79), and has the alternate form *bi* which it shares with Cameroonian: *Bro' Rabbit biluk fo' see* 'Brer Rabbit looked to see'; *I bee' tell you I could dibe* 'I told

you I could dive' (Stewart 1919, 395)." Hancock does not provide any data
from Gullah that show the auxiliary *da* functioning as a reduced form of *did*.
In his view, what appears on the surface as a single phonetic form *da* may be
derived from two different structures, one the auxiliary *da* in its progressive/
iterative/habitual functions, the other a reduced form of the English morpheme
did, functioning as an auxiliary replacing the creole auxiliary *bin.*

I do not agree that perfective *da* in sentences 57–61 represents a reduced
form of English *did,* and I cite two arguments to support my position. One has
to do with how *did* replacement supposedly occurs in the creole verbal system.
Bickerton has proposed a developmental pattern that explains how the creole
auxiliary *bin* is replaced by the English morpheme *did.* This will be briefly
outlined below, but we will find that the Gullah data do not totally coincide
with Bickerton's expectations. This raises doubt that the auxiliary *da* in the
perfective structures above is a reduced form of *did.*

The second argument concerns the use of the auxiliary *a* in the Gullah verb
phrase. There have been no observations of this auxiliary verb in previous
studies of Gullah. The importance of this auxiliary verb lies in the fact that
its functions and meanings are not unlike those of auxiliary *da.* I will argue
here that *a* is a variant or offshoot of the auxiliary *da* and that this development
reinforces the functions and meanings of *da* in the Gullah verbal system.

Arguments Against da *Being Derived from English* Did

In his discussion of *did* in the creole grammar of anglophone Atlantic creole
languages, Hancock (1987, 292) says that "the presence or absence of *bin*
(discussed in, e.g., Bickerton, 1967: 65–66, 1975: 45–47) results in a grammatical distinction which is not everywhere the same. *Did* or *di* replaces *bin* in
acrolectally-shifting Guyanese and Jamaican; only 19th century texts for Barbadian have *bin,* also true for Black English: a text from Virginia dated 1836
includes *is you been ax yo' mammy?* and *That ah brindle steer been broke into
our fence* (Anon., 1836:43)."

According to Hancock, *did* in the creole grammar of Guyanese Creole and
Jamaican Creole, and presumably also Gullah, is the result of a shift from
the grammar of the creole (the basilect) up the creole continuum toward the
associated superstrate language (the acrolect). *Did* replaces the basilectal form
bin and thus represents part of the intermediate grammar (the mesolect) between the basilect and the acrolect in this developmental phase. Hancock does
not illustrate how *did* replaces *bin* in the creole verbal system, but I assume

that he has adopted Bickerton's proposal for this development in Guyanese Creole English (he references Bickerton in the above quotation describing this language shift). Bickerton (1975) proposes that a creole, in merging with its lexifier language, first replaces its creole forms with forms from the lexifier language. The new forms initially assume the original function of the creole forms that have been replaced but later undergo restructuring in function and meaning until they approximate the linguistic targets in the lexifier language.

The English morpheme *did* underwent such a development in the creole verbal system, according to Bickerton, functioning as a replacement of the creole auxiliary *bin*. The implication is that a creole that has *bin* as an auxiliary in its verbal system will naturally undergo this replacement. Bickerton illustrates how this happened in Guyanese Creole English. According to Hancock, the presence of *did* (or a reduced variant *da*) in Gullah suggests that it followed the same line of development. Bickerton's description of what happened in Guyanese is briefly outlined as follows.

The auxiliary *bin*, or one of its phonetic variants (*ben, wen,* etc.), is found in most English-related creoles (Gullah, Guyanese Creole English, Krio, Jamaican Creole, etc.). It is commonly described as an anterior auxiliary marking the uninflected lexical verb for anterior meaning. The functions of the auxiliary *bin* are conditioned by what Bickerton proposes as a stative/nonstative distinction of the creole verb phrase. That is, whereas the continuative/iterative meanings expressed by the auxiliary *da* are restricted to a nonstative verb sense, the anterior meaning expressed by *bin* is determined by whether the verb phrase is stative or nonstative.

Bickerton argues that the auxiliary verb *bin* used with stative verbs conveys a simple past-tense meaning; with nonstatives it conveys a past-in-the-past meaning. The latter applies whether or not the past perfect is used in the English translations. Two of his examples from Guyanese Creole English illustrate this distinction (1975, 35).

62. *dem bin gat wan lil haus.*
     'They had one little house' (simple past).
63. *dem bin gatu get we an kom dis said, lef di ples an get we, bikaz terabl ting bin hapn wid dem chiren.*
     'They had to get away and come over here, leave the place and get away, because terrible things had happened to their children.' (The use of *bin* in 62 shows that *bin* occurs with stative verbs; thus, *bin* indicates simple past meaning. The use of *bin* here shows its function with a nonstative verb; therefore, *bin* indicates past-in-the-past meaning.)

I examined the uses of *bin* in Gullah to see how closely they coincide with Bickerton's observations of this auxiliary in Guyanese. Below are some examples of the auxiliary in Gullah.

64. *ai bin sɛn em wan taim ta fain aut hau mač ai ow.* (EH)
   'I had sent the papers [in] one time [before] to find out how much [money] I [still] owed.'
65. *i gat wan a dem tiŋ wat yu bin æsk mi fa læs nait.* (EH)
   'He had [on] one of those things [Band-Aids] that you asked/had asked me for last night.'
66. *æn if ai bin æks em di ada de wat di wɛta gon du . . .* (EH)
   'and if I had asked him the other day what the weather was going to do [be like] . . .'
67. *ai bin no zækli hu tif em æfta ai hir.* (EH)
   'I knew exactly who stole [the guns] after I heard [who it was].'
68. *yu bin sii ini?* (DG)
   'You saw any [light]?' (The speaker is asking me if I saw any light when I went down to a section on the island called Land's End where a light is supposed to be visible at certain times of the night.

These uses of *bin* closely resemble Bickerton's description of the auxiliary verb in Guyanese. In both languages, *bin* with nonstatives indicates past-in-the-past meaning; with statives it indicates past meaning. Of the two, Bickerton considers the occurrence of *bin* with statives to be more common. Based on my data, however, *bin* appears to be more common with nonstatives in Gullah.

Bickerton proposes that in decreolization, creole forms are first replaced by new forms from the lexifier language. With respect to *bin,* in the early stage of development this form vacates the creole grammar, and the syntactic slot left open is taken by the English morpheme *did*, with *did* taking the functions left vacant by *bin* rather than retaining any of its English functions and meanings.

During its replacement by *did,* however, *bin* is not deleted immediately from the creole grammar. When first acquired, *did* is used alongside *bin* with the original functions of the latter. The two morphemes *bin* and *did* alternate in the grammar, with *did* gradually taking over the functions of *bin*. Bickerton illustrates this with examples from Guyanese Creole English (1975, 70).

69. *wi bin tretn, yu no, wi did fraikn laik kowad.*
   'We were threatened, you know, we were frightened like cowards.'
70. *ai biliiv iz dats wai shi di sen.*
   'I believe that's why she sent [it].'

I found no evidence in Gullah of the replacement of *bin* by *did*. This seems surprising in light of the fact that the Gullah data show the acquisition of the English inflectional *-ing* affix as well as a number of other acrolectal features. It would seem that if the replacement of *bin* by the English morpheme *did* is important, there would be some examples of this. This is not to argue that such a development has not taken place in Gullah, only that my extensive research of the Gullah language found no instances where *did* appeared to assume the functions of *bin*. To my knowledge, no other researchers who have studied Gullah have observed it either.

Bickerton explains this discrepancy by saying that the proposed stative/ nonstative distinction that occurs with *bin* is reversed in the *did* + verb constructions. That is, among heavy *bin* users, *bin* occurs more frequently with statives, but the occurrences of *did* in *bin* functions are with nonstatives.

Although I found no cases of the replacement of *bin* by *did*, let us assume for the sake of discussion that such a replacement occurred in Gullah. If it did, then *did* could occur in slots held by *bin*, according to Bickerton's proposed development. Sentences 71–75 illustrate this replacement.

71. *ai sɛ B——, yu *bin* sii B——?
    'I say B——, you been see B——?'
72. *æn dæt gæl *bin* tɛk dæt ples æn sɛl em tə ə krækə den.
    'and that girl been take that place and sell it to a cracker then.'
73. *ai fiil laik dæt tʊŋ *bin* kræk den . . . ɪt jɛs *bin* cracked den.
    'I feel like that thing been crack then . . . it just been crack then.'
74. *kaz ai *bin* yɪə somɪn hɪə ai en no.
    ''cause I been hear somethin here I ain't know.'
75. *dæt stoom *bin* staat an sætde nait æn . . .
    'That storm been start on Saturday night and . . .'

My Gullah informants considered these sentences unacceptable within these contexts,[7] refusing to substitute *bin* in the slot occupied by *da*. This suggests that *da* in sentences 57–61 does not represent a reduced variant of the English morpheme *did*. The difference between *da* and *bin* is shown by sentences 57 and 68.

In 57 the auxiliary verb is *də;* in 68 it is *bɪn*. Both are followed by the same lexical verb *see*. In 57 we observed that *da* cannot be replaced with *bin*. On the other hand, according to some informants, *da* cannot replace *bin* in 68. The use of *did* in the latter was equally unacceptable (e.g., *yu *did* si eni?). The inability of *da* and *bin* to replace one another argues that they do not share the same function in Gullah.

Da and *bin* can be further distinguished semantically. According to informants, *da* in 57 denotes a situation in the past that has present relevance, while *bin* in 68 denotes a situation that took place and was completed in the past before some other past time orientation. Thus, to interchange the two auxiliaries would change the contextual reference of a sentence.

The auxiliaries also differ prosodically. In sentences 57–61, *da* is produced with a higher pitch than is *bin* in sentences 64–68. This and previous evidence support my position that *da* in examples 57–61 does not represent *di*, a reduced variant of *did*.

Some informants, however, did accept the substitution of *did* for *bin* in 64 and 67. But in these examples, *did* does not behave like *bin* in having an anterior function; rather, its function is not unlike *did* as an auxiliary in English when used as an emphatic affirmative.

There were other situations in which *did* occurred in Gullah but could not substitute for *bin*. For instance, *did* is used as a negator of *bin* + verb structures, an example of which is 76:

76. ai didn *bin* no moni so gud ∪in dem taimz bʌt mai hasban šo mi æn tɛl
    mi. (EH)
    'I didn't know [about] money so good in those times but my husband
    showed me and told me [about money; e.g., how to count money].'

In this example, *didn* functions as a negator of *bin* + verb, a function like that of English *didn't*. Here *did* is employed as an operator to carry negation (it may have other syntactic functions elsewhere). In this case, *did* does not represent a replacement for *bin* but functions along with *bin*. Bickerton found that the replacement of *bin* by *did* occurs with nonstative verb senses. If, as he claims, *bin* is more often used with stative verbs, then his replacement appears to apply to the less common rather than the more typical function of auxiliary *bin* in the creole grammar.

We have suggested that *did* inherits the functions of *bin,* but there is one point on which the two forms differ strikingly.. . . . The distribution of fifty-two *bin* occurrences in the recordings with regard to the stative–non-stative distinction was thirty-nine stative, thirteen non-stative: i.e. 75% of *bin*-occurrences were with statives. The figure for *did* exactly reverses this distribution. Of forty-eight occurrences, nine only are stative, a further three possibly interpretable as stative, and the remaining thirty-six clearly non-stative: i.e. 75% of *did*-occurrences are with *non*-statives. (Bickerton 1975, 72)

But why would *did,* if its function is merely to assume the syntactic slot vacated by *bin* (both in function and meaning), reorder the functions of *bin* in any way? If this replacement is possible, then it seems that *did* does not simply appear in the syntactic slot vacated by *bin,* retaining its functions and meanings. If *did* simply replaces *bin,* then it would not be necessary for *did* to reorder what is really a crucial syntactic function of *bin* (its occurrence with stative verbs).

Let us suppose that this linguistic development operates in accordance with Bickerton's proposal and that *did* in its replacement of *bin* reorders its syntactic function from stative to nonstative verb senses. This development would not hold with respect to the examples with perfective *da* cited above (sentences 57–61), since *da* in these structures is used more with a stative than a nonstative sense. If *da* in these cases is really a reduced form of *did,* then its presence in the Gullah grammar is in opposition to Bickerton's proposed development, which states that *did*'s occurrence is with a nonstative verb sense.

The use of *bin* and the use of *da* as a presumed reduced form of *did* in Gullah are not in accord with Bickerton's description of these verbs and their functions. This inconsistency suggests that the use of *da* as a perfective must not be confused with *did* but must be viewed as a separate development unto itself.

The second argument against *da* as a reduced form of *did* has to do with the use of the auxiliary verb *a,* phonetically [ə], in the Gullah verb phrase. As I mentioned earlier, there are no citations of this verb in the literature on Gullah. It functions like *da,* both as an auxiliary and as a main verb. Some examples I found of the verb *a* used as an auxiliary denoting an event in progress or in duration are shown below.

77. *o hi jɛs a sɛ dæt jɛs so. hi jɛs a sɛ dæt jɛs so.* (GB)
    Oh, he just is saying that just so. He just is saying that just so. [He's just saying that but he really doesn't mean it.]'
78. *"yu en kol?" ai sɛ "no, yaal a primp."* (ER)
    '[They said], "You aren't cold?" I said, "No, y'all are primping." ' (The speaker is referring to a situation in which she wore the proper clothing for the cold weather but the others did not.)
79. *bʌt ai tink de jɛs a fʌn.* (EH)
    'But I thought they just were funning. [But I thought they were just joking.]'

These examples show that the Gullah auxiliary verb *a* denotes a situation in progress, similar to both Gullah *da* and English *be.* It is used in verb phrases with uninflected verbs (i.e., without the *-ing*) and indicates both past and present temporal reference, like *da* but unlike *be*. Thus, these examples show that *a* is similar to the verb *da* in its typical function as a durative or continuative marker in the prototypical creole TMA system.

Like the verb *da*, *a* can occur with a verb inflected with *-ing*.

80. *yaal a fʌnin*. (ER)
   'Y'all are funning [joking].'

The verb *a* in sentence 80 is not restricted to the action verbs *come* and *go*, as was observed for *da*. Thus, the idea that the action verbs *come* and *go* occurring with the inflected *-ing* and the auxiliary *da* were acquired in their inflected forms may not be fully justified.

There are other cases in which a form of the English auxiliary verb *be* (i.e., *ain't*) is used with the Gullah auxiliary *a*.

81. *kaz ai din no nau til F—— en a pen in di haus nau*. (EH)
   '[Be]cause I didn't know now until [you told me that] F—— isn't painting in the house now.'

Gullah speakers use *ain't* to negate *a* + V structures in much the same way as they use *ain't* to negate *da* + V structures. I found no constructions in Gullah in which *ain't* (or a form of *be*) co-occurred with *da* and a verb inflected with *-ing*, as in **ain't* + *da* + V + *-ing*. However, there were constructions in which the verb *a* was used with the English verb *was* (a form of *be*) along with a main verb inflected with *-ing*.

82. *sɛ ši waz a kamin yɛstəde de æn* . . . (EH)
   '[She] said [that] she was coming yesterday and . . .'

With regard to auxiliary verb *da*, the patterns used to convey the progressive include *da* + V, *da* + V + *-ing*, and *be* + *da* + V, but not **be* + *da* + V + *-ing*. The patterns used to convey this same meaning with the verb *a* include *a* + V, *a* + V + *-ing*, *be* + *a* + V, and *be* + *a* + V + *-ing*.

These examples illustrate some of the ways Gullah speakers use the auxiliary *a* to express progressive meaning; however, this is not the only way *a* functions as an auxiliary verb in Gullah. Consider sentences 83 and 84:

83. *ši kiip a tɛl mi al dem tiŋ, sɛ* . . . (EH)
   'She keeps telling me all those things, saying . . .'
84. *en no wud bin ta wasa wen piipl a baan wud stob, bʌt nau* . . . (DG)
   'ain't no wood was to Wassaw [Island] when people used to burn wood stove, but now . . . [There wasn't any wood on Wassaw Island when people used to cook on wood stoves, but now . . .]'

Example 83 shows that the verb *a* can convey iterative meaning, and in example 84 *a* denotes habitual meaning; these functions were also observed of the auxiliary verb *da*. As with the verb *da*, there appear to be no restrictions on temporal reference. That is, *a* is used in iterative and habitual situations with past and present temporal reference.

The discussion thus far indicates that the Gullah verb *a*, like *da*, can express events that are in progress or are habitual and iterative. But as with *da*, too, there does not appear to be a term that would embrace these functions and include others found in Gullah, as with sentence 85.

85. *P—— kam rait in hir di ata de æn a sɛn im in.* (EH)
    'P—— came right in here [the house] the other day and sent them [the papers] in [for me].'

This example shows that auxiliary *a*, like *da*, can express a completed situation. The question now is whether we want to consider *a* used in this way to be a reduced variant of the English morpheme *did*. Before determining this, let us consider some other functions of auxiliary *a*.

86. *hi a bi hir təmaro.* (EH)
    'He will be here tomorrow.'
87. *if hi en sii mi hi a kam in dæt ruum fə han mi.* (GB)
    'If he didn't see me, he would come in that room to hunt [look] for me.'

Sentence 86 shows that auxiliary *a* can convey futurity, as was also observed of *da*. In 87, *a* functions as a modal in a conditional clause. In addition to its function as an auxiliary, *a*, like *da*, functions as a main verb (i.e., as a copula). Consider the following examples:

88. *i jɛs a fʌn fə wi.* (EH)
    'It just was [a lot of] fun for us.' (The context in which the speaker uttered this statement does not indicate a situation in progress.)
89. *M—— waif a dɛ nau yu no.* (GB)
    'M——'s wife is dead now, you know.'

These examples show the verb *a* in Gullah functioning as a main verb followed by an adjective complement. I found other examples of this verb with noun and adverb complements. Again, these functions of *a* are not unlike those of *da*.

It seems surprising that none of these functions of *a* has shown up in previous studies of Gullah. It is possible that the occurrence of this verb is a recent development that occurred after Turner conducted his study of Gullah. There are numerous examples of this verb in my data, suggesting that it is very productive in the Gullah verb system. An important question here is how this verb use came about.

My hypothesis is that the verb *a* is an allomorph of the verb *da*. Its occurrence in the verb phrase may be the result of phonological reduction—the deletion of the initial consonant. This would not be unique to Gullah; other creoles (e.g., Jamaican) also show variant morphs for this verb.[8] Once *a* appeared in the verb system, it began to assume some of the functions of *da*. An example showing the two items being used interchangeably is given below.

90. *ši sɛ ši din hæv di haat ta sɛ natin mač . . . sɛ ši tiŋ ɛvatiŋ iz nais. æn B——jɛs a tɛl ha, "wat yu da sɛ? hau yu en da sɛ natin?"* (EH)
    'She said [that] she didn't have the heart to say nothing much. . . . [She] said [that] she thinks everything [that was said in the meeting] is nice. And B—— just told her, "What are you saying? How [come] you aren't saying nothing?" '
91. *de en a fʌs wit mi bʌt de da fʌs wit wan nata.* (EH)
    'They weren't fussing with me but they were fussing with one another.'

It is not clear what specific functions, if any, *a* assumes in the Gullah verb phrase, although its function as a modal denoting futurity and other modal meanings appear to be more common than those of *da*. In short, it appears that *a* is moving toward a target that cannot be English because its final output is not present in the grammar of English.

Variation in the use of the auxiliary verb *da* in contemporary Gullah presented here differs from observations in earlier Gullah studies and from the traditional view of this auxiliary verb described in the creole literature. My data show that auxiliary *da* denotes situations that are in progress or are habitual and iterative. These functions were also observed for *da* by earlier researchers who studied Gullah, and *da* is used in this way in the prototypical creole TMA system. My findings differ, however, in demonstrating the function of *da* as a perfective. This function of *da* is not reported in earlier studies of Gullah, nor is it found in the prototypical creole TMA system.

Hancock's thesis that *da* replaced the basilectal form *bin* (→ *did*) is not supported by my data. He has presented no contemporary Gullah data that show the use of *da* as a reduced form of *did*; nor does he provide any contemporary data that show *did* functioning as an allomorph of the auxiliary *bin*. Earlier studies of Gullah also do not provide any data to support his view. Hancock's idea that this replacement occurred is based on Bickerton's proposal that such a development occurred in other English-related creoles in the process of de-creolization, but my data on *da, did,* and *bin* do not support this proposed development.

Notes

The Gullah data used in this study come from my dissertation. Ian Hancock, Salikoko Mufwene, and Charles Bird provided many helpful discussions of the verb *da* in Gullah, and Michael Montgomery made numerous comments on an earlier draft of this essay; however, I assume full responsibility for any shortcomings.

1. *Gullah* is the name commonly used in the literature to refer to the speech of African Americans living in the Sea Islands along the southeastern Atlantic coastline from South Carolina to Jacksonville, Florida, and the adjacent mainland cities. At the local level the term *Geechee* is often used.

2. Hawaiian Creole English differs from the other English-related creoles in its phonetic form of this auxiliary verb. The aspect auxiliary in HCE is *stay.*

3. Turner based his analysis of Gullah on his field research of the Gullah language conducted in the South Carolina and Georgia Sea Islands and bordering mainland cities in the 1930s. His study represents the most comprehensive analysis of this language to date.

4. I have made the following adjustments to Turner's phonetic representation of these examples. For his voiceless palatal stop [c], I use the voiceless palatal affricate [č]; for the voiced palatal stop [J], the voiced velar stop [g] is used; the lowercase [ɑ] is used for the turned A [ɐ] and turned script A [ɒ]; and the iota [ι] is used for the small capital [ɪ].

5. I have modified Jones-Jackson's phonetic description of the Gullah examples for ease of presentation. The voiceless palatal fricative [š] is used here in place of her voiceless palato-alveolar fricative [ʃ]. The voiceless labiodental fricative [f] is used in place of the voiceless bilabial fricative [ɸ]. And the voiced apico-alveolar trill [r] is used for the voiced alveolar frictionless continuant.

6. *Ain't* is generally viewed as a nonstandard contraction of *am not, is not, are not, has not,* and *have not.* In Gullah it seems to function as a general negator and is used with both auxiliary and main verbs.

7. Relying on my knowledge of Gullah, I also consider sentences 71–75 to be unacceptable structures in Gullah.

8. Jamaican Creole English is very similar to Gullah in its use of the auxiliary *a* (see Cassidy 1961a).

Flexibility and Creativity in Afro-American English

Peter A. Roberts

The terms *creolization* and *decreolization* have become famous in the analysis
of Afro-American dialects and beyond.[1] Not only have these terms diverted a
lot of energy into speculative arguments, but by asserting that Afro-Americans
are on a unidimensional path toward a standard language, they overlook the
flexibility and contrasts that are necessary and normal in natural language and
human relationships. In this paper I address these shortcomings in three ways:
first, I throw some light on the function and meaning of *fu* in early Afro-
American English; second, I propose a relationship between the verbs *be* and
de; and third, I account for the contrast between the use and nonuse of certain function words. Then, I will relate these three arguments to the notions of
linguistic flexibility and language development.

I will not refer directly to most of the extensive literature on these subjects,
only to specific pertinent claims. I will support my analysis with examples from
Gullah stories recorded and published in 1919 by Sadie Stewart. Although these
have not been extensively used, I find them to be of great linguistic interest. The
forms *be* and *fu* have received great attention in the analysis of Afro-American
English because they are thought to characterize the language of the speakers.
A better understanding of their function and development therefore should lead
to a better overall appreciation of the structure of varieties of Afro-American
speech.

Fu

Whereas *be* is famous in American Black English, *fu* (also spelled *fi, fo'*, or *fa*)
is famous in Caribbean Creole English, made so by Derek Bickerton, in whose
every work its functions are selected to show an evolutionary relationship to
to. I have pointed out elsewhere (Roberts 1980) that *fu* is more complicated
than it is usually made out to be and that Caribbean creole speakers, when they
know that the context is not appropriate for the stigmatized form *fu*, in certain
structures change it to *mus*. For example:

1. *she tell yo fu come*   = 2. *she tell you mus come*, or
                                3. *she tell you mus to come*
4. *she tell you no fu come* = 5. *she tell you mus dont come*, or
                                6. *she tell you mus to dont come*

This clearly indicates that *fu* is not semantically empty or simply an infinitive marker as it is in the Standard English equivalents below.

 7. She told you to come.
 8. She told you not to come.

Just as it is misleading to equate *fu* + verb with Standard English *to* + verb, one cannot equate *fu* + noun/pronoun with Standard English *for/to* + noun/pronoun. In Jamaican and other varieties of Caribbean speech, *fu* is used before nouns and pronouns as a strong possessive form, as in the following:

 9. *fu mi book* 'my book'
10. *mi book* 'my book'
11. *fu John book* 'John's book'
12. *John book* 'John's book'

Lorenzo Dow Turner (1949, 212) claims that in Gullah, *fa* (his spelling of the form) is African derived and is used before another verb with the meaning " 'intend to,' 'choose to,' 'must' or 'should.' " Used in this way, *fa* can be translated easily by the verb or auxiliary equivalent given by Turner (1949), which tends to make *fa* conform structurally with English (and Romance) syntax in a way that *mus* in sentences 2 and 3 and *fu* in 9 and 11 do not.

A closer examination of other Gullah sentences (S. Stewart 1919, 394–96) shows, however, that there is not always conformity with English syntax (Stewart spells the form *fo'*):

13. *Mr. Terrapin say, "Well, which one can run de fas'est, Mr. Deer?" "I can't fo' say, . . ."*
14. *Bro' Rabbit say, "I dunno, Bro' Wolf, but I know I ain't eat um. Some one mus' fo' tief it whil' we been a-dibe."*
15. *Den him slip back in de bucket, an' say, "Bro' Wolf, ain't you fo' ready to come town agin?"*
16. *Bro' Wolf and Bro' Rabbit come out de water and mek fo' de house. Bro' Rabbit fo' tell Bro' Wolf to sha' de tallow.*
17. *Nex' day de man come 'long an' ketch Bro' Rabbit playin' de same trick. De man fo' look at Bro' Rabbit an' say, "I can't trus' you."*

In fact, it seems impossible to give a meaning to *fo'* in the above sentences, but that is only because the syntax of Turner's equivalents ('intend to,' 'choose to,' etc.) does not fit. The same is true of the following Barbadian sentences.[2]

18. *He fa to put it there*
    'He has to put it there.'
19. *If I did know, I wen fa tell you*
    'If I did know, I wouldn't tell you.'

The function and meaning of *fo'* /*fa* in sentences 13–19 become clearer, however, when one relates these forms to *fu* in sentences 9 and 11. The full context of the sentences clearly corroborates the idea of strong form and definiteness that is semantically related to the common idea in *mus* in sentences 2, 3, 5, and 6, and in Turner's 'must,' 'intend,' 'choose,' and 'should.'

Don Winford (1984, 20), after giving a comprehensive analysis of *fi* (his spelling) in Caribbean English Creole, concludes with a diagram of the uses of *fi* in which *directional, benefactive, possessive,* and *purposive* are listed as prenominal functions; and *futurity, intentional, obligation,* and *purposive* are preverbal functions. And he suggests a basic semantic link between all of them.

My conclusions are that whether or not one links all the uses of *fu*/*fi*/*fa*/*fo'*, in some of its uses in Afro-American speech it is semantically primary (with a meaning of focus, force, definiteness, obligation), that it has a greater freedom of syntactic occurrence than before infinitive verbs only, and that in its early basic function it coincides only accidentally with English syntax.

Be

It is important to recall first of all that *be* is not mentioned or analyzed as a verb or verb auxiliary in Gullah in Turner (1949). At first, it seems that a probable explanation of this is that *be* was not yet a prominent feature of Gullah when Turner was conducting his research. This is clearly not so, however, as can be seen in the stories recorded by Sadie Stewart (1919). Another explanation, one that Turner himself alludes to as a problem for early researchers in Gullah territory, is that Gullah speakers produced only a certain form of speech for outsiders. This explanation is not inconsistent with the kinds of texts given as samples of Gullah in Turner (1949), which tend to be of the same style.

In much of the literature on American Black English, *be* as a verb (e.g., *He be sick*) and *be* as a verb auxiliary (i.e., *be* + verb + *-ing,* as in *She be waiting on the bus*) are seldom differentiated. In fact, they are presented in this way (e.g., in Rickford 1980, 1986) specifically to establish their semantic unity and common evolution. John Rickford puts forward the idea that *be* may have developed from *does be* and so links Gullah and the Caribbean creoles, which use *does* rather than *be* for the same semantic purpose. Rickford uses the following as examples of types of sentences in which *does* and *be* coexisted before one or the other evolved in Black English and Caribbean creoles, respectively:

20. *He does be working.*
21. *He does be sick.*
22. *He does be in the club.*

Rickford proposes this historical development to link *does* and *be* used together to express habitual or iterative realities.

The syntactic difference between *be* verb and *be* auxiliary is quite clear in Standard English, in that whereas *be* verb stands alone, *be* auxiliary is inseparable from *-ing* (i.e., *be* + *-ing* is a discontinuous morpheme). Historically, the form *be* (as opposed to *am, is, are,* etc.) as a copula verb is more frequent in older English, a form that can be used to support its present-day use in American Black English when the verb is followed by an adverb or adjective. However, one would have to appeal to (1) reduction of a longer structure (e.g., *does be eating* → *be eating*) and (2) a later stage of the development toward Standard English in order to explain *be* + *-ing*. The problem is that *be* + verb—that is, without *-ing,*—occurs in the early recorded Gullah stories, as in, for example (Stewart 1919), the following:

23. *Bro' Rabbit tell Bro' Wolf, "Let's go down to de crik side an' see which one can dibe de longis'." Bro' Rabbit and Bro' Wolf be gone.*
24. *Ebber nown den Bro' Rabbit bi luk fo' see ef Bro' Wolf been acomin'.*
25. *Bro' Wolf, I bee' tell you I could dibe de longis'."*

Semantically, as is the case with most other verb particles in Caribbean creoles, no one meaning can be given to *be,* and it is misleading to try to give a special history for iterative *be* by itself. It would be perverse, for example, to claim that in the following, *I be hungree* unqualified by an adverb means 'I am always hungry.'

26. *"Mornin', Bro' Fox!" "Mornin', Bro' Wolf!" "Want sumpin' fo' eat?" "Yah, beca'se I bee' hungree."*

The same is the case with *be* in sentence 23, in which there is clearly no idea of repetition or continuity. In fact, there is no clear semantic distinction between durative *be*, iterative *be*, and other uses of *be* in the multitude of uses for *be* in American Black English.

My conclusion is that in Gullah, and probably in other varieties of Afro-American speech, *de, be*, and *is* (*is, am, are*) are in a multidimensional relationship involving idiosyncratic, stylistic, and evolutionary variation. In short, the forms are generally interchangeable, and there is no need to posit a reduction of longer constructions such as *does + be*. This substitutability is supported by semantic factors identified by Turner, who says that "there is usually no special form to indicate whether or not the action is continuous. The practice of the Gullah speaker is to select the simplest form of the verb, before which he may or may not place the word *de: ai go* or *ai de go* may mean any of the following: 'I go,' 'I went,' 'I am going,' 'I was going,' 'I shall go,' or even 'I had gone' " (1949, 225). Turner also says that "the tense of the verb in each sentence is determined by the context out of which the sentence is taken" (1949, 213).

The variation between *de, be*, and *is* is idiosyncratic because Gullah speakers choose one or the other of these variants unpredictably. In the broader perspective this has turned out to be regional variation in that Caribbean English uses *de* and American Black English *be*.

Be and *is* are invariable for person and number in their nonstandard usage (i.e., *I be, you be, they be; I is, you is, they is*) but conform increasingly to standard variation (i.e., *I am, you are, they are, it is*) according to speaker and formality of context. This is social variation. The form *de* may be said to be West African in origin, *be* and *is* to represent change in form without great change in syntactic structure, *be + -ing* to be an approximation to English, and *am, is,* and *are* to be Standard English. This constitutes evolutionary change. The fact that a Gullah speaker can elect to use any one of the variants in a given situation indicates that there is stylistic variation. This kind of variation is not to be regarded simply as a result of constraints of discourse; it represents real choice on the part of the speaker.

Semantic variation in this case means that the form is used both precisely and imprecisely. *De*, as Turner points out, can be used in most contexts (as can *be/is*), but it is used more often to express continuous or durative aspect (and iterative secondly) than it is for the other tenses or aspects. This kind of variation (imprecise-precise) is typical of the zero particle, negative markers, prepositions, and other features of Caribbean creoles. It is also typical of many function words in major world languages such as English. (Compare, for example, the many meanings of the word *in* occurring in any book and the meaning of the word in isolation.) Further semantic complication sets in as nonstandard *be* approaches standard *be* (e.g., *will be, would be, will be* + *-ing, may be,* etc.).

An attendant proposal that I would like to make with regard to the *de* [də]-*be* relationship is that the habitual or iterative meaning of *de/be* is integrally related to the suffix *-z,* which is used for specificity or disambiguation in the imprecise-precise relationship in the use of variants. Note the contrast in the following pairs of sentences:

27. *It be that way*
28. *It bes that way* (American Black English)

29. *I de [də] work*
30. *I dez [dəz] work* (Gullah and Caribbean creole)

31. *I de work*
32. *I z work* (Caribbean creole)

33. *I work*
34. *I works* (Caribbean creole)

Dəz (*d* + *əz*) may appear today as a separate, viable, and durable form because it has had phonetic support from Standard English *does.* On the other hand, *bes* seems sporadic because it has had no such phonetic support from Standard English. The morphology of the two, however, seems to be the same. Although Rickford (1980) suggests that *z,* as in sentence 32 above, has probably been misinterpreted in the literature for *is* and that it is really a case of phonetic erosion of *does* (i.e., *dəz* → *iz* → *z*), there is no way to prove conclusively that *dəz* historically precedes *z* in this type of sentence.

Də

Turner (1949, 225) claims that the form *də* has no specific meaning and gives no reason why Gullah speakers use it as opposed to not using it. Such an analysis presents two problems: optionality and meaning. The notion of free variation has been disputed in linguistics, although essentially in the context of choice between one form and another rather than between a form and zero; and in the analysis of Afro-American dialects such variation is additionally linked to a process of evolution. For example, William Labov (1969) relates what he calls "contraction" and "deletion" to linguistic contexts (i.e., a form is more likely to contract and disappear in one phonetic environment than in another). In Labov (1971) the analysis is one of statistically significant variability (i.e., a speaker will show in all relevant occurrences of variation a certain preference for one form over another). Bickerton (1973) takes up the notion of statistically significant preference and explains it in terms of the speaker's stage of evolution in relation to acrolect and basilect.

Analyses of variation that concentrate on statistics and evolution pay little attention to the intention of the speaker and other normal factors in human communication. There is nothing evolutionary involved when a speaker in topicalizing chooses to use or not use the topicalizer, as in the following:

35. *a my own that : my own that* (Jamaican)
    'that is mine'
36. *and da him save me : and him save me* (Gullah)
    'he saved me'

or *fu* in possessive phrases

37. *fu mi book : mi book*
    'my book'

or *bin* in

38. *he bin eat : he eat.*

In relation to the analysis of the verb specifically, the contrastive type of grid set up for the Afro-American verb particle or auxiliary (i.e., realis: irrealis, past: future, continuative: punctual, etc.) will become vaguer and vaguer and will eventually collapse because it presents the Afro-American world of aspect and tense in a narrow and specialized manner. For instance, the Afro-American speaker who says (in answer to the question Where's Tom?), *Oh, he done bin long gone,* might not mean any more than another who answers, *He gone,* with the last word drawn out. Attempts to put *done, bin,* and *gone* into slots and relate them simply to tense and aspect categories like perfective, past, and remote overlook the flexibility of Afro-American speech. Although Elaine Tarone (1972) points out that there is a wider pitch range in black speech in that higher pitches, more patterns of rising final intonation, and greater use of a falsetto register occur, these features have not been generally treated as an integral part of linguistic competence and as equivalents of morphological and syntactic strategies for signaling meaning either in black speech itself or in other varieties of speech.

In addition to those already given for multidimensional variation, some of the obvious variables involved in the use and nonuse of function words are (a) discourse contrasts, (b) speaker personality (e.g., the combination *done bin long* would never be used by some speakers), and (c) performative factors (e.g., relating incidents, stories; philosophizing). In short, the linguistic situation we have been considering is one in which there are (1) fewer forms, (2) presumably the same number of meanings to be covered, (3) greater optionality in the use of forms, and (4) a linguistic system dominated by oral informal rather than written formal factors of communication. In such a situation, to identify verb particles and match them to predetermined aspects and tenses, no matter how ingeniously, is to underrepresent the communicative system of Afro-American speech. The nature of the communicative system is more crucial in Afro-American speech not because it is restricted to Afro-American speech but because taxis, explicitness, redundancy, and contrasts in form have become normal in the English language itself as a result of a long history of written and non-face-to-face communication as well as through normative teaching in English, which is not the case in Afro-American speech. Optionality and meaning are directly related to syntactic ellipsis and phonological suprasegmentals, which in turn are related to the two basic notions in the presentation of information: focus and presupposition.

In the first section of this paper I indicate that the semantic content of the lexical item *fu* can cause that item to be used in varying syntactic positions, creating structures that are not a part of English and Romance languages and so seem unusual to speakers of these languages. It is difficult to assess the extent to which this is either language creativity or the retention of a native language. In the second section I identify a basic grammatical strategy in which the forms change and at the same time relationships become more complex. In the third section I highlight nonverbal linguistic factors and their relationship to meaning and the nature of the communicative system. There is no doubt that such different developments were required for normal human language flexibility to replace those lost in the West African languages and not acquired in English. The three sections therefore illustrate aspects of creativity in Afro-American English and show that Afro-American English is a flexible *system*, not simply a stage on the way to a Standard English goal.

Notes

1. I use the term *Afro-American* to encompass varieties of English in the United States and in the Caribbean.
2. These sentences were recorded in the Saint Philip area of Barbados, which is generally associated with nonstandard speech.

Componentiality and the Creole Matrix:
The Southwest English Contribution

Ian F. Hancock

Acknowledgment of the importance of social and linguistic variables in the formation of creole languages is not new (see, e.g., Reinecke 1937; Hymes 1971; or Whinnom 1971, 1981). There is still, however, a substantial body of thought that accepts, with little or no modification, the monogenetic notion that all of the various anglophone creoles—including Sea Island Creole, Jamaican Creole, and Saramaccan—around the Atlantic share an earlier common ancestor, which lost its creole features to a greater or lesser extent in each area after being taken there.

There are also a number of exponents of the polygenetic hypothesis, which maintains that each creole developed independently in its own location. I reject this approach in its most extreme form, although it is a popular one among the universalists. Interestingly, one of the most ardent proponents of this hypothesis was the first to attempt a reconstruction of the proto-form of the creole (Hall 1966, 118–19). It is my contention that there are valid arguments on both sides of the monogenetic versus polygenetic argument but that neither extreme is sufficient in itself to account for the contemporary character and distribution of the anglophone Atlantic creoles.

Starting in a formalized way with Cassidy (1961b), the hypothesis based on the presumed existence of a single common ancestor has since been elaborated to incorporate decreolization and also the relexification hypothesis. This presumed ancestor was, in fact, alluded to much earlier by George Philip Krapp, who believed that "two hundred years ago, all the Negroes in America must have spoken a language very similar to Gullah" (1924, 193). Half a century later, J. L. Dillard wondered whether that distant ancestor wasn't even "closer to Saramaccan" (1975, 96). Peter Wood called Gullah "the roots of Black English" (1974a, 167); more recently, John Holm has written of Black English in terms of its being "a descendant of an earlier creole English, but [one which is] now approaching the norms of the standard through centuries of contact" (1983a, 17). John Baugh's "own linguistic research suggests historical linguistic roots that link black street speech [in the United States] with Jamaican creole" (1983, 21). It is not surprising that North American creolists should be concerned with Gullah and Black English in particular; but their observations simply reflect a widespread belief that differences across time and space between the creoles resulted when an earlier, "deep" creole began a process of assimilation with English because of contact with it, in different places and at different rates. John D. Roy has given renewed impetus to the argument for a common proto-creole ancestor originating in Barbados, not only for the western Atlantic anglophone creoles but for those spoken on the Guinea coast of Africa as well (1985).

Rather than viewing the development of these creoles from the vantage of either the monogeneticist or the polygeneticist-universalist extremes, I want instead to discuss their development componentially—that is, in terms of the components, or ingredients, present in the formative situation for each. I regard each creole as the result of a complex of historical and social factors that were present during the earliest decades of its formation and which had a direct bearing on the nature of the coming together of three broad components: the African, the creole, and the English. I have discussed these elsewhere (e.g., in Hancock 1986b, 1988) but will summarize the first two briefly here. The third I shall deal with in more detail.

The African Component

Samuel Stoney and Gertrude Shelby (1930, xi), Lou Lichtveld (1954, 53), and Ian Hancock and Peter Gingiss (1975) have all discussed the possibility of an African-derived lingua franca providing a model for the European-derived creoles, but while the contribution of such a language to the initial contact situation on the Upper Guinea coast seems probable, there is not enough evidence of its hypothesized form to consider it as a factor in the creolization process outside Africa. A recent argument for a specific African-language substratum underlying the West African anglophone creoles has been made by Gabriel Manessay (1985, 138), who believes we can suppose that there existed, if not a vehicular variety of Yoruba, at least a trade language strongly influenced by it, which was in use along a large portion of the Guinea coast and of which the Nigero-Cameroonian Creole could be an elaborated form. The Krio of Sierra Leone, which constitutes a distant, more recently transplanted, enclave of this, incorporates features from the Africans liberated before they reached the Americas, and from blacks repatriated from there.

The African component consisted of many hundreds of languages which

differed from place to place, depending on where in Africa the slaves originated. Although there were wide differences in lexicon, forcing the retention
of one predominant lexical source, languages from the same areas of Africa
generally shared a high rate of semantic correlation. This is one important area
in which the anglophone creoles differ from metropolitan English (i.e., any
native variety of noncreole English), and it has a major bearing on problems
creole speakers have in the English-language classroom.

A number of scholars have emphasized the Africanness of the creoles while
minimizing other influences, although their motivation has sometimes been
subjective. Others, like Holm, while giving non-African linguistic influences
their due, have equated the "degree of creolization" with the extent of "influence from African language" (Holm 1983a, 15). Morgan Dalphinis (1985, 47)
states this even more bluntly: "Creolization [is] the use of any of the African/
Creole grammatical features [and] is taken as a positive measure of 'creolization' in the speech of all speakers." There is no African language whose
structure matches that of any creole. Many structural similarities exist, but
they are eclectic. They turn up in the deep structures of all sorts of languages,
including English, and it is not necessary to get too imaginative in trying to
account for them. Some of the features most typically referred to in arguing
for the Africanness of the creoles may in fact be superstratal; that is, they were
acquired after the creole had become established, as a result of later migra-
tions into the area. The pluralizing postnominal -dem (as in de masa dem 'the
masters') is one such feature. Although Yoruba and Akan are ritually elicited
to illustrate various creole structures, neither pluralizes with the third-person
pronoun in this position; only the Manding languages do this, and pre-1800
samples give no evidence of this feature's existence in Guinea Coast Creole
English then. Nor do any of the earliest-attested Western Hemisphere creoles—
Sranan, Djuka, or Saramaccan—pluralize in this way. Manessy, who undertook a study of pluralization in a number of Atlantic creoles of various lexical
bases, concludes that "it is, then, apparent to us that only Yoruba offers a
plausible model for the mode of pluralizing [i.e., with a pre- and/or postposi-
tioned third-person plural pronominal form] here examined" (1985, 138; my
translation).

In Hancock (1986b) I deal with creolization as a slowly evolving process,
not an instantaneous one. While metropolitanization, or the replacement of
creole features by those from the coexistent metropolitan language, is a factor of change, creolization too can continue beyond the formative period; the
development of pluralizing -dem in some creoles is an example of this. It is
a mistake to accept "decreolization" unquestioningly; changes can occur in a

creole that are not modeled on the lexifier language; for example, the anterior marker *bin* has been replaced by *woz* in Panamanian (*a woz hav plenti moni*) and by *had* in Bay Islands Creole (*shi had ded*).

The Creole Component

Elsewhere I have presented evidence that an anglophone creole developed in Upper Guinea during the seventeenth century (Hancock 1986b). This came to be the first language of the Creole communities along the coast and the second language of the grumettoes who worked for them and for the coastal Europeans as middlemen in the slave trade. At least some of the Africans who were brought to the Americas had acquired a knowledge of this creole in Africa before being transported (Hancock 1986b). We can never know how many learned some creole in this way, or how many learned it from others after their arrival in the New World; that it spread in order for African to communicate with African rather than for African to communicate with European, however, we do know; and we know that so pervasive was it that today it is the mother tongue of millions of speakers.

We can assume that transmission was most intense between 1650 and 1700. As the efficiency and volume of the slave trade increased, enslaved people's access to Guinea Coast Creole English and the time necessary to acquire it decreased. A slave's linguistic exposure in the various parts of the Caribbean was to locally modifying varieties, not the dialects of the African coast, but individuals would nevertheless have continued assimilating the new language. A steadily decreasing minority of the Africans being transported would have known any Creole before they left Africa, but its small numerical representation was offset by its widespread applicability and practical use. Whatever the extent of Guinea Coast Creole English may have been at the height of its transmission, after its introduction into the different colonial areas it continued to develop independently. The linking factor of the Creole component was sufficiently strong, however, to allow us to treat the modern creole languages dealt with here as being on one level genetically related. We can assume that commonly shared core Africanisms, such as the second-person plural pronoun *una* and English-derived grammatical morphemes such as *bin, de, go,* and *don,* were a part of Guinea Coast Creole English. I have said elsewhere that the only alternative is coincidence, and the very high rate of shared forms of this kind make this logistically improbable.

Factors affecting this development include the proportion of African-language speakers to Creole speakers across the first two or three decades and the extent to which the crystallizing linguistic system of the locally born Creole speakers fed back into the Creole pool and itself came to serve as a model. Each environment differed in terms of the existing social relationships, terrain, and so on. Some communities were subject to population movements in or out, or may have been disrupted by natural factors. All these things contributed to the different linguistic outcomes in each place, differences that began to take shape from the outset. It is facile to explain creoles in terms of different rates of decreolization operating on a single, early, pan-Atlantic anglophone creole. If this were true, we would expect eighteenth-century Black English to resemble modern Gullah, and eighteenth-century Gullah to resemble modern basilectal Jamaican, and eighteenth-century Jamaican to resemble modern Sranan. The few samples we have of those languages from that time make it quite evident that this was not the case.

The English Component

Interest in the English base of the anglophone creoles began to grow in the 1980s, and several very respectable studies are now available (e.g., Niles 1980; Harris 1985; Rickford 1986; G. Bailey and Ross 1988). The extremist view of the influence of the anglophone component eliminates other components completely. Sixty years ago, George Philip Krapp felt it "safe to say that not a single detail of Negro pronunciation or of Negro syntax can be proved to have any other than an English origin" (1924, 191). This is the approach now being taken by Edgar Schneider, who believes that "Black English is derived almost completely from . . . British English folk speech" (1981, 358). Robert Hall, referring to the genetic classification of Haitian Creole French, says it should be "classed among the Romance languages, specifically among the northern group of the Gallo-Romance branch" (1953, 12–13); and Beryl Bailey maintains that Jamaican Creole English "bears direct genetic relationship to the midland and northern 17th and 18th century provincial [British] dialects" (1962, 39). Statements like these simply show that no satisfactory hypothesis is available to account for the origin, and hence the genetic affiliation, of these languages, (both Hall and, especially, Bailey devote considerable space to creoles' non-European aspects as well). Some proponents of the Africanist position have demonstrated similarly extreme attitudes. Indeed, Richard Allsopp believes that "the African forced immigrant to the new world came equipped with an advantage . . . namely a native, perhaps *genetic*, conditioning in the selection and most effective use of linguistic essentials . . . in the variety of English produced" (1983, 20; my emphasis). Suzanne Sylvain concludes her study of Haitian Creole with the oft-quoted observation that it is "French cast in an African syntactic mould and, since we generally classify languages in terms of their syntactic parent, Ewe with a French vocabulary" (1936, 178). This is essentially the position taken by Mervyn Alleyne (1980, 174), who concludes his chapter on creole origins by saying that "it seems that Afro-American would have to be viewed as a 'simplification' of Kwa."

The earlier disregard of the African component in black speech—discussed, for example, by Lorenzo Dow Turner (1949, 1–14)—was due not only to social prejudices that operated against the efforts of linguists to acknowledge that the Afro-American had any heritage of his own but also to a general lack of scholarship in the area of African linguistics. To some extent, a similar lack of scholarship among creolists in English dialectology, as well as perhaps some reactionary emotionalism, has led to the downplaying until quite recently of the English contribution.

Most attention has focused on the Irish influence on the anglophone creoles, originally stimulated by the similar function of *be* in Hiberno-English and Black English. Lawrence Davis seems to have been the first to have considered this from the creolist's perspective: he questioned whether any "creole features existed in the speech of Whites," referring to "the use of be with durative aspect in the speech of certain areas of Ireland" (1971, 93). He found this line of pursuit unproductive, however, and it was left to John Rickford (1974, 1986) and John Harris (1985) to continue research in this area. Their very valuable work is still in progress. Both writers have also devoted some space to the southwestern British dialects, the group I deal with here.

G. L. Brook notes that the earliest Hiberno-English texts have "many points in common with the dialects of South-West England" (1963, 111), although Alan Bliss indicates that this medieval source had probably died out by the seventeenth century (1979, 317–18). According to Harris, the English (i.e., non-Scottish) colonists in the north of Ireland came "mostly from the northwest Midlands and the south-west of England" (1984, 115). The historical connections between Hiberno-English and the southwestern British dialects have still to be fully dealt with; A. L. Beier writes of a population movement in the other direction and shows that "the Irish provided the single largest contingent of vagrants in Devon and Cornwall in the 1630s" (1985, 34). Given the large-scale transportation of settlers from such southwestern centers as Plymouth and Bristol, as well as from Ireland itself, it is not surprising that both dialects shared equally significant roles in the metropolitan English component, especially in the Caribbean. Norma Niles, writing about the settlement of Barbados, says: "In summary, the seventeenth century southwestern dialect as spoken by the inhabitants of the counties of Somerset, Cornwall, Devon, Dorset and the Isle of Wight was the language brought to Barbados by the majority of English immigrants at that period" (1980, 48).

Niles's table (1980, 77) indicates that 13,500 of the 22,000 transportees to the Barbadian colony by the 1670s were from the Southwest, the balance originating from all other parts of Britain and Ireland. It is not safe to assume that all those transported from a particular area spoke the dialect of that area; as Beier (and Hancock 1988) have shown, many transportees from England spoke Hiberno-English, and it is possible that their influence was greater, linguistically, than the figures indicate. Holm's analysis of the sources of Nicaraguan English Creole (1978, 82–95) gives 12 percent of the overall number of regionalisms as having parallels in southwestern dialects, as against 7.5 percent for Hiberno-English (but 24 percent for Scottish dialects). My own breakdown for Krio (1971, 125–26) gives 20 to 30 percent each to the Southwest and Scotland, but only 0.5 percent to Ireland. For Krio, I found between 30 and 40 percent of the general (i.e., nonregional) English items to have phonological forms shared by the southwestern dialects.

This paper is largely the result of my reading a small book of stories written in one southwestern dialect, that of Cornwall. I deal principally with just one sample text, chosen at random from this collection, and look at a few of the characteristics it shares with the Atlantic anglophone creoles. Where relevant, I have included parallel examples from other parts of the same book. The book, *Echoes from Carn, Cove and Cromlech*, was published in 1935 and is a collection of short stories by "Nicky Trevaylor," the pseudonym of Thomas Newall, that appeared regularly in the *Western Weekly News* at the turn of the century. The dialect is that of the far west of Cornwall—of Mousehole, St. Just, Praa Sands, and Penzance—and while its history indicates that a "completely different type of English [from that of eastern Cornwall, Devon, etc.] predominates here" (Wakelin 1984, 195), the dialect shares a sufficient number of features with the other dialects from this part of Britain to allow us to treat them together. I bought the book in Penzance a number of years ago, at which time I was assured by local speakers of the dialect that it is an exceptionally faithful reproduction of the speech of the area as it was around 1900. The features I discuss here are identified by page and line numbers with illustrative text; only the page number is given for examples taken from other chapters in the same book. Many examples are from one story in the collection, "A Braa' Quate Boay," which appears on pages 37–43 in the original and is reprinted in the appendix to this chapter.

Phonologically, there are a number of examples that suggest a source for the anglophone creole forms. Thus *feer* (1. 107) and *weer* (11. 265, 266) for 'fair' and 'wear' reflect the raising typical of the West Indian dialects (/fiir/, /wiir/) and of Krio (/fia/, /wia/). Similarly, the diphthong written *aa* (phonetically [ɛə]) in *paashunce* (1. 46) and *waasted* (1. 180) is closer to the Caribbean /ie/ (/niem/, /pieshans/, etc.) than to the Standard English [eɪ]; a falling offglide is also evident in *soa* 'so' (1. 64) and *s'poase* (/suo/, /spuoz/) (1. 33), and labialization in *boay* 'boy' (/bwai/) (1. 30). Other similarities include *stoody* 'steady' (1. 109), *be'n* 'been' (11. 210, 215), *la* 'law' (1. 204), *shart* 'shirt' (1. 216), and *onder* 'under' (1. 50); and acquired initial aspiration is evident in, for example, *harm-cheer* 'armchair' (1. 50), *haoutside* 'outside' (1. 57), *hunyan* 'onion' (1. 174), *hup* 'up' (1. 189), and *hart* 'art' (1. 218). Other examples are found in Matthews (1939).

Lexically, we find dialect forms such as *axin'* 'asking' (1. 224), *chuck'd* 'blocked up' (1. 162) (cf. Krio *chok-op*, Jamaican *chak*), *lev'* 'leave' (1. 38) (cf. Krio, Gullah, etc., *lef* 'leave'), *ha'* 'have' (1. 298) (general Antilles, Gullah), *thankee* 'thank you' (1. 291), *ef* 'if' (1. 30), *Chressmess* 'Christmas' (p. 58), *maaken' 'aste* 'hurrying up' (p. 54), *gether* 'gather' (p. 17), *coss* 'abuse' (p. 24), *a'ter* 'after' (p. 23), *gi'* 'give' (p. 59), *a'redee* 'already' (p. 8), *taek-taek-taeken'* 'chattering' (p. 8) (cf. Sranan *tak'-taki*, earlier Krio *talkee-talkee* 'chattering'), *yalla* 'yellow' (pp. 33, 68), *'quatten* 'squatting' (p. 10), *liard* 'liar' (p. 26), *marcy* 'mercy' (p. 19), *t'morra* 'tomorrow' (p. 19), *'umboog* 'trouble' (p. 22), *farks* 'forks' (p. 17), *cheeny* 'china' (p. 16), *clemb* 'climb' (p. 21), *joomp* 'jump' (p. 22), *sho!* 'goodness!' [an exclamation] (p. 53), *guarnsee* 'sweater' (p. 27), *beetif'l* 'beautiful' (p. 27), *cover-sloot* 'overalls' (p. 28), *buccaboo* 'mischievous person' (p. 28), *fittee* 'able to' (p. 56), *by'mby* 'soon' (p. 53), *fergi'* 'forgive' (p. 33), *r'member* 'remind' (p. 71), *drap* 'drop' (p. 10), *kittle* 'kettle' (p. 10), and *bore his jaw* 'pierce his cheek' (p. 11). Other southwestern items (not Cornish specifically) in Krio include *brok* 'break,' *danda* 'dandruff,' *frosh* 'effervesce,' *galut* 'burly,' *gladi* 'glad,' *jonk* 'chunk' (segment of fruit), *krabit* 'miserly,' *leys* 'lazy,' *loboloboh* 'lump of fat,' *los* 'lose,' *monchi* 'deride,' *raizin-bomp* 'acne,' *wol-wef* 'wrasse fish,' *yeri* 'hear,' and *yangeyangeh* 'irritable, fussy' (Holm lists others for the Miskito Coast; see 1978, 84–86).

Grammatical forms include *how* for 'why' (1. 37): *'Aow 'sn't ee fix up the booard* 'Why don't you fix up the board,' commonly occurring in Krio (*au yu noh dey mek di bowd?*); *it is* (*tes*) for 'there is/are' (11. 26, 32): *'Tes some wan t' the' dooar* 'There's someone at the door' (cf. the same use in American Black English). The same word is used as highlighter in *'Tes K'ziah Boynes d' want ee* '[It's] Hezekiah Boynes [who] wants you' (p. 32) (cf. Antilles *iz Ezikaya waant yu)*. The function of aspectual *do* is the southwestern feature most often referred to in works on creole structure, although no acknowledgment has been made of *do*'s functional differences in southwestern British dialect and in creole. In the dialect texts, at least four functions occur: progressive, *w'ile 'e d' fillee* 'while he's filling [it]' (p. 68); punctual, *I d' want t' ax' ee a quesyen* 'I want to ask you a question' (p. 31); habitual, *I d' b'leeve oall I d' 'eear* 'I believe all I hear' (p. 20); and imperative, *Oul' th' jaw, do, Lizzee* 'Please stop talking, Lizzy' (p. 58). These functions are not found neatly transferred into the creoles; indeed, they differ in creoles from area to area. This is evident in the equivalents of these four sentences, given here in a West African, a western Caribbean, an eastern Caribbean, and a North American creole (Krio, Jamaican, Kittitian, and Gullah), respectively:

Krio
  wais i dey fulop am
  a wan aks yu wan kweshon
  a kin bilif ol weytin a kin yeri
  set yu mot, du
Jamaican
  wais im a ful i
  mi wan aaks yu a kweshan
  mi biliib all wa mi iir
  shet yu mout, du
Saint Kitts
  wail i a ful am
  mi waan aaks yu a kweshan
  mi doz biliiv aal wa mi doz hea
  shet yu mout, du
Gullah
  wail i də ful em ap
  a daz waan fə aaks yu a kweshchən
  a de bliib ɔl dat a də yedi
  shet yu mout, du

According to Peter Trudgill (1986, 70–71), hyperdialectism is leading to generalization of the functions of *do* in the southwestern dialects, a process that may have already begun a century ago, to judge from the texts used here.

Past action is marked in the text with both *did* and *have*: *The Temanite ded b'long to* 'The Temanite used to' (p. 11), *th' Queeryans do s'poase th' boanses ded b'long to a helk* 'the antiquarians suppose that the bones belonged to an

elk' (p. 18), *'Enry 'ave shut aout* 'Henry shut out' (p. 14). Neither form occurs
in West Africa, but both are found in the North American and Caribbean creoles. Habitual aspect is marked with *a-* in *'e doan't a beer to miss a night,* 'he
can't bear to miss a night' (p. 9), *I've a keept 'n* 'I've kept it' (p. 7), *The w'iles
I'm a-doen' et* 'while I'm doing it' (p. 10), and *I've a-gote* 'I've got' (p. 17). In
the eastern Caribbean and Gullah, the particle *a* (or *da*) has a similar function
that overlaps its function as a progressive marker; in the western Caribbean
only the progressive is marked with *(d)a.* The form itself may be the result
of the collapse in the creoles of both *d'* and *a* from the metropolitan dialects.
The function of the Cornish English verbal suffix *-i* indicating repeated action
(*diggee, 'arkee, yearee,* etc.) has not been transferred into the creoles, although
some forms suggest its phonological retention; for example, Sranan *diki, arki,*
Krio *yeri,* 'dig,' 'hark,' 'hear.' Norman Rogers writes of the southwestern pronunciation of such verbs as *carry* as *carr,* "probably a case of over-correction,
taking off a -y that was part of the word, not the free infinitive ending" (1979,
37–38). In Krio we find *ker* and *ber* for both 'carry' and 'bury.'

Another marker, which turns up in both Krio and Gullah but not elsewhere,
is the indicator of habitual action *blan(t)* (< *belang t'* < *belong to;* cf. similar
usage in Tidewater United States); in southwestern dialect it occurs in *'e . . .
do b'long smawken' cigars* 'he usually smokes cigars' (p. 14), *dead boays d'
usu'lly b'long . . . fer t' lev' no fut-prents* 'dead boys don't usually leave foot-
prints' (11. 122–23), *Billee, 'ome, d' b'long gwine long weth 'e's sister, Jaanee*
'Billy, at home, usually goes with his sister Janey' (p. 27), and *aurs 'n' yours
d' oallus b'long t' smooder t'gethar!* 'ours and yours usually smother [i.e., get
blocked up] together' (11. 164–65). In Krio these sentences would be *i blant
smowk siga, deydey boboh noh blant lef non fut-mak, Bili, to wi, blant go wit in
sista Jeyni,* and *wi yown en yu yown blant chok-op towgeda.* The generalized
prepositional use of *'pon* occurs in *laafen' 'pon thet* 'laughing at that' (p. 15),
'pon th' haoutside 'on the outside' (11. 56–57), and *t' luk 'pon tha* 'to look at
you' (1. 83); compare creole *luk pan yu, laf pan yu,* and so on.

Infinitives are found with *for to* in this text (11. 87, 88) rather than simply
for, the marker in common creole. In Britain today, *for* alone is found only
in part of northern Cornwall and the northern half of Devonshire, and in the
area around Liverpool (significantly, these two regions were major points of
embarkation to Africa and the West Indies; see Orton et al. 1967–68, S3).
Wright includes such examples as *I baint gwain vor let you habm, Maister zend
me down vor tell ee,* and *the wheelwright's here for mend the cart* (1898–1905,
2:452) in the *English Dialect Dictionary.*

Several examples of the third-person subject pronoun *a* or *aw* turn up in the Anglo-Cornish text: *aw eddn' no wan 'pon th' roof* 'it [i.e. there] isn't anyone on the roof' (1. 29), *I d' moas'ly think 'aow that aw es* 'I mostly think that's how he is' (1. 64), *I'm thinkan' aw 'll be 'is awn fau't* 'I'm thinking that it'll be his own fault' (ll. 146–47), *wos aw, 'en?* 'was it, then?' (1. 156), *Wheere'st aw be'n to sence, un?* 'Where has he been to since, then?' (ll. 213–14), *es aw?* 'is it?' (1. 205). There is one instance of *'e* for 'it': *'t laist not fust gwain off, 'e wadn'* 'at least, not at first it wasn't' (ll. 157–58); and one of *om* for 'it': *moas' hexlant fer th' brown-ti-tes I d' b'long t' find om* 'most excellent for the bronchitis, I usually find it' (ll. 174–75). These, and the form *en* or *'n* for the third-person singular object (human and nonhuman masculine, and inanimate crafted), the form *ee* or *'e* for the second-person singular subject, *me* as possessive, and *we* and *she* as object pronoun all have parallels in the creoles: *shut 'n 'ome 'pon th' haoutside* 'lock it on the outside' (ll. 56–57), *not a pass'l o' gab wed'n* 'not a lot of talk with him' (ll. 143–44), *you wud faal in wed'n to wance* 'you'd get along with him right away' (1. 145), *I d' wish 'n well* 'I wish him well' (1. 150), *Taake 'n wi'ee 'n, an' weer 'n as aw es* 'Take it with you then, and wear it as it is' (1. 266), *ef aw'll do fer 'n, 'e's welkom to 'n,* 'if it'll do for him, he's welcome to it' (1. 273), *'Tes K'ziah Boynes d' want ee* 'Hezekiah Boynes wants you' (1. 32), *me boot* 'my boot' (1. 239), *quate people like we* 'civil people like us' (1. 153), *t' do 'eere 'long we* 'to do here with us' (p. 21) *a wadn' no trooble t' she* 'it was no trouble to her' (p. 17), *carr, aout woss 'pon um* 'take out what's on it' (p. 66), *a goold noogetty pin in 'um* 'a gold nugget pin in it' (p. 14).

In one case, *um* occurs in subject position: *ded um diggy ar no?* 'did he dig or not?' (p. 17). In the creoles this form is restricted to Barbadian and Guyanese (discussed further in Hancock 1988, for sentence 4 therein).

Possibly the model for the Suriname group's possessive construction noun + *for* + noun is the dialect's noun + *of* + noun, which occurs frequently in the texts: *th' piyetee ob'm* 'his piety' (p. 9), *th' buzzum ob'm* 'its bosom' (p. 14), *th' graazen' rights ob'm* 'its grazing rights' (p. 16), *th' pawket ob'm* 'its pocket' (p. 44), *Gawd bless th' dear aul' faace av 'ee* 'God bless your dear old face' (p. 59), *th' taail-end av 'er* 'her tail end' (p. 23). *Of* does not occur in the Suriname creoles, nor in the West African dialects.

Passing to mean 'excepting' occurs once, in *Nawthen into 'er pooer in'ards, passen' av a yepmee Bicklig's loaf* 'Nothing in her poor belly excepting a half-penny Bicklig's loaf' (p. 12). In Krio (but apparently no other creole), 'except' is also translated by *pass;* this sentence would read *natin noh dey na in po beleh pas wan eypni yown Bicklig lowf.* Multiple negation, found in all nonstandard metropolitan dialects and all of the anglophone creoles, occurs in *no 'osses t' ait no 'ay, ner no hoates,* 'no horses to eat any hay or oats' (p. 21).

The kind of regional dialect source analysis that has been started for the West African and Caribbean creoles needs to be undertaken for the Suriname group too; the Sranan pronouns for 'you,' 'he,' and 'him' are also *i, a,* and *en,* and may have originated in the English of the Southwest, although Mandinka also has the same forms for the first two of these pronouns. *Om* object 'it' (see above) occurs in Nevis, Saint Kitts, Antigua, and Saint Vincent. Finally, there are a few instances of negation with preverbal *no: you no 'caount t' maak a fool av yerself* 'you don't need to make a fool of yourself' (p. 34), *she no need t' do et* 'she doesn't need to do it' (p. 12), *aw no need t' go flyan' daown me throat* 'he doesn't need to go flying down my throat' (11. 223–24).

A more exhaustive examination of this text and the others in the same collection turns up many more similarities; enough have been given here, however, to indicate that the southwestern regional dialects occupied an important place in the metropolitan component during the formative period of the Atlantic anglophone creoles. In addition to the linguistic evidence, we may cite cultural similarities such as the children's game of "gaays" described on pages 25–26, reminiscent of the Sierra Leonean and Jamaican "moonshine baby," in which pieces of broken china are used to outline figures on the ground. Some creole folk beliefs appear to have West Country origins also, such as that which holds that cutting a child's fingernails with scissors will make him grow up to be a thief (E. Wright 1914, 265). Only by extracting the Irish, Scottish, Southwestern English, and other elements in these languages and analyzing them in the framework of the social and historical circumstances that gave rise to each in each area can we hope to understand the processes that led to the creolization of English.

Appendix: "A Braa' Quate Boay"

1 "Tap-tap! tap-tap! Rat-tat-tat-tat!" Theophilus
2 Trevorrow sat on his three-legged stool and hammered a
3 patching-piece of damped leather on his lapstone.
4 The workshop of the village shoemaker was not only a
5 home of industry; it served the purposes of the scattered
6 villagers in a variety of ways, for the shoemaker's stool at
7 the window facing the main road was an excellent observation
8 point. Theophilus was therefore the trusty depositary of
9 messages and admonitions of all sorts; and seldom would the
10 doctor or the post-girl, the 'bus-drivers, or the school-
11 attendance officer pass the shoemaker's shop without a half-
12 halt and a glance of inquiry at the little second-storey
13 lattice window.
14 In the evenings—especially during the long winter
15 evenings—Theophilus seldom lacked company; for the shop then
16 became the rendezvous of the socially-inclined neighbours—
17 miners, farm-hands, and a fair sprinkling of the village-
18 elders whose days of toil were for the most part past. These
19 old cronies would group themselves about the stove—a rude
20 iron structure placed near the centre of the room, and having
21 a pipe-flue leading through the roof; while the younger
22 denizens would lounge on benches, boxes and forms. The only
23 approach was by way of an outside flight of granite steps at
24 the house-end, communicating direct with the high-road.
25 "Tap-tap! Tap-tap! Tap-tap-tap-tap!!"
26 "I d' moas' think 'tes some wan t' th' dooar, Thophy,"
27 said Mister Bill with a tired drawl, his hands clasped round
28 his bent knee, and his gaze on the rafters.
29 "Shoor aw eddn' no wan 'pon th' roof, Mister Bill?—
30 Awp'm 'broadth' dooar, wan o' yo' boays,—ef you're
31 waakan'!"
32 " 'Tes K'ziah Boynes d' want ee, Mais'r 'Vurraw."
33 "Want me?—no s'poase, Edwert John; (tap-tap!-tap!)—
34 moore likelier t' be th' self, sonnay.—Come'st in K-ziah;
35 nobody 'eere edd' gwain' t' ait ee, maid! (tip-tap!)—

From Nicky Trevaylor, *Echoes from Carn, Cove, and Cromlech* (St. Ives: J. Lanham).

36   come'st in an' see 'aow purty Edwert John c'n thraw spears
37   t' th' targit! (tap!—tap-tap!)—"Aow 'sn't ee fix up th'
38   booard, yo' boays back theere, an' lev' th' maid pick aout
39   th' bes' shot (tap—tap!) fer a shiner? Haw!—nawthan' av
40   no soort you haa'n't gote 'baout ee, yo' boays!"
41   "Es feyther's boots done, Mais'r 'Vurraw, plaise?" said
42   Keziah from the doorway.
43   "Done!—my deear maid! w'y—feyther's boots was done an'
44   double-done 'foore I clump't them time-'foore-laast! Done!!
45   Tell feyther, m' dear, oall them theere boots es good fer es
46   taichan' shoo-maakers t' larn paashunse (tap-tap!).
47   "Iss K'ziah (b' quate, yo' boays back theer, 'r elst
48   auver they stipses you goes!—haa'n't ee gote no manners,
49   un!)—iss maid, I done them. W'eere ded I putt Benny's—I
50   moas' think 'aow they're in onder your harm-cheer, Mister
51   Bill: sheft auver 'aaf meenut', aul' fella'."
52   Mister Bill vacated the upturned bucket, whence
53   Trevorrow produced a sorry-looking pair of patched boots.
54   "Good riddance to ee," said he, handing them to the
55   girl—"not you I doan't mane, K'ziah—aunly feyther's boots.
56   Awp'm dooar fer 'er, Edwert John; an'—shut 'n 'ome 'pon th'
57   haoutside ef 'tes auver mooch bacca-swawk 'eere t' soot tha!
58   Saame to ee, K'ziah. An' luk—mind thee maake Edwert John
59   carr' they boots fer tha!"
60   Mister Bill still gazed at the rafters.
61   "I d' think—ha—that Edwert John es a braa' tidy lad
62   comin' awaay, ha—Thophy," drawled he.
63   "Iss, iss, th' boay 'll do vury well, Mister Bill."
64   "A quate lad ar—ha soa I d' moas'ly think 'aow that aw
65   es, Thoph'lus."
66   "Me 'n' you es av wan mind, Mister Bill. (Tip-tip-tap!
67   Tippety-tap!!) Gote anything in yer mind p'tickler agin th'
68   boay, Mister Bill?"
69   "Well—n-noa. Nice lad—h'm—quate lad th' chap es."
70   "Taake yer time, Mister Bill (tippy-tap!) we gote a long
71   ebemen' afoore es. No need fer tha' t' do no vi'lence t'
72   yar thoughts, not t' your time o' life. Quate lad, Mister
73   Bill (tat-at-at-at)—vury."
74   "Th' boay's feyther wos a braa' quate man—h'm—in 'is
75   time, too, I moas' think."
76   "An' 'is gran'fer likewise, Mister Bill."
77   "Trew, Thoph'lus—trew. Never 'eeard nawthan' agin 'is

78   gran'fer nuther: quate people—ha—right 'long."
79   The shoemaker set down his hammer and took up knife and
80   whetstone. With a preparatory spit upon the latter he half
81   turned round on his stool.
82   "Mister Bill," said he, sharpening his knife in the
83   pauses—"any wan wud saay t' luk 'pon tha that *thee* wes't a
84   quate man (tss—tss! tss—tss! tss—tss!); but m' deear out;
85   fella (tss—tss)—ef they shud aunly c'me up t' shop, 'eere,
86   an' 'ark t' tha (tss—tss—tss!) givin' of yer heloquance weth
87   sooch a roosh (tss—tss!) they mit go fur fer t' oalter theer
88   'pinyans—ha? You shud auft fer t' taake things stoodier an'
89   aisier t' your time o' life, Mister Bill, 'pend 'pon ut."
90   Mister Bill evinced his appreciation of the wholesome
91   and timely warning by shifting his clasp to the other knee
92   and transferring his gaze from the rafters to the shelf of
93   leather above the shoemaker's head.
94   "H-ha—I moas' think as 'aow 'tes a braa' daal av
95   trewth, h'm, in wot you're tellan', Thoph'lus. Av cou'se we
96   d' oall av es knaw, a-ha, that we shan't be 'eere fer hever;
97   an' some'aow I d' think, h'm, that 'tes hev'ry man's dooty,
98   like, fer t' live s' long 's 'e can; fer they d' tell me,
99   ha, that you gote t' be a braa long time dead.—Trewly a
100   nice quate boay, Thoph'lus."
101   Trevorrow ceased sharpening his knife, and with an
102   innocent glance, collected the mute wish of the shop, as he
103   fitted the piece of hammered leather to the sole of a
104   child's shoe.
105   "Pr'ceed on, Mister Bill," said the shoemaker, "we're
106   oall 'arkan'. Sart'nly th' boay eddn' 'eere t' taake up fer
107   'isself; saame time we d' knaw you're a feer man. ('Oosh yer
108   clatter theere, yo' boays, an' pass auver th' pitcher t'
109   Mister Bill, wan av ee.) Drink up an' stoody yerself, Mister
110   Bill, no need t' be afear'd ob'm, 'e's aunly fresh draw'd
111   fr'm th' peeth 'day moornan'."
112   "I s'poase you doan't think Thoph'lus, 'aow that 'tes
113   sooch a thing—h'm—as fer a boay t' be *too* quate, naow?"
114   "Aw noa, Mister Bill, aunly a dead wan."
115   The shoemaker turned to the window seat, littered over
116   with sundry small tools, scraps of leather, wooden shoe-
117   pegs, round-headed hobs, toe-plates, and heel-irons, bits of
118   wax, and various other odds and ends—and trimmed his smoky
119   little lamp. Mister Bill quaffed a leisurely draught from

120 the pitcher.
121 "I doan't 'ardly think, sim' me," resumed Mister Bill,
122 resettling himself, "as 'aow dead boays d' usu'lly b'long,
123 like-a-thing, fer t' lev no fut-prents t' spaik av, a-h'm."
124 "Fut-prents, Mister Bill?"
125 "Fut-prents was wot I 'looded to, Thoph'lus."
126 "Boay's fut-prents, Mister Bill?"
127 "Th' saame, Thoph'lus, 'thout I'm mooch d'caived."
128 "Zackly soa, Mister Bill. Braa' whist job fer we
129 shoomaakers ef they ded, oul' fella!"
130 Trevorrow threw the little shoe on the pile of the
131 mended, and picked up the next from that of the maimed. It
132 chanced to be a stout boot, recently mended, from which the
133 "cue" or heel-iron had been roughly wrenched—exposing the
134 new piece of bed-leather. He glanced quickly up at Mister
135 Bill, whose glance as quickly shifted from the boot to the
136 overhead shelf.
137 "Rum thing," said the shoemaker, *sotto voce,* examining
138 the boot curiously; adding, as he put it underneath his
139 stool, "Later on," and turning his attention to other repair
140 items.
141 "Pity you dedn't c'me up t' shop laast ebemen', Mister
142 Bill. Th' noo p'leeceman drop'd in fer a bit o' wile—
143 (tap tap!)—braa' smairt, tidy young fella, I sh'd s'poase.
144 Not a passl' o' gab wed'n—a quate soort av a chap, Mister
145 Bill: you wud faal in wed'n to wance, I d' knaw you wud.—
146 Tidy lookan' g'eat youngstar 'e es, too; I'm thinkan' aw 'll
147 be 'is awn fau't ef 'e doan't carr' off wan av aur maadens
148 fer 'is missus,—weth s' mooch av aur awn chaps gone t' S'th
149 Af'ca!"
150 "I doan' knaw, ha, but wot I d' wish 'n well, Thoph'lus;
151 f'r oal I haan't 'ad th' plezhar av maakan' 'is 'quaantance,
152 h'm, not as yit. Doan see 'aow aw shudn' prospar 'n' git
153 fat, a-h'm,—'eere 'long weth quate people like we."
154 "Tap!—Tap-tap!—Tap!"
155 "—Yer brown-ti-tes troublan' av tha laast ebemen',
156 Mister Bill, wos aw, 'en?"
157 "Noa Thoph'lus, aw noa, a-ha—h'm;—'t laist not fust
158 gwain' off, 'e wadn'."
159 "Thoft I 'eard tha caughan' braa' 'n' loosty when I went
160 indooars, thass oall."
161 "Iss. 'Mse, I wor a bit troobled wed'n fer a braa' spur.

162 Aur oul' chimley gote kind o' chuck'd like—back kitchan
163 wan."
164 "Aw!—aow's that, 'en, wender?—Aurs dedn't an' aurs 'n'
165 yours d' oallus b'long t' smooder t'gethar!—Wadn't no
166 wes'ly wind nuther, laas' night—wos aw?"
167 "Noa—aw noa, nar aw warn't, Thoph'lus."
168 "Straange, Mister Bill!—Caan't be fer want av clanen';
169 fer aw wadn' but laas' week you sot fire to 'n—was aw?"
170 "Aunly laas' week, Thoph'lus. Laas' We'nsday."
171 "P'r'aps a brick 've gote athurt th' flew?"
172 "N-noa. Edn' like that theere, 't oall-h'm. Y'see—my
173 oul' wumman wus t' th' fireplaace fryan' av a pan av tripe
174 an' a hunyan ar two—h'm—a-ha—moas' hexlant fer th' brown-
175 ti-tes I d' b'long t' find om—w'en daown come a braa' size
176 tubban, daown chimley, slap 'n th' pan, 'knaw; an' aw scat
177 th' tripe flyan' aout auver th' floo-er 'n oall d'reckshuns,
178 an th' hunyans likewise—a braa' dirty coadle, shoor 'nough!"
179 "Deear, deear, Mister Bill—wot 'r' 'e tellan' av!—oall
180 th' tripe 'n' hunyans clane waasted like 'at theere, jis'
181 w'en . . ."
182 "Noa, Thoph'lus—aw warn't waasted nuther, 'zactly; fer
183 me 'n' th' oul' wumman 'n' th' cat, h'm—stroogl't, like,
184 'tween es fer t' maade a meal ob'm aaft'w'rds. I'm gwain a
185 bit 'foore m' stoory, f'r oall. W'en th' tripe 'n' traade
186 flied like 'at theere, I thoft—h'm—that I 'eeard a soort
187 av a scraapen' kind av a nooise 'pon th' slats av th' roof,
188 luk; so I quately awp'md th' back dooar (aw wor 'pon th'
189 letch, 'knaw), mainin' fer to try fer t' see, ef I cud, wot
190 wus hup theere. But wot fust ketcht me heye wes a peer av
191 boots—'ha right 'long-side th' waater-bar'l—h'm."
192 "Peer av *boots,* Mister Bill—ha!"
193 "—Peer av boots, Thoph'lus. Soa I tuk 'n' creept onder
194 th' winder an' raitcht footh an' tuk wan o' thum, yo."
195 "—Aaf meenut, Mister Bill—'ould on 'aaf meenut,"
196 interrupted the shoemaker; "—I moas' think I 'eeard a stap
197 'pon th' stipses!"
198 The door opened, and in came Edward John, who took a
199 seat well in the shade.
200 Mister Bill was clasping his knee, his steady gaze on
201 the rafters—a picture of elderly innocence. Trevorrow, at
202 the lifting of the latch deftly half-wheeled on his stool
203 and was busy with an old shoe.

204 "La!" said he, looking back over his shoulder,—"thass
205 never Hedwert c'me back a'ready, es aw?—Thee hassn't 'ad
206 mooch av a spell t'night 'en, boay! (Tippy-tap! tap-tap!)—
207 K'ziah's people eddn' mooch fer nawthan' in th' waay av
208 suppers, so I've 'eeard tell.—Es th' 'booses come aout long
209 yit, Edwert, dust tha knaw?"
210 "Noa yo', doan' knaw nawthan' 'bout thum. Haan't be'n
211 aout-long, 't oall."
212 "Theess' went aout-'long w'en theess' went fr'm 'eere
213 oall right 'en, boay! (Tip-tap-tap!)—Wheere'st aw b'en to
214 sence, un?"
215 "Nawthan' do wi' thee wheere I be'n to, s'poase—es aw?"
216 "Haw—haw!—Kip yer shart on, boay—kip yer shart on!
217 No need fer ee t' git roosty 'baout ut, 't oall! W'y we be'n
218 'eere tellan' ov wot a quate boay thee hart, too!—an' naow
219 'eere thee hart thrawing moock auver thy awn pickshur!—I'm
220 'shaamed o' thee, boay!—artn't thee, Mister Bill?"
221 H'm—I doan' knaw 'ardly as to that nuther, Thoph'lus.
222 Hedwert John 's a quate boay 'nough f'r oall I d' knaw."
223 "So aw es, Mister Bill. Is fye—so aw es; aunly aw no
224 need t' go flyan' daown me throat fer aunly mere-ly axin'
225 ob'm 'baout th' 'booses, see!"
226 "Wadn' fer that 't oall, Thophy, an' thee knaw ut," said
227 the youth.
228 W'y boay—I'll lev ut weth Mister Bill, 'eere, ef I
229 dedn' aunly . . ."
230 "—Doan't matter nawthan' t' Mister Bill, nar noa
231 huther Mister Bill: I d' knaw wot thee said, pardner."
232 "Come-come, Edwert John!—Ef you aunly comed back 'gean
233 t' maake a stir . . ."
234 "I—I eddn' come back t' maake no stir, nawthan' o' th'
235 soort, see that, too!"
236 "Noa?—p'r'aps yo' wudn' mind levvin' av es knaw wot you
237 *ded* come back fer, 'en—as you're s' pert 'bout et?"
238 "Thee'st knaw s' well 's me wot I'm come back fer. I d'
239 want me boot fer t' carr' 'ome wi' me."
240 "Paashunse guide me—so thee dost, boay! Naame o'
241 Deear!—'eere av we party be'n chat, chat, chat, 'bout wot
242 a quate young chap Edwert John es,—an' ef I haan't be'n 'n'
243 fergote oall 'bout puttan' 'is boot t' rights fer 'n!"
244 And Trevorrow reached beneath his stool and withdrew the
245 boot. In a twinkling he placed the last between his knees

246 and fitted the boot thereon; turned out a box of heel-irons
247 on the bench, and began to sort them out—only to reject
248 each one as he fingered it.
249 "Drat th oul' cues!" said he, thumping his left palm
250 with his right fist; "ef I dedn' fit th' vury laast peer av
251 them-size cues on they vury peer o' boots av thine aunly
252 this week, booay! Give es th' saame wan; 'e'll do full s'
253 well 's a noo wan."
254 "Haan't gote 'n."
255 "Aw,—thasss a poor job, un'—wheere 's aw to?"
256 "Lost'nt."
257 "Chuckle-'ead!—wheere ded ee lost 'n to, 'en?"
258 "Chuckle-'ead th'self, cumrade!—Ef I knaw'd wheere I
259 lost 'n to, I sh'd knaw wheere t' find 'n to, shudn' I?"
260 "Iss, s'poase, Maister Wisdom! But theere, 'tes a pity
261 oall th' same; fer noan av theuse 'ere cues, waan't fit 'n,
262 an' so I caan't do 'n fer ee t'night, m' sonny boay.
263 Ows'mever—I'll sent in t' P'nzaance weth th' 'booss for
264 some moore t'morra."
265 "I d' want t' weer 'n t'morra, man!"
266 "—Taake 'n wi'ee 'n, an' weer 'n as aw es!" And the
267 shoemaker whipped the boot off the last and flung it across
268 to its owner.
269 Mister Bill spread his hands on his knees, and, throwing
270 one shoulder into a most accommodating expression, said—
271 "W'y a-h'm—I b'lieve I gote a cue 'eere 'n me 'awkut,
272 Thoph'lus, that mit meet th' caase. Edwert John's a braa'
273 quate boay—'ha,—an' ef aw'll do fer 'n 'e's welkom to 'n.
274 'Eere aw es, Thoph'lus."
275 "Thank ee, oul' fella.—Oo sh'd 'a' thoft to find Mister
276 Bill carr'in' raoun' sich traade in 'is pawkut!—carr' 'n
277 fer *luck* s'poase, Mister Bill—ha?—Thraw auver th' boot,
278 Hedwert John."
279 The last was again put into position, the boot put
280 thereon, and—"Blest ef aw doan't fit 'n like a cork 'n a
281 bottle, Mister Bill!—Wheere'st a git'n to, oul' fella?"
282 "Well yo'—eh, h'm—I foun' a boot put theere 'long-side
283 aur bar'l, h'm—an' I tuk 'n indooars 'n gote th' pinchars
284 an' haled th' cue haout ob'm—'ha—an' putt 'n in me pawkut
285 fer *luck,* as you d' saay, Thoph'lus. Will aw do, think?"
286 "Do!—Saame 's ef aw wor maade fer'n!—aunly luk 'eere!"
287 And in a trice the heel-iron was re-fixed. Tossing the boot

288 to its owner, Theophilus said, "Theere thee hart, Edwert
289 John. Hey? Aw, no need t' thank *me,* boay; Mister Bill 's
290 th' wan for ee to thank, 'blaw."
291 "Thankee, Mister Bill," said the thoroughly discomfited
292 youth.
293 "I'm shoor, Mister Bill," said the shoemaker, rising and
294 unstrapping his apron, "I'm shoor ef you d' want a kindness
295 done ti' ee any time, you aunly gote t' lev Edwert John knaw
296 ut."
297 "I d' b'lieve ut, Thoph'lus—I d' b'lieve ut.—Ef you
298 gote a mind t' c'me in 'n' ha' a bit av supper wi' me 'n'
299 th' oul' wumman—I sh'd like t' 'ave a bit 'o chat wi' ee.
300 Edwert John. I d' knaw ee fer a braa quate boay—h'm!—an'
301 I doan't s'poase you'll turn yer noase hup to a plaate av
302 tripe 'n' hunyans: will ee come?"
303 And as the kindly old man and the shame-faced youth rose
304 to go out together Theophilus Trevorrow diplomatically
305 turned out the lamp!

Let the Church Say "Amen": The Language of Religious Rituals in Coastal South Carolina

Patricia Jones-Jackson

This paper investigates the most prestigious and sophisticated variety of language in African-American communities, especially in the Sea Islands, the language used in religious rituals by the clergy and some members of the congregation in black churches. Indisputably, the church has been and remains the most powerful force in these communities, and the most prolific black public speakers—including Jesse Jackson, Barbara Jordan, and Martin Luther King, Jr.—have adopted the speaking styles used in the church. Yet, few studies have compared the speech used in the home and less formal environments with that used in the church and similar formal settings. Such a comparison will be only one part of this paper, however; my primary objective is to discuss the language of religious rituals in the Sea Island coastal areas of the South Atlantic United States to determine what linguistic features contribute to the process sometimes called the "evocation of the spirit."

I choose the language of this ritual process because its speakers must possess extraordinary rhetorical skills to achieve this evocation, and, contrary to expectations, the most accomplished speakers in many black congregations have little, if any, formal academic background. Unfortunately, the technical nature of descriptive linguistic studies has led many readers to conclude that language skills are not highly valued in the black community. On the contrary, outstanding rhetorical skills are praised, practiced, and deeply venerated as essential for effective speakers and learned individuals. The question, then, is What is the source of this linguistic eloquence? Most of these speakers have never heard of Cicero or Quintillian, yet their speech embodies Ciceronian and Quintillianesque ornaments of style capable of divinely inspiring and passionately persuading a congregation to respond with rapturous and joyous replies. More important, their speech is filled with electrifying stylistic devices used judiciously throughout to induce the rhythmic incantation so imperative to the evocation.

Linguistic energy is not created for its own sake. It is essential to creating an environment for the embodiment of the Divine, the evocation of the spirit. In this paper I will analyze the language of this ritual, both verbal and nonverbal, to determine what gives it tenacity, homogeneity, and mass appeal.

The religious evocation, or "calling up," process is far from unique to the coastal areas of South Carolina and Georgia. It has been observed in African cults, in Haitian voodoo, in Cuban santería, in Jamaican pocomania, in Brazilian macumba, in Winti cults of Guyana, on the Sea Islands, and in black churches throughout the United States. Again, linguistic energy is not created for its own sake. Through this energy, God, the Divine, is actually evoked and is thought to become embodied in certain members of the congregation. It is through this release of religious energy that African-derived religious practices differ most from European-derived ones. In most European-derived religious services and rituals, the congregation sits quietly and thinks of the Divine in abstract terms. To worshippers on the Sea Islands, however, the Divine is a concrete entity whose presence can be created by a master rhetorician and a responsive audience; but for this mutual "call and response," or verbal interplay, to occur, there must be mutual respect and an understanding of roles. The minister must speak in the language of his congregation and choose imagery unique to the environment of his listeners. He may, for example, ask a blessing that the Holy Spirit "touch each and every heart so that their spirits shine like a crab's back in the rain." To further illustrate his knowledge and acceptance of the rural lives of his coastal parishioners, the minister may pray that the members of the congregation would strive to "plant the children's feet deep down in the soil like the mighty Angel Oak tree so that they won't be rooted by the storms of life." The members of the congregation, knowing their roles well, encourage the minister to continue his "warming words" by replying and calling out cries of agreement until the whole church is one mass of spiritual energy.

Some writers, both black and white, have denounced such overt religious expressions as barbaric and uncouth (see Bastide 1978; Carter 1976; Mbiti 1970; Jahn 1961). Yet the homogeneity of such practices among the masses has ensured their cohesiveness and widespread survival throughout the New World. In the past there have been efforts to eradicate these emotional religious practices. Protestant and some Puritan groups in America, for example, restricted their slaves' personal lives much more than did their Catholic counterparts in the West Indies or South America. Some Protestants considered it their duty to educate their slaves into being better human beings, and this meant teaching them to be ashamed of their African beliefs and practices. Baptist and Methodist slave holders took a different approach, stressing practical maxims and an intimate, personal relationship with God. Their teachings were in many instances commensurate with the concept of a personal "Chi," or Deity, with whom the African slaves were already familiar. On the surface, this familiarity won the Baptists and Methodists more converts, but on a deeper level, the slaves may have shaped and reinterpreted the European religious practices to fit their traditional mode of worship (Joyner 1984). Even in 1838, Kidder and Fletcher, for example, stressed the point that the "Mohammedan slaves did not abjure their faith even when they were baptized," and said that slaves continued to practice their own religion although they considered themselves Christians (Bastide 1978, 128).

The Africanized religious practices transcended every faith. Regarding Catholicism, Roger Bastide (1978, 142) says that "although catholicism in imposing itself on African religion adulterated it, it is only fair to say, in the beginning at any rate, it was African religion that adulterated catholicism." Efforts made by parish priests in Brazil and elsewhere to force blacks to abandon religious practices such as dances, overt calls and responses, and shouting were futile. In 1917, shouting was prohibited by ordinance in Trinidad and Tobago because it was not considered austere, but the practices continued just the same.

African-derived overt religious expression continues to survive in the 1980s in North, Central, and South America. The homogeneity of this expression regardless of the location or the language in which the rituals are performed indicates that certain requirements are being met in the evocation of the spirit. The ritual begins with a song, such as the *akuko iwate nti* in Igbo, which is designed to create the right mood for the experience. The selected song may be a hymn of Christian European origin, but it is usually modified to a jubilee and given the Africanized timbre, rhythm, emphasis, and harmony (Jahn 1961, 224). Once the mood is created, the speaker may begin a prayer or sermon. To be effective, the speaker must know the kind of oratory that inspires his congregation, and he must have the ability to string beautifully constructed phrases together to produce concrete images and create the chanting rhythm and tone characteristic of African-derived religious rituals. Once the rhythm is established, it is maintained through various techniques, the most important of which is the reply from the audience. Some speakers are able to excite and evoke feelings of the Divine through their energetic diction and tone alone. Others intensify the mood by tapping with a stick, drumming with a chair, pausing strategically, swaying back and forth, or using gestures and movements, all of which have become associated with the ritual.

Gestures and movements are as important as the message itself, and certain gestures have become associated with certain speech performances. To an outsider, for example, a minister wiping his perspiring brow has little significance beyond the obvious, but to an African-derived congregation, that gesture is uniquely loaded with semiotic functions. It is used only at tense moments, and never until the congregation is completely involved in the service and is replying enthusiastically. Wiping the brow means that "I [the minister] am ablaze with the 'word,' and I am perspiring from heat generated from within." The gesture is inappropriate if used in other parts of the service. But during tense moments, a minister may make strategic pauses. He stops preaching, wipes his perspiring brow, walks over to the Amen corner, leans over the railing, shakes his head, and says: "My brothers, I ain't think you bina know what I de come for tell you today!" To this the men in the Amen corner will shout out: "Sho! Sho! We de know! Sho!" This series of movements is performed not only to see whether the listeners are attuned to the service but also to release pent-up tension by allowing the congregation to participate actively in the service.

Capturing an Oral Tradition

The prayers and sermons in contemporary African-American Baptist and Methodist churches have changed little over the past two hundred years. The speakers change, but the formula for expressing the oral tradition of religious exhortation does not. The prayers contain a fixed arrangement which helps perpetuate the oral tradition. The formulaic opening begins with a quote from the Bible, a poem, or, more traditionally, a quote from *the Lord's Prayer*. Generally, the minister selects a member of the congregation to give the opening prayer. The speaker called on by the minister doesn't know beforehand that he or she will be asked to pray. Thus, the quotation serves to give the speaker time to collect his or her thoughts. The speaker is at liberty to alter the quotation to his or her own specification, and often the alteration is more descriptive than the original. But oral tradition does not require that a prayer be invariant or that one remember it exactly like the written version; quite the contrary. The speaker is expected to use poetic license and to add an original touch and creativity. For instance, the section of *the Lord's Prayer* that says "For thine is the kingdom, the power, and the glory" may be changed to "O Lord that thine may be our kingdom. We (are) expecting your kingdom to be a poor sinner's glory!"

After the quotation, the speaker begins his personal prayer. This prayer signals the beginning of a structured oration with a poem, line of appeal, and peroration. This beginning functions as a salutation to God in grand rhetoric

commensurate with the solemnity and propriety of the occasion. It enables the
speaker to express humility as a servant of God. Using such words as *mutable*
and *impermanent* (words the speaker may seldom, if ever, use in daily conversation, formal or informal, yet which are part of his religious vocabulary to be
recalled at will), the speaker does not presume to be as fortunate as the "foxes
of the forest," or the "birds of the air." He projects himself as a mere waif asking for mercy with his knees bent in humility, and the rest of the congregation
responds to him:

> Master, it's no lower
> Could I come this evening   *No!*
> Excepting my knees are down at the floor   *Floor!*
> Guilty heart within
> Crying Guilty! and already condemned   *Condemned!*
> Crying to you this evening, Jesus
> For mercy   *Yeah! Uh Hum!*
> While mercy can reach
> As you say the foxes of the forest got hole   *Yes!*
> And then the birds of the air has nest
> Master, we are poor son of man   *Pray now!*
> No where to lay down weary head . . .

The rhythm and the tone are usually set in the speaker's salutation to God,
after which he begins his appeal and inquiry. This appeal, or plea, follows a set
sequence. The number of pleas will depend on the occasion and the number of
items for which the speaker is asking for consideration. If he makes an appeal
for himself, he usually makes it the very last item in his prayer. Often, each
appeal begins with a traditional expression such as "And then, then, my God!
We ask . . ."; or "O you, you this evening, my heavenly Father, we ask . . ."
The pleas are likewise concluded with a traditional expression such as "Have
mercy if thou on us so please!" ("Grant this plea only if it is your desire.")
In addition to clarifying the organization of the prayers, these phrases, perhaps more than others, help to sustain the increasing force and rhythm of the
prayers. The peroration may vary. Most prayers, however, end with the quotation. "Somewhere Lord, Job declare. The weak shall cease in trouble and the
soul find rest."

Contrary to what many outsiders view as mere combinations of shouts,
moans, and exclamations such as "Yea Lordy!" and "Have mercy!" the prayers
and sermons of those truly gifted in the technique have few, if any, tags, stut-
ters, screams, or cries. Since the prayers and sermons are persuasive in their

appeal, it is for the listeners to get carried away with the beauty and phrasing of the speaker, and it is for the listeners to shout out "Amen!" Even the most unsophisticated prayers have a moving power when given by those gifted in the technique. The following is an excerpt from a slave prayer delivered by an elderly woman described as "an old Negro woman, apparently of the lowest type," who wore over the white wool on her head a dingy handkerchief, and who walked a mile and a half to church. The recorder (Harold Carter), unaccustomed to the language, says, "I reproduce the prayer as nearly as I can recollect it, changing some of the idioms to make it intelligible" (Carter 1976, 48). The excerpt from "Aunt Jane's Prayer" begins with the traditional salutation:

> Dear Massa Jesus, we all uns beg Ooner [you] come make us a call dis yere day. We is nutting but poor Ethiopian women and people ain't tink much 'bout we. We ain't trust any of dem great Massa, great too much dan Massa Linkum, you aint shame to care for we African people.
>
> Come to we, dear Massa Jesus. De sun, he hot too much, de road am dat long and boggy [sandy] and we ain't go no buggy for send and fetch Ooner. But Massa, you 'member how you walked dat hard walk up Calvary and ain't weary but tink about we all day way. We know you ain't weary for to come to we. We pick out de torns, de prickles, de brier, de back-slidin' and de quarrel and de sin out of yor path so dey shan't hurt Ooner or pierce feet no more. (Carter 1976, 49)

The creole syntax of this prayer takes little away from the readability and distracts nothing from the quiet beauty of the speaker's thoughts. A primary characteristic of prayers and sermons in African-American churches is that they are performed in the language of the community. The rural references in Aunt Jane's prayers vary little from the prayers and sermons given today on the Sea Islands and elsewhere. The "boggy" roads attest to the tortuous path that many congregation members have traveled to make it to the morning services; the briars and thorns attest metaphorically to the pricks and stabs that most of the members have received not only in their feet but in their daily lives as well. The words of the prayer are chosen specifically to soothe the listeners' minds and to provide a salve to the wounds of their consciences. Thus, the words are everything; they touch the listeners' lives and give them temporary solace from the outside world. So when the members of the congregation scream out their despair in unison to the speaker's call, they are doing more than practicing an ancient African ritual; they are replying to the words of a speaker who is gifted in a rhetorical technique, who knows how to "join the words" to provide the kind of emotional release that members of African-American congregations go to church to experience.

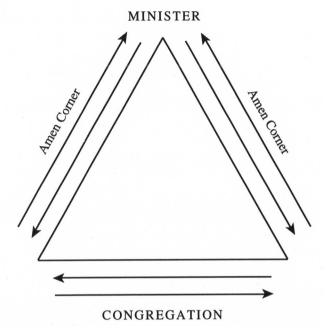

MINISTER

Figure 1. Call and response relationship in African-derived congregations.

Figure 1 illustrates the symbiotic relationship between the minister and congregation members in many African-derived church services. The minister has at his disposal a repertoire of regulatory functions which he uses to control the flow of his sermon. At the same time, the congregation and the members of the Amen corner encourage and provide reciprocal responses, sometimes directly related to the signals sent out by the minister. For the process to be effective and for the "evocation of the spirit" to occur, verbal and nonverbal interactions must be synchronized and harmonic. Each call from the minister requires an appropriate response from the congregation. Each gesture carries a coded message, and each sender and receiver (if both are a part of the exchange) is aware of the signals, which are a part of the church or "group" repertoire.

A few researchers (Carter 1976; Pipes 1951; Asante 1970) suggest that a few respondents in African-American congregations may not understand or accept what the speakers say, that they are instead responding to the contagious rhythm and cadence established by the call from the speaker and the response from the audience. I take exception to this claim. Usually church members who practice the type of ritual described here come from an oral tradition where none of the prayers and few of the sermons are written. Herein lies much of their inventiveness. Many of the prayers and sermons rival T. S. Eliot's *The Waste Land* in their elaborate allusions to works of literature. The most outstanding prayers are alive with prolific imagery, maxims, puns, understatements, and cultural references which the audience understands and responds to with enthusiasm. Since the rituals are not written, potential candidates must be attentive to detail to master the technique. More important, it does not matter whether the congregation listens to every word. What does matter is that the energetic force is created through the rhythm of the words. Only those who are known to have the gift of knowing how to "join the words" are asked to pray.

The sermons, on the other hand, are delivered by ministers and preachers, some ordained, some not. A minister may be ordained but still not have been "gifted with the silver trumpet," the speaking technique. The most effective ministers know the language and know how to use it to meet the spiritual needs of their congregation; they take their sermons directly from the Bible but select the proper biblical images to appeal and relate to their listeners' lives. The concept of a "good preacher" transcends race, creed, and educational background. One of the saddest events in a church community occurs when one of its members goes off to college or a divinity school and returns unable to preach, unable to join his words and make his prayers and sermons beautiful, alive with elaborate allusions and cultural references which only his congregation can understand. The good minister in some communities knows that his congregation is passionate and likes to be moved. He must know how to move them well, how to inspire them and make them respond to his every word and phrase until the Holy Spirit is completely evoked and the shouts and cries are the evidence that something has "touched" the souls of some of the listeners.

Those who denounce such services as mere performances or religious shows, not useful for teaching the congregation about the Bible or how to live in this modern world, may not have listened closely to the words of one gifted in the prayer and sermon techniques. Gifted pastors teach their congregations to seek the Divine within themselves and inspire them to look forward to coming every Sunday to feel its presence. So the answer to the question of what keeps the "spirit" alive is not simple. Religious language and overt exhortation are the driving force that gives the members cohesiveness (and can be inspired in them only by one of their own skilled in the technique). The language and style of delivery form a linguistic ritual which hits at the heart of the people's existence and keeps their spirit alive. Through this evocation process, they can come in contact with the Divine and actually experience its presence through the creation of that certain mood—mass ecstasy, pocomania, voodoo, or otherwise.

A Sermon

Below I will give an excerpt from a long sermon delivered by Rev. Renty Pinckney, a native of Yonges Island, South Carolina. Transcribing a sermon presents the religious language in its social context but, as might be expected, obscures many of the linguistic features unique to the Sea Island and coastal areas. The excerpt is from the end of a sermon given at the New Jerusalem Methodist Church on Wadmalaw Island, South Carolina, in June 1980. Since the excerpt is from the end of the sermon, it does not exemplify the manner in which he developed his theme, "God as the Bread of Life," but it does reveal Rev. Pinckney's creativity in joining scattered allusions from the Bible into a cohesive whole.

Though it is not my intent to thoroughly analyze the creole features in the speaker's language, one cannot help observing that the language of the sermon places the speaker somewhere on a continuum of features between English and Creole (the mesolect). While it is true that religious oratory may not be subject to the constraints of day-to-day speech, this speaker sprinkles enough of the creole syntax throughout his sermon for his parishioners, educated and uneducated alike, to accept him as a member of their speech community. Though subtle, the wording of the sermon is far less creole when the speaker uses biblical passages stored in his memory than when he uses phrases from his daily speech repertoire. Yet, features of the islands as well as of the coastal areas of Georgia, South Carolina, and Florida do show up even when the speaker paraphrases a quote. For example, the speaker deletes the *-ed* morpheme on most verbs, as in *Sometime you gone be toss; To be call a city;* and *When he look at Jesus.* Yet, the fact that he uses *-ed* with other verbs in similar contexts suggests that he knows the rules of Standard English and respects the expectation of his listeners who desire that he use, or at least approximate, a form of it and speak the prestigious language of the church.

Though this speaker is a native of the Sea Islands of South Carolina, he does not use the more stigmatized features of the basilect (Standard Creole) such as the preverbs *de, ben, bina,* and *don* (cf. the excerpt from "Aunt Jane's Prayer"). In his desire to use the elevated language of the church and to avoid the creole, however, he often hypercorrects himself by choosing the incorrect verb, as in *He are on the bank this morning.* He might have said, *i de here in the bank this morning,* but he would have been using the language of the common folk and not that of the minister. Even in the improper context, the verb *are* is preferred to the creole verb *de,* but again, only within the confines of the church.

Other features characteristic of the creole, but less stigmatized, are the speaker's nonuse, or at least inconsistent use, of the possessive pronouns, as in *All power in he hand;* the inconsistent use of the nominative case pronoun *we* in the objective case, as in *Got power for we* in one line, yet the use in its Standard English context in *He's able to feed us* in the very next line. The interplay of English and Creole features in the sermon is the subject of another essay that discusses where this speaker may fall on a linguistic continuum. For the purposes of this essay, however, the syntax of the wording is secondary to the linguistic energy. While the words of the sermon are captured below, and the congregation's replies appear alongside in italic type, the rhythm and force necessary for the evocation process escape. Readers cannot see the subtle gestures, pauses, blinks, stances, and other nonverbal interplay that contribute to the effectiveness of the spiritual evocation process; nor can they hear the speaker call out or experience the force with which the audience responds. The necessary linguistic energy, like the spiritual energy, cannot be, and perhaps was never intended to be, captured on the page.

THE BREAD OF LIFE

God is the Bread of Life
God will feed you when you get hungry   *O Yes! I know he will.*
     All right! Yeah. Amen! Yes Sir!

Look on the mountain
Beside the hill of Galilee   *My Lord!*

Watch his disciple
Riding on the Sea   *Yeah! Uh huh!*

Tossing by the wind and rain   *Yeah. Come up*

Going over the Sea of Temptation   *Uh um*

Brother I don't know
But I begin to think
In this Christian life   *Yes!*

Sometime you gone be toss   *Yes, Yeah!*

By the wind of life   *Yes, my Lord!*

The wind gonna blow you
From one side to the other   *Yes!*

On this Christian journey

The way ain't gonna be easy on us children   *No!*

And the disciple as they was going across   *Oh yes sir! Yeah*

The wind was tossing
As they was going over to Cana   *All right!*

The King was on the safe [same] side   *Uh hum*
To the Sea of Galilee   *All right*

To the land Goshen
It was so sufficient size   *Yeah, Right!*
To be call a city   *Yeah*
It was close to the seashore   *Shore! Yes!*

One-half mile long
Quarter of a mile wide   *Yes Sir!*

Brother I know
Jesus would be so glad   *So pleased!*

There he was among them
Brotheren of our Lord
And his disciple   *Yes! Yes, sir*

The Gospel!   *Oh yes*
Of John was formed in writing   *Writing*

Jesus was Towhead   *All right*

They begin to wonder brother   *Yeah!*

How is this could be   *Yeah!*

We left him on the other shore   *Yeah*
But this morning we are here   *Yes, here. My Lord!*

Jesus don't have a boat   *Boat*

Don't have a airplane   *Ah hah! Yeas!*

Here he are on the bank this morning   *Yes sir*

Yea God!   *Yea God!*

What a fortune   *Amen!*

All the power in he hand   *Oh Yeah!*
Got power for we
When we get hungry   *Yea!*
He's able to feed us   *Yeah. Yes sir*

O Lord!
Come to tell you children   *Yes!*
Jesus! is the Bread of Life   *Jesus!*

My brotheren   *My God!*
Come to him   *All right!*
Come to him   *Yeah!*
He feed you when you get hungry   *All right*

He will be on the Ark   *Yeah!*

Yea God!   *My God*

Upon the mountain someone said
Jesus said: *Yeah!*

If you come to me
I'll give you water   *Water*

In dry land   *Dry land!*

O Lordy!
Jesus is the Bread of Life   *Yes!*

How do you know   *Uh huh!*

He's the Bread of Life?   *Yeah!*

When he begins to speak   *Yeah!*

He's the Bread of Life, brotheren   *Yeah!*

O Lordy!
I begin to think back   *Yeah!*

In Moses time
when he said   *Yeah!*

God feed them   *Oh yeah!*
With manna from on Heaven
My brother!   *All right yeah!*

I was out in the wilderness
Didn't have nothing to eat   *Uh huh*

God feed them   *My Lord!*

With manna from on high   *Yes!*

To stop a little while [pause]

I be able to preach for you   *Yeah! All right*

If you feed me with bread   *Yeah! All right*

I be able to call him   *Yeah*

If you feed me with that bread   *Yes*

O Lordy!   *O Lord!*

I be able to pick up   *Yeah!*

Pick up my brother   *All right. Yes!*

Who is down in the ditch this morning   *Oh yeah!*

If you feed me this morning   *Yes! Lord*

I be able to call   *Yea Lord*

The lost sinner home   *Yeah!*

Oh Lordy!
Jesus!
Is the Bread of Life   *Yeah*

God knows
Somebody look   *Yes*

Back in space of time   *Yes!*

Saw Jesus
Coming through
Seventy-two generations   *Yes. Uh huh*

One said:
When he look at Jesus   *Oh Yes!*

Yea God!   *Yea God!*

His feet   *All right*

Look like polish brass   *Yeah!*

Eye look
Like a consuming fire   *Consuming fire*

Hair look
Like lamb wool   *Lamb wool*

Pressing the wine press   *Yeah!*

All by himself   *By himself*

Coming down to the gate   *Yeah!*

To let you and I
Have a right   *Right*

To the Tree of Life
O Lordy!   *Oh Lordy!*

Jesus is alive   *All right!*

My brothers   *Yes!*

When I get hungry   *Ah Yeah!*

My soul get hungry
I go to Him   *Yeah. All right!*

And say unto Him   *Yeah. That's right!*

God I want you
Feed me with the Bread of Life   *Yes!*

Feed me   *Feed me!*

Till I want no more   *Want no more!*

Then at last   *At last!*

In this old world   *Yes! This old world Thank you! At last.*
        Yes sir. Step right on up. All right.
[long pause]
Brother, I don't know about you, friend   *Yes*

But I begin to sing   *Yeah!*

Deep down in my heart   *All right! Sir!*

But Jesus is the Bread of Life   *Uh huh! All right!*

Great God!   *Yes!*

Some how   *Some how. Yeah!*

Some way   *Some way!*

That same Jesus   *That same Jesus!*

One day   *Yes!*

I look down   *Yes sir!*

Into the old pit   *Yeah! All right!*

A little wretch
Like me was
My brother   *Yeah!*

Stoop down   *Stoop down!*

And lift me up   *Lift me up!*

Take my feet
Out of the mucky mire   *Yeah!*

Climb up on
Rock of Eternal ages
Establish my goings   *Yeah!*

Say unto me   *Yeah! Amen!*

I want you   *All right!*

To go out into the world   *Yeah!*

Tell men and women   *Yeah!*

I said:
I was dead
But I'm alive, brotheren   *I'm alive!*

Tell them I said: *Yeah. All right!*

When they get hungry   *Yeah!*

If they would come to me   *Yeah!*

I would feed them   *I will feed them. Yes!*

Tell them I said: *Yes*

When they get lonely
Don't have a friend   *A friend*

I will be a friend for them   *Yeah*

Tell them I said: *Yeah*

When all bodies   *Yeah*
Walk off from them
And put he name on every milepost   *Oh Lord!*

I'll be right there with them   *Yeah!*
Tell them I said: *Yeah!*

When mother father   *Yeah!*
Forsake you   *Oh Yeah*

I be by your side   *By your side*

O Lordy!
And when you come   *Come Jesus!*

To the end of your journey   *Yeah!*

And you are weary   *Weary!*

Of life, my brother   *Yeah!*

Old battle is won   *Won!*

I'll be right there   *Be right there!*

When the time come
My God Almighty!   *My Lord*

Gonna call the angel   *Yeah!*

Take care   *Oh yeah!*
I want you to

Stand around   *Oh yeah!*

The throne this morning   *Oh yes*

Want you to sing   *Yeah!*

As you ever sing before
Somebody who will come out   *Yeah!*

From Jerusalem   *Yeah!*

[Crying out]: I know   *All right!*

Back yonder   *Yonder*

In yonder world   *Yonder world*
I cry some Sunday

A charge   *Jesus! A charge I have! Right.*

To glorify   *Glorify!*
My brother   *My brother!*

I don't know
But I look across
In the Amen corner   *Corner*

See somebody   *Yeah!*

Who cry out:
One day   *Yeah!*

I saw the lighthouse   *Yeah!*

O Lordy!   *Oh yeah, my Lord*

I wanna be there!   *Oh yeah!*

I wanna be there!   *Oh yeah!*

I wanna be there!   *Oh yeah, oh yes! I wanna be there!*

Over yonder [long pause] . . .

I wanna view the beauty land
Where God Eternal Glory   *Eternal Glory!*

Where all wicked   *Wicked*

Shall cease   *Cease, cease!*

All weary soul   *Yes Lord! All weary soul!*

Shall be at rest   *Rest!*

Jesus said:
I am the Bread   *I am the Bread. The Bread. I am the Bread*
Of Life

Let us Pray   *All right! Yes sir! Yes Lord! Let us Pray!*

Spirits of Our Ancestors:
Basket Traditions in the Carolinas

Dale Rosengarten

> In basketry we must feel ourselves linked by a common everyday
> object to our remote antecedents. At a time when the habits, beliefs,
> and institutions inherited from the past are being destroyed by our
> technological society, baskets impose a recognition of our own
> moment as a part of history and prehistory, as a continuation of all
> natural history.
> —Ed Rossbach, *Baskets as Textile Art* (1973, 12)

The basket traditions of the Carolinas derive from three continents: North America, Europe, and Africa. Prominent among these traditions are the plaited river cane baskets of southeastern Indian tribes; the split oak, wickerware, and coiled straw of English, Irish, Scots, Scotch-Irish, and German settlers; and the coiled sea grass of Low Country African Americans. Although these peoples have been in close contact in America for more than three hundred years, their basketry remains remarkably distinct. Apart from one notable exception— European splintwork, which was adopted quickly by both Native American and black basket makers—techniques and forms were not widely shared. Baskets produced today by Cherokees in western North Carolina, by African Americans in Mount Pleasant, South Carolina, and by southern highlanders of European stock demonstrate the tenacity of ancestral traditions.

Basketry is an ancient craft. It originated in many areas at about the same time and reached a high level of development in all civilizations. The first basket makers in the Western Hemisphere were descended from bands of hunters who had migrated from Asia tens of thousands of years earlier. When these nomadic peoples began making carriers of entwined tree limbs or shelters of lashed saplings we cannot say. Plant fibers are so perishable that they are preserved only under exceptional conditions. Hence, "baskets are among the most

133

short-lived of all human-made containers" (Sieber 1980, 285), in contrast to stone and pottery, which are the most durable.[1]

Native American Traditions in the Southeast

In southeastern North America, people started making baskets in the Archaic period, a prehistoric era that began in some localities as early as 8000 B.C. As the last glaciers receded and certain large mammals—such as the mammoth, mastodon, and bison—became extinct, hunters turned to gathering, fishing, and, eventually, cultivation. During the Woodland period, in the first millennium before Christ, tribal peoples developed a complex material culture. Besides basketry, they made pottery, fur clothing, bows and arrows, musical instruments, and many other objects (White 1979, 28). By the time the first Europeans landed in the Americas, native cultures had flourished, declined, and risen again. "Columbus did not discover a new world," commented historian J. H. Parry, "he established contact between two worlds, both already old" (Jennings 1975, 39).

In the Southeast, plaiting was the dominant basketry technique; west of the Mississippi River, coiling and twining prevailed. In all tribes, basket making was women's work, practiced mainly during the winter while the able-bodied men were hunting. Baskets were designed for specific purposes: harvest baskets for gathering; chests for storage; burden baskets for carrying heavy loads; winnowing trays, threshing baskets, sifters, sieves, seed beaters, and corn and acorn washers; tightly coiled or double-woven baskets for cooking, boiling water, brewing beverages, and washing and dyeing clothes; fancy baskets for holding ceremonial objects or trinkets; cradles and hats; trays for gambling games; traps for fish and birds; and mats for bedding and shrouds (White 1979, 195–97; see Figure 1). Although coarse weaves characterized basketry traps and walls, Native Americans also produced baskets so fine they resembled cloth.

In 1540, the Spanish explorer Hernando de Soto found the Cherokees living in pole houses built of straight saplings covered with plaited mats of cane (Hamel and Chiltoskey 1982, 18). All southeastern tribes made extensive use of cane (*Arundinaria gigantea*), an abundant native plant of the bamboo family. Cane stalks were split and used as building material and for making baskets of all kinds. For hunters, cane provided traps and weapons, including knives, blowguns, arrows, and shields. Sections of the plant were employed also as pipes, flageolets, and conduits for air or braids of hair (Swanton 1946, 244–45).

Split river cane was the traditional material for single- and double-woven

Figure 1. Woman with a pack basket, Eastern Cherokee, North Carolina, 1904. (Courtesy of the National Museum of the American Indian, Smithsonian Institution)

Figure 2. Cherokee double-weave rivercane basket, 1725. Sir Hans Sloan Collection. (British Museum)

containers (see Figure 2). The Cherokees "made the handsomest baskets I ever saw, considering their materials," wrote James Adair in 1775. Adair, who traded and worked among southeastern Indians for more than thirty-five years, observes that the Cherokees split the large swamp canes into "long, thin, narrow splinters" which they dyed several colors and wove with double warps and wefts so that "both the inside and outside are covered with a beautiful variety of pleasing figures." In the past, Adair remarks, Cherokee baskets were "so highly esteemed . . . for domestic usefulness, beauty, and skillful variety, that a large nest of them cost upwards of a moidoire [a Portuguese coin]" (Swanton 1946, 604; cf. Leftwich 1970, 9–13; Bookout, n.d., 32).

Cane weaving may have originated with the Chitimacha people of Louisiana and radiated north and east to the Choctaw, Creek, and Cherokee tribes (Lamb 1962, 126). The Chitimacha used extremely narrow cane splints to create complex, abstract, curvilinear patterns. Cherokee designs were simpler and more rectilinear. A recent hallmark of the Cherokee cane basket is a thin oak hoop bound to the rim with hickory fiber, a feature shared only by the Catawbas among southeastern tribes (Leftwich 1970, 15).

Leaves, bark, roots, and seedpods of many plants supplied dyestuff, and contemporary weavers still rely on four: walnut, butternut, bloodroot, and yellowroot. Urine and wood ash lye were used as mordants for setting the color; alum was introduced more recently for the same purpose.

Twilled designs on cane baskets and mats portrayed important tribal symbols. Woven mats hanging in Cherokee council houses bore traditional motifs which may have indicated where each of the seven clans should sit (Hamel and Chiltoskey 1982, 10). Although many designs—and a great deal else—were lost during the tragic Cherokee Removal of 1838, Native American basket makers still include in their work symbolic patterns such as Flowing Water, Arrow Point, Chief's Coffin, Cross on the Hill, Man in the Coffin, Chief's Daughters, Broken Heart, and Indian Arc (Leftwich 1970, 48–56).

Reputable authorities contend that southeastern basket makers did not practice hardwood splintwork before European contact. Splint basketry, according to art historian Christian Feest, was "plainly post-European since iron implements are needed to obtain thin and regular hardwood splints" (Feest 1980, 107). The conventional wisdom that Indian basket makers began to use white oak "when metal tools became available" (Hamel and Chiltoskey 1982, 19) has been challenged recently, however. The recovery of prepared oak splints from an archaeological site (ca. 1450) in Hamilton County, Tennessee, suggests that "the advent of wood splint basketry in the region predates European contact" (Duggan and Riggs 1991, 25).

Alternate theories explaining the introduction of splintwork into the Southeast argue that it came from South America or from the Southwest, where, before A.D. 700, sandals and ring baskets were made of plaited yucca-leaf splints (Teleki 1975, 19). In the Northeast, too, where Indian basket makers split ash by pounding the wood so that it separates along its growth rings, the origin of splint basketry is in dispute (McBride 1990, 10–11).

We know that in the historical period Native Americans used hardwood splints to make fish baskets, heavy wares, mats, and sieves. A rare early reference to the Cherokees' use of oak splints comes from the naturalist William Bartram, who traveled through Cherokee country just before the American Revolution. The Indians' council or town house, he reports, was furnished with "sophas . . . covered with mats or carpets, very curiously made of thin splints of Ash or Oak, woven or platted together" (Bartram 1928, 298). By the mid-nineteenth century, Cherokee basket makers had fully incorporated white oak into their repertory, using European tools and techniques to make narrow oak splints, which they dyed with native dyes and wove into basket patterns that have been handed down for generations (Sarah H. Hill, pers. comm., June 1, 1993). Adapting both their river cane and white oak basketry to the tastes of Anglo-American customers, Cherokee weavers added handles to traditional forms and by 1880 were experimenting with commercial dyes (Duggan and Riggs 1991, 31, 35).

Japanese honeysuckle became popular among the Cherokees after World

War I. More recently Cherokee weavers began making decorative pieces from glossy maple splints. Traditional double-woven river cane baskets, however, claim the honor of being the oldest type and the most difficult to make, and they command the highest prices in today's market.

Basket Making among the Lumbees

The Indians of Robeson County, North Carolina, who have taken the name Lumbee after the "brooding, mercurial" Lumber, or Lumbee, River at the headwaters of the Pee Dee, accommodated very early to European ways (Dial and Eliades 1975, xiii–xiv).[2] When Scottish immigrants encountered them in the upper reaches of the Cape Fear Valley in the early 1730s, they were already speaking English, living in simple houses, and farming in the European manner (Dial and Eliades 1975, 1).[3] Most likely they were also making baskets in the European style, including ribbed white oak melon, or gizzard, baskets and egg baskets. Baskets of these types were made by John Oxendine during the Civil War, "down in the swamps," where he was hiding from Confederate scouts who were impressing Native Americans to work on the docks at Wilmington (Janie Maynard Locklear, pers. comm., May 29, 1985; Locklear recalls her mother telling her that her great-grandfather's large gizzard basket at one time would hold water).

By the mid-1930s, basket traditions among the Indian people of Robeson County seemed threatened with extinction. In a summary of information written for the Bureau of Indian Affairs, Joseph Brooks reports only a few old people making baskets (Wesley White, pers. comm., May 15, 1985). Among the Lumbees, now numbering some 40,000 people, at least one basket maker, Cleveland Jacobs of Pembroke, was still weaving with white oak in the late 1980s. He learned the craft as a "little bitty boy" from his grandfather and picked it up again when he lost his sight. Jacobs also made baskets of flat river cane and was one of the few Robeson County Indians familiar with the tradition of coiled grass basketry practiced through the first decades of the twentieth century. Jacobs called the grass he used for this "wire grass." It was found on sandhills in open areas on the banks of rivers and grows about three feet tall— "purty stuff"—but it was "all burned out some years ago" and is no longer available for basket making (Cleveland Jacobs, pers. comm., May 15, 1985).

Among the few surviving examples of coiled baskets preserved in Lumbee families are the nineteenth-century sweet grass sewing basket illustrated in Figure 3 and a smaller sewing basket made by Meritha Bell in 1923 from "wild grass" wrapped with tobacco twine, which is on permanent loan to the Native

Figure 3. Lumbee Indian sewing basket, Maxton, N.C., c. 1900. H. 13½″ (34.3 cm), D. 17¾″ (45.1 cm). Coiled sweetgrass. (Courtesy of Joe E. A. Wilkinson)

American Resource Center at Pembroke State University (Linda E. Oxendine, pers. comm., May 29, 1985).

Arrival of European Traditions

Along with the immigrants from northern England, Scotland, Ireland, and Wales who arrived on the Atlantic seaboard between 1700 and 1850 came their basketry tradition of flat, plaited splintwork, which may itself have been introduced to the British Isles centuries earlier by Scandinavian invaders (Stephenson 1977, 3). Wickerwork is also native to Anglo-Saxon and Celtic peoples, and to Germans as well. German-speaking immigrants, mainly from the Rhine Valley but also from southeastern Europe, brought with them down the Great Wagon Road their ancient heritage of coiled rye baskets—a tradition that dates back at least twelve thousand years and is still practiced today.

Frontier farmers adapted Old World forms to New World materials. First in Pennsylvania and later in southern Appalachia, the traditional willow (several species, especially *Salix purpurea*) used to make wicker baskets was replicated with whittled rods of white oak (*Quercus alba*). The weaving splint of coiled straw basketry was fashioned also from oak or, occasionally, from ash or hickory. Flat splint baskets, too, were made almost exclusively of oak.

American basket makers reproduced traditional European tools such as the shaving horse, used by mountain basket and chair makers to cut out their splints, or "splits," as they are called in the southern highlands (Eaton 1937, 37).[4] German tools for making splints retained their German names: *schnitzelbank* for the shaving horse and *schnitzelmesser* for the draw knife, a viselike instrument used to refine the rough *schienes* until they are smooth and thin (Lasansky 1979, 29–30).

Surviving remnants of old English terminology include *osiers* for willow shoots, *sallow* or *sally* for willow, *withe* for switch, and *slype* meaning "to slice to a point" (Stephenson 1977, 30). Names of basket forms also reflected their country of origin. From Germany came the terms *orsch backe* for the ribbed-style cheek or buttock basket, *stroh karreb* for the straw basket, *warrik karreb* for the market basket, and *back karreb* for the bread-raising basket (Lasansky 1979, 10, 12, 35, 40, 41).[5] In Scotland, the hen basket, which Allen Eaton calls the Carolina basket, is known as an Ose basket or Skye hen basket, for the Isle of Skye where it was commonly made. Some writers have suggested that its origins are Scandinavian, but "in Sweden, the basket is known as 'The Scotch Basket' " (Dorothy Wright, in Stephenson 1977, 14).

Baskets took their names most often from their shapes or uses. A family associated with a particular form might give its name to a basket, as in the case of Rector, Purvis, Moore, and Aunt Lydia baskets (Eaton 1937, 169–70). Gathering baskets ranged from small berry and flower baskets to larger egg and melon baskets, the latter named for their shape rather than their contents.

Large field baskets usually were made of white oak splints and came in one- or two-bushel sizes; they were reinforced on the bottom with heavy strips called shoes. Storage baskets were designed for specific items such as feathers, clothes, or apples. Carrying baskets were made in a wide variety of shapes and sizes with many types of handles, including wrapped, twisted, and carved. Cross handles formed the central rib of the basket or were lashed to the rim. Nineteenth-century baskets used in food preparation included drying trays, cheese or curd baskets, winnowing fans, sieves, funnels, and bread-raising baskets. Among common household forms were key, sewing, miniature or toy, picnic, pie, and provender baskets. Special shapes were fashioned to carry birds, house honey bees, and trap fish.

Baskets also provided a means of measurement. Egg baskets were made to hold a certain number of dozens. Peck and bushel baskets were constructed in standard sizes, though not always the same standard. Sue Stephenson describes a bushel basket she found in West Virginia that was larger than a bushel. An elderly man explained to her that it was "one them old Scotch bushels; the Scotch people around here used a bigger bushel sometimes" (possibly a "firlot," used in Scotland to measure oats and barley, and equal to one and a half times the Winchester bushel; Stephenson 1977, 20).

No systematic study has been made of European basket traditions in the Carolinas comparable to Jeannette Lasansky's superb monograph on Pennsylvania basketry, *Willow, Oak, and Rye.* Such a study is long overdue. Lasansky provides some guidelines, however, to regional features. White oak, she reports, is the predominant material used by all European-American basket makers. Willow and rye straw are particularly common in German settlements in Virginia, Missouri, Ohio, North Carolina, and Iowa. Ash and hickory are used in New England and the southern highlands, but not in Pennsylvania. Spoke-constructed baskets are made of willow in Pennsylvania, the Midwest, and the South, but flat oak splints are customary in New York and New England. The modified melon-shaped basket is more often found in Pennsylvania than its counterpart, the cheek, or *orsch backe,* ribbed style, which is standard in southern Appalachia. "Plaited flat splint baskets are ubiquitous" (Lasansky 1979, 10).

Native American and African-American basket makers readily adopted from European settlers the sturdy rib construction for eel and fish traps; field, market, and feed baskets; laundry hampers; and picnic baskets. Thereafter, ribbing techniques and forms were exchanged among people of different cultures, sometimes through intermarriage. Clarence Baggett, for example, a fourth-generation white oak rib-basket weaver of Grandin, Missouri, claims that his grandfather learned to make baskets from his North Carolina Cherokee mother (*Ozarks Mountaineer,* cited in Teleki 1975, 27).

Black South Carolinians continued to make cotton baskets and even oak rice fanners in the twentieth century,[6] and today a few African-American basket makers—mainly in the Up Country—work in white oak (Stanton and Cowan 1988). On the coastal plain in West Andrews, South Carolina, Rollin McCutcheon weaves huge corn baskets, square clothes hampers, and two sizes of market baskets, just as his father and grandfather did (Rollin and Etta Mae McCutcheon, pers. comm., February 26, 1991; see Figure 4). Leon Berry, of Mecklenburg County, North Carolina, was one of the last African-American

Figure 4. Rollin McCutcheon, West Andrews, S.C., September 1993.
(Photograph by Dale Rosengarten)

basket makers in his area making cotton hampers. "Plenty of people round here
make baskets, but they all dead 'bout," Berry told folklorist Glenn Hinson in
the late 1970s, attributing the young generation's disinterest in basket making
to lack of patience. "If you ain't got good patience, you ain't gonna fool with
it. I have four boys I raised, and none of 'em will make a basket. Not nary a
one of 'em. Well, they say that's too slow for them. Seems like people now just
aren't patient" (Hinson 1979, 57).

   In no culture was basket making regarded as a specialized craft or were basket makers accorded artisan status. At one time, basket making "was nothing
more than a common household skill—not at all in the class with cooperage,
for example" (Stephenson 1977, 30). On a detailed list of manual occupations
in Charleston in 1848, only one basket maker, a white man, is included in the
catchall category "other mechanics" (Phillips 1918, 403).

   Making baskets was a routine farm chore for family members, and sometimes hired hands, during the long winter evenings. In some towns and cities,
baskets were mass produced by "companies" where the various tasks were
divided among several workers. For example, in Charleston, South Carolina,
in 1882, two basket and willowware establishments, with a combined capital
of $2,500, employed five hands and produced $3,000 worth of baskets (South

Figure 5. Basket with cover, western North Carolina, c. 1850. H. 15½″
(39.4 cm), D. 21″ (53.3 cm). Coiled rye straw. (Courtesy of Old Salem Inc.,
Winston-Salem, N.C.)

Carolina State Board of Agriculture 1883, 682). Nevertheless, the process
"always involved hand work, even after the introduction of machines which
steamed the willow, made veneer, or stapled rims" (Lasansky 1979, 4).

The coiled basketry practiced by northern Europeans utilized the straw of
their staple grains. Wheat straw and occasionally corn fodder were used as the
foundation material in some baskets, but rye straw (*Secale cereale*) was preferred because of the length of its fiber and its reputation for resisting rot and
repelling rats (Lasansky 1979, 35; see Figure 5).

Thrifty German farmers used a bone or iron awl to insert thin oak weavers
through coils of straw in the construction of storage hampers, bee skeps, bread-
raising baskets, and trays with openwork borders (Lasansky 1979, 36).[7] Less
common forms included winnowing fans, sewing baskets, and gathering and
market baskets. Storage hampers reached monumental size. Made of coils up
to an inch in diameter, some stood three feet tall and were almost as wide.
Straw was a more economical material for bee skeps than either wood or glass,
and straw hives were warmer in winter and cooler in summer (Lasansky 1979,
46; quoted from *Farmers' Guide* 1838).[8]

The bread-raising basket was perhaps the most common coiled form. In its shape and material the rye straw basket symbolized the bread dough it was meant to hold. Generally round, ten to twelve inches wide and four to six inches deep, the basket was lined with a cloth that had been dusted with corn-meal or white flour and then set near the oven while the bread was rising. For that reason, surviving examples frequently have burn marks. When the dough was ready to bake, it was turned out of the basket onto a long-handled flat wood or iron paddle called a pie peel, or *backoffe-schiesser* (see Figure 6). The bread-raising basket went out of use in the twentieth century, "replaced by the larger wooden dough trays, metal pans, and eventually, store-bought bread" (Lasansky 1979, 42).

Coiled straw baskets were made in all German settlements; they differed only in the kind of straw employed and the occasional use of ash, hickory, or twine as binding material. American examples from the eighteenth and nine-teenth centuries closely resemble their Old World antecedents of the sixteenth and seventeenth centuries.

German immigrants were by no means a homogeneous group; they included Moravians, Mennonites, Amish, Dunkards, Schwenkfelders, Lutherans, and Huguenots. What these people had in common was the poverty induced by the Thirty Years' War and their fervent religious dissent (Murtagh 1967, 3). Unlike earlier German-speaking settlers, who came mainly from the Rhine Valley, the United Brethren had roots in Bohemia-Moravia in western Czechoslovakia. Among the Moravians, to a greater degree than among other German immi-grants, religious and secular lives merged. The people were craftsmen who regarded their labors as under the direct guidance of the Lord. This simple "heart" religion carried over into the domestic economy (Griffin 1981, 1) and inspired their basketry. Sturdy Moravian baskets were in the mainstream of the German tradition and bore an affinity to the massive brick and stone architec-ture of Moravian towns.

In 1753, an advance guard of Brethren left their settlement in Bethlehem, Pennsylvania, and established a new community in *Wachau,* or Wachovia, a 98,985-acre tract they had purchased in central North Carolina. Two ministers, a carpenter, a cooper, a millwright, a tanner, a tailor, a shoemaker, a surgeon, a baker, and a farmer led the way (Murtagh 1967, 112). At Bethabara, the Brethren's first village in Wachovia, a blacksmith was injured while shingling a roof, and he was put to work making baskets and sieves while he recuperated (Dan Freas, pers. comm., May 31, 1985). Although basket making did not have the status of a trade, it was clearly important to the life of the community.

Through their missions the Moravians came in contact with Native Ameri-

Figure 6. Bread-raising baskets, Berks County, Pa., early twentieth century. (Courtesy of Schwenkfelder Library, Pennsburg, Pa. Photo by H. Winslow Fegley.)

cans. Indeed, they taught Cherokees and Catawbas such crafts as blacksmithing and carpentry; in turn, they adopted the native agricultural techniques necessary for survival in their new home. They also had contact with African Americans, first in Savannah, Georgia, which was their port of entry into America, and later in their congregation towns, where the church owned slaves whom it hired out to members (Dan Freas, pers. comm., May 14 and 31, 1985). Brimming with religious assurance, the Brethren eagerly proselytized among both Indians and blacks. How Moravian material culture was influenced by contact with these other peoples is unclear. Despite formal similarities between the coiled rye baskets German settlers made in western North Carolina and the coiled sea grass baskets Africans made on the coast, there is no evidence linking the two traditions.

The African Element

Africans were present in the Carolina colony from the first days of European settlement. The Proprietors—eight English lords empowered to grant land in the new colony—intended to populate Carolina with "seasoned" planters and slaves who would produce a commodity to be consumed abroad. The first settlers came from the West Indies, especially Barbados, where declining productivity and the consolidation of landholdings impelled planters to look for opportunities elsewhere. After twenty years of experimentation with possible staples, Carolina colonists found that rice could be grown economically near inland swamps. As rice production expanded, so did the importation of African slaves. As early as 1710, Africans outnumbered Europeans. "Carolina," remarked a Swiss newcomer named Samuel Dyssli in 1737, "looks more like a negro country than a country settled by white people" (quoted in Wood 1974a, 132).

The Africans who were carried in chains to the New World knew more about planting, harvesting, and preparing rice than did their masters. Some 43 percent of the slaves imported during the eighteenth century came from regions of Africa where rice was an important crop (Littlefield 1981, 113). The agricultural technology of rice production, especially in the early decades of settlement, was distinctly African. It included what has become the most famous form of the Low Country basket, the fanner, a wide winnowing tray used to "fan" rice; that is, to throw the threshed grain into the air or drop it from a basket held aloft into another basket, allowing the wind to blow away the chaff (see Figure 7).

The basketry of the various African tribes was as diverse as that of Native American peoples. Fences, granaries, reedwork, thatching, traps, and heavy

Figure 7. Mrs. Rebecca Green "fanning" rice, St. Helena Island, S.C., c. 1909. (Southern Historical Collection, University of North Carolina Library, Chapel Hill, N.C., with permission from Penn Center, Inc., St. Helena Island, S.C. Photo by Leigh Richmond Miner.)

field baskets tended to be made by men; mats, smaller baskets for storing and serving food, and fancy baskets generally were made by women (Trowell and Wachsmann 1953, 134).[9] Though coiled grass baskets were made throughout Africa, Low Country baskets are most closely related to those of Senegambia, the Congo, and Angola (Twining 1978, 167; Vlach 1978, 16).

The earliest known documentation of rice fanners in South Carolina appears in a Charleston County register of wills and inventories. Fanners were listed among the personal effects of Noah Serre on May 18, 1730, and of Joseph Wilkinson on June 10, 1745 (G. Day 1978, 21).[10] The oldest artifact of coiled basketry is a fragment excavated from the bottom of a privy at the Heyward-Washington house in Charleston. It probably dates from the Revolutionary period (Elaine Herold, pers. comm., May 10, 1985).[11] As more waterlogged sites are studied, even older examples of both basketry and textiles most likely will be found (Leland Ferguson, pers. comm., April 26, 1985).

It is logical to assume that Low Country fanners were used to process the first crops of rice raised in the New World—possibly as early as 1672—although the colonists did not manage to produce a "plausible yield" until the 1690s. Even then, Governor James Glen later admitted, they remained "ignorant for some years how to clean it" (quoted in Wood 1974a, 58). In other words, planters did not have a commercially efficient way to mill the grain. When production moved from the swamps to the tidal rivers after the American Revolution, the age-old implements—the flail, mortar and pestle, and winnowing basket—continued in use (see Clifton 1978, xi, n. 7).

The function of separating the chaff from the grain was eventually assumed by winnowing houses. Raised on posts about fifteen feet high, these structures had a grating in the floor through which the threshed and pounded seed was dropped. Along with such innovations as the Louisiana process for granulating sugar, mills for pounding and threshing rice, and Eli Whitney's cotton gin, winnowing houses should be regarded as part of the broad advance in technology that revolutionized the processing of staple crops. Historians have not determined precisely when these structures were introduced, but by the nineteenth century winnowing houses were present on all Low Country rice plantations (Clifton 1978, xxiv).

Old methods nevertheless persisted alongside the new. Rarely does one see a drawing or photograph of a winnowing house without noticing a basket somewhere in the picture. And long after methods of irrigating the fields and cleaning the rice had become mechanized, African Americans continued to use mortars, pestles, and fanners in the slave quarters to prepare the rough rice they were issued as rations and rewards.

Fanners served some unexpected functions as well. A watercolor painted by

Alice Ravenel Huger Smith in the 1930s, depicting "The Plantation Street" of a Carolina rice plantation of the 1850s, shows Negro babies "sunning in blanket-padded 'fanner baskets' supervised by a 'mauma,' or nurse" (Sass 1936)—an image Smith's father recalled vividly from his youth on a Combahee River rice plantation. "On fine days," he says, "there might be seen on the open ground in front of the sickhouse, which doubled as a nursery, a large number of 'fanner-baskets,' and on each basket a folded blanket, and on each blanket a baby" (D. Smith 1950, 15).

Two other Low Country memoirs written in the early twentieth century and based on recollections of antebellum society provide graphic descriptions of African-American basketry. David Doar was a boy living on a Santee River plantation when the Civil War began. His family had been cultivating rice for four generations. Doar recalls baskets made "out of river rushes cured and sewed with white oak strips." Besides fanners, plantation "handicraftsmen" coiled "small baskets with handles which the women used, and out of a finer kind of grass, sewed with palmetto or oak strip, a very neat sewing-basket, some of them three-storied; that is, one on top of the other, each resting on the cover of the one below and getting smaller as they went up" (Doar 1936, 33–34).

Although Doar implies that plantation basket making was dominated by men, Elizabeth Allston Pringle, in *Chronicles of Chicora Wood,* tells of Maria, an outstanding woman weaver. Maria, who came from a royal family in Africa, was taken in battle by an enemy tribe and sold into slavery with her kinsmen Tom and Prince. "Maum Maria made wonderful baskets and wove beautiful rugs from the rushes that grew along Long Cane Creek," says Pringle. These "three quite remarkable, tall, fine-looking, and very intelligent Africans . . . occupied an important place in my mother's recollections of her early childhood" (Pringle 1940, 53–54).

References to basketry from the pre–Civil War years tend to be more cut-and-dried. On August 27, 1836, for example, a Low Country planter named Thomas Walter Peyre reported (and indexed!) in his journal, "Jacob and Jim getting stuff for baskets. Jacob was occupied 3 weeks in making baskets" (Peyre, Journal). Once the rice was threshed and ready for pounding and winnowing, dozens of fanner baskets were issued. On Argyle Plantation on the Savannah River, for example, beginning in November, as many as fifty-three hands were engaged in "thrashing and winnowing rice." These workers appear only as numbers on the daily entry but are listed by name, under the heading "Disbursement of tools and baskets," at the end of the overseer's report (Potter, Journal).

The Civil War brought mass destruction to the Low Country rice kingdom.

When cultivation resumed, it was on a new basis. The fields frequently were leased and the work was done by freed men and women for wages, for a share of the crop, or under the "two-day system" in which the workers exchanged their labor for a few acres of land for their own use, plus living quarters and fuel.

Planters made valiant efforts to revive rice production after the war, but the plantations never fully recovered. Competition from new colonial economies in Southeast Asia and from large, efficient rice tracts in Louisiana and Texas contributed to the downfall of rice planting in the Low Country. Rice operations that managed to struggle past 1890 were dealt fatal blows by the hurricanes that ripped the shoreline and flooded low-lying fields in 1893, 1894, 1898, 1906, 1910, 1911, and 1916.

What did all these events and trends mean for the coiled basket? The wartime destruction of threshing and pounding mills and the liberation of the work force allowed black people to practice a kind of subsistence agriculture in which baskets were an essential part of the technology. Many former slaves managed to acquire farms, and even as late as the mid-1900s small quantities of rice were planted and processed in the traditional way. The craft of basket making persisted wherever black families were able to hold onto their land. Both coiled and splintwork baskets were made for household use, and some were sold to local farmers on order. People carried their produce to market in baskets. By 1900, a minor genre of street vendor photography had emerged, featuring black women and children with large coiled baskets poised on their heads "in the manner of their African ancestors" (Vlach 1978, 13; see Figure 8).

The practice of bearing loads on the head, which "tends to give a better balance to the body and thus makes the load easier to carry" (Ross and Walker 1979, 134, n. 20), distinguishes the African-American form from the Native American "burden basket" strapped to the back by a "tump line" across the bearer's forehead or shoulders, and from the European-American hand-carried market basket. "Head tote" baskets, fanners, and storage baskets were made most often of black rush (*Juncus roemarianus*)—an abundant salt marsh plant commonly called bulrush, "rushel," or needlegrass. In utilitarian basketry of the plantation period, durability and quick construction were primary values. Splints made from white oak or the stem of a saw palmetto frond (*Serenoa repens*) are much stronger than the strips of palm leaf (*Sabal palmetto*) used to sew contemporary baskets. An interlocking stitch also distinguishes agricultural baskets from baskets made for lighter uses.

Coiled baskets with handles began appearing in the twentieth century. A contemporary sewing basket in the Smithsonian Institution's collection adds a cross handle and a conical lid to a traditional basket body (see Figure 9). Earlier

Figure 8. Street vendor, Charleston, S.C., early twentieth century. (South Carolina Historical Society, Charleston, S.C. Photo, *Annie with a ga'den on e head,* by G. W. Johnson.)

hybrids—bulrush baskets with wood strap handles lashed onto the sides—suggest a borrowing from European splintwork styles. Examples of this unusual type were made at the Penn Normal, Industrial, and Agricultural School on St. Helena Island, South Carolina, by Alfred Graham and his protégés and were photographed by Leigh Richmond Miner in the early 1900s. Miner's photographs, published in Edith M. Dabbs's *Face of an Island,* provide a rich pictorial record of the baskets made and used on St. Helena.

Figure 9. Sewing basket by Mary Jane Manigault, Mt. Pleasant, S.C., 1971. H. 16″ (40.6 cm), D. 13¼″ (33.7 cm). Coiled sweetgrass and longleaf pine needles. (Smithsonian Institution, National Museum of American History, Division of Community Life)

Figure 10. Basketry class of Alfred Graham, Penn School, St. Helena Island, S.C., 1905. (Southern Historical Collection, University of North Carolina Library, Chapel Hill, N.C., with permission from Penn Center, Inc., St. Helena Island, S.C.)

"Native Island Basketry" was an important part of Penn's curriculum from 1904 through World War II (see Figure 10). By teaching basket making to boys and by selling baskets for local people who made them at home, the school encouraged the survival of what administrators proudly described as an African craft. "This is the only real Negro craft inherited from African forefathers and is so beautiful and useful it seems important to preserve it," proclaimed Penn School's *annual report* for 1930. "These baskets were useful in the field in plantation days and have been adapted for home use" (Penn 1929–30, 12–14).

Penn's promotion of bulrush basketry began during the Arts and Crafts era and continued through the rise of black nationalism and the rural handicraft revival of the 1920s and 1930s (Bookout n.d., 40–42)[12]—movements that all endorsed, in varying degrees, the virtues of tradition, craftsmanship, and ethnic identification. Penn's purposes were also commercial. The school sold baskets through mail orders and through craft shops in Charleston, Philadelphia, and Boston, earning a small but significant income both for the school and for local farm families, who used the money to pay taxes on their land and homes.

During these same years, black people from James, Johns, Yonges, and

Edisto islands, and from Mt. Pleasant, east of Charleston, would carry vegetables and flowers, fish, fishing nets, jars of oysters, pelts, and occasionally baskets to the city to sell (K. Day 1983, 15; Henry Yaschik, pers. comm., May 21, 1992). By 1945, however, the making of bulrush work baskets had almost ceased. Only in Mt. Pleasant were basket "sewers," as they called themselves, able to tap a market that could sustain the craft. There, as early as World War I, basket making had expanded, primarily among women, although boys as well as girls learned to sew and men gathered materials in the woods and marshes.

Instead of the bulrush and palmetto "butt" used for work baskets, Mt. Pleasant "show baskets" were made of sweetgrass (*Muhlenbergia filipes* and *M. capillaris*) sewn with strips of palm leaf and decorated with rust-colored needles from the longleaf pine (*Pinus palustris*). New shapes proliferated, influenced in part by Charleston retail merchants who commissioned particular styles from the basket sewers and at times introduced nontraditional elements such as colored plastic strips to replace the natural palmetto (Rosengarten 1987, 31–34).

Around 1930, with the paving of Highway 17, the construction of the Cooper River Bridge, and the consequent increase in traffic, Mt. Pleasant sewers began displaying their wares on the road (see Figure 11). As Charleston became more of a tourist town, sales picked up and roadside stands multiplied; today they number more than sixty.

Mt. Pleasant baskets present a case of the evolution in America of an ancient tribal craft from a tool of plantation agriculture to a modern folk art produced for sale. Contrasting the recent demise of the Low Country basket on the Sea Islands with its endurance in Mt. Pleasant provides clues to why basket making traditions persist in some situations and die in others.

On the Sea Islands, despite the efforts of the Penn School to develop a national market, the craft remained tied to a farm economy. When rice and corn were no longer grown for home use and commercial farmers began employing machines or migrant laborers outfitted with factory-made baskets and crates to harvest the crop, the coiled grass basket went out of use. Now, not only craft traditions but traditional communities themselves are threatened with extinction. Like the Native Americans who were driven off their lands by expanding white settlement, the Sea Islanders are facing wholesale removal under the onslaught of resort development. "Developers come in and roll over whoever is there," says Emory Campbell, the current director of Penn Center. "We have given up on trying to protect the shrimp and crab because we, the black native population of these islands, have become the new endangered species" (Campbell 1984).

Figure 11. Viola Jefferson, basket stand on U.S. Route 17, near Mt. Pleasant, S.C., 1938. (Photo by Bluford Muir.)

In Mt. Pleasant the immediate future of Low Country basketry seems secure. Because of their long history of entrepreneurial activity and their proximity to a scenic city and a major north-south artery, basket makers have been able to take advantage of a growing market for their work. Souvenir hunters and collectors of folk art are willing to pay enough to make basket sewing worthwhile as a source of supplementary income. But as the local economy expands and offers better opportunities for black women, basket making may not be able to compete as an economic activity.

The craft may then survive among older women to whom baskets are meaningful in ways the market cannot fathom. It may also survive as art, as a means of expression for gifted individuals who have perfected a technique and invented forms that spring from a deep appreciation of their tradition and from exposure to outside aesthetic influences. The idealist and the artist who carry on the tradition will have eclipsed the basket's historic context of provincialism and primitivism. Continuing the tradition of basket making into the twenty-first century is a challenge to people's capacity for patience and devotion and a test of their will to be agents in the preservation of their culture.

Notes

I gratefully acknowledge the contributions of the following informants: Gregory Day, San Francisco, Calif.; Leland Ferguson, Anthropology Department, University of South Carolina, Columbia, S.C.; Dan Freas, Curator of Crafts, Old Salem, Inc., Winston-Salem, N.C.; Elaine Herold, Anthropology Department, State University College, Buffalo, N.Y.; Sarah H. Hill, Atlanta, Ga.; Cleveland Jacobs, Pembroke, N.C.; Janie Maynard Locklear, Pembroke, N.C.; Rollin and Etta Mae McCutcheon, West Andrews, S.C.; Linda E. Oxendine, Native American Resource Center, Pembroke State University, Pembroke, N.C.; Wesley White, Pembroke, N.C.; and Henry Yaschik, Charleston, S.C.

1. Archaeologists working in desert regions and protected sites have found very old specimens of North American basketry. Recent excavations at Meadowcroft Rockshelter in southwestern Pennsylvania, for example, have uncovered a remnant of simple plaiting approximately twelve thousand years old, and another fragment, possibly nineteen thousand years old, which may have been part of a plaited basket. If so, "it is not only the oldest known basket from eastern North America but, indeed, the oldest basketry now known in the world" (J. M. Adovasio, in Schiffer 1984, 20).

2. The Lumbee Indians officially adopted their name in 1953. They have been known, at various times in the past, as the Croatan Indians, the Indians of Robeson County, and the Cherokee Indians of Robeson County.

3. How these Indians had come to live in this isolated area surrounded by swamps, what language they originally spoke, and how they came to adopt English as their only tongue have long been subjects of historical speculation. The Lumbees have been linked to Hatteras Indians of the Outer Banks, the Eastern Sioux, the powerful Cherokee, and the Tuscarora. It is also possible, as Adolph Dial and David Eliades (1975) forcefully argue, that among the Lumbees' English ancestors were survivors of Sir Walter Raleigh's lost colony of Roanoke.

4. Eaton traces the shaving horse back to Shropshire, England, where it was still used in the 1930s to make "spelks" and "trugs" for local baskets.

5. Alternate spellings of *karreb* include *karib, korrob, korrup,* and *korb.*

6. From interviews with Joseph and Evelyina Foreman, Mt. Pleasant, S.C., February 23, 1985; and Maggie Manigault, Mt. Pleasant, S.C., March 23, 1985.

Tapes, transcripts, and field notes from the Lowcountry Basket Project are available at McKissick Museum, University of South Carolina, Columbia.

7. An awl is used to make an opening in the coil for the weaver, or binding material, to pass through. In the coiled work of all cultures, awls were traditionally made of bone. In Germany they were made from antlers. Southern highlanders used "a rear leg bone of an old horse" and made a second tool from "a straight section of a cow horn . . . for shaping the coils of straw" (Stephenson 1977, 37). Native Americans used a deer leg bone. Africans used a cow rib or monkey bone. Low Country African Americans formerly made awls from cow or hog ribs; basket makers still call the tool a "bone," though it is now fashioned from a teaspoon handle or a twenty-penny nail, hammered flat and filed smooth.

8. "Often daubed with mud for more insulation, the rye coil bee skep, used for centuries in Europe and England, was the common hive before 1850 when the improved wooden box stacked hive replaced it" (Lasansky 1979, 46). Gloria Teleki claims that straw hives were outlawed because they "harbored or helped spread apiary diseases" (Teleki 1979, 63).

9. Baskets figure prominently in the folktales of African peoples, sometimes illuminating the sexual division of labor; see, for example, Ross and Walker (1979, 441, 448, 484).

10. In an earlier will, the abbreviation "fann." may have signified "fanners" (Greg Day, pers. comm., June 3, 1985).

11. Herold conducted this excavation for the Charleston Museum in the early 1970s.

12. See Bookout (n.d., 40–42) for an analysis of how these movements affected Appalachian basketry.

Lorenzo Dow Turner's
Early Work on Gullah

Michael Montgomery

In June 1932, a young American black linguist, born in northeastern North Carolina and educated at Howard, Harvard, and the University of Chicago, ventured into the remote reaches of the Georgia and South Carolina Sea Islands to begin the first scientific investigation of Gullah, or Sea Island Creole. Lorenzo Dow Turner had developed a keen curiosity about the speech of his students from the coastal areas while teaching at South Carolina State College in Orangeburg, sixty miles up-country, during the summer of 1929. Three years later, supported by a research grant and armed with an interview questionnaire, he began the task of collecting and studying Sea Island speech (Wade-Lewis 1988, 8).

In 1930, at the suggestion of Hans Kurath, Turner had attended the Linguistic Society of America's Summer Linguistic Institute and taken Kurath's course in American English; in 1931, the year in which he became the society's first black member, Turner attended a second summer institute, taking "Les Problemes de la Preparation d'un Atlas Linguistique," a course offered by the European linguistic geographers J. Jud and P. Scheuermeier. At these institutes the focus of attention and excitement was the launching of the Linguistic Atlas of New England (LANE), the first stage of the larger Linguistic Atlas of the United States and Canada (LAUSC) project, and the composition and testing of the final questionnaire for LANE (Hanley 1931, 92–93). Turner studied under Kurath, the recently appointed director of LAUSC, and other members of the atlas team, learning about linguistic atlas work—its approach of interviewing informants with a uniform, eight-hundred-item questionnaire spanning a wide range of lexical and phonological items and a scattering of grammatical items as well, and its goal to survey systematically the English spoken in North America. The end product of the atlas work, it was hoped, would be not only published maps displaying regional variation in American speech habits but, more important, comparable responses for the same questionnaire items. This data would allow researchers to determine the degree of distinctiveness of the speech of particular areas such as the Sea Islands.

158

American linguists in the early 1930s knew about Gullah, but indirectly. Their main sources of information were the writings of Reed Smith, Ambrose Gonzales, John Bennett, and Guy Johnson, none of whom was a linguist and none of whom provided the kind of dispassionate and systematic data that might begin to relate Gullah to mainland varieties of speech or provide clues to its history. Given their orientation of trying to trace connections between American and British dialects, the staff of LAUSC no doubt believed that the Sea Islands might be an important relic area to study and Gullah a potential source of relic forms from earlier stages of English. This must have fueled the interest that had already been kindled in Turner to study Gullah more closely. Exactly how it came about is not clear, but by the summer of 1932 Lorenzo Dow Turner had funds from the American Council of Learned Societies, principal sponsor of the linguistic atlas, to begin fieldwork on the Sea Islands using an atlas questionnaire.[1]

During the next year Turner completed the first systematic series of interviews of Gullah speakers ever carried out by an American linguist and embarked on an investigation that was to become his life's work, leading to the publication of *Africanisms in the Gullah Dialect* nearly two decades later (1949). In that initial year of research, Turner conducted twenty-one interviews with Gullah speakers on the Sea Island coast, twelve in South Carolina and nine in Georgia. In each of seven areas he interviewed three individuals—on Johns, Wadmalaw, Edisto, and St. Helena islands in South Carolina, and in Georgia on Sapelo and St. Simons islands and on Harris Neck and Brewer's Neck, part of a peninsular mainland area. In each of the seven areas, two of the informants were "above sixty years of age and one [was] between forty and sixty" (Turner 1949, xiii–xiv).

Turner most likely revisited these twenty-one individuals (who are listed as his "Principal Gullah Informants" on page 291 of *Africanisms*) during the course of his more extensive work on Gullah in later years and got to know them intimately, since most of the "Gullah Texts" (stories, testimonies, recollections, etc., pp. 254–89 of *Africanisms*) were collected from them. In his book Turner tells us almost nothing about these individuals, giving only their names and their localities; they are listed below in the Appendix, along with their locality, age, sex, level of education, and literacy (this information was noted by Turner on the personal data sheet on the first page of each field notebook he used in his interviews).

A look at the personal data shows that nearly all twenty-one informants for the field records were what J. K. Chambers and Peter Trudgill (1980, 33) call NORMs (nonmobile older rural males) and might call NORFs (nonmobile older rural females), which was typical for linguistic atlas–type investigations.

All were extreme in their lack of education (thirteen had no schooling), low level of literacy, and age (thirteen were over seventy-five). None had traveled outside their immediate vicinity except for very brief periods, and all but one were native, and had parents who were native, to the immediate area.[2] None were descendants of Up Country blacks who had migrated to the Sea Islands following the Civil War. Indeed, most of them were born before the war.

The field records from these interviews represent Turner's earliest Gullah material. Each record is a notebook about 105 pages long, 2 pages of which provide personal information on and a brief characterization of the subject's personality and pronunciation, followed by 103 pages of phonetic transcriptions of individual items. These twenty-one records have heretofore not been analyzed for the light they might shed on a number of important scholarly questions (outside of an unpublished paper by Raven McDavid, 1952). The records were published by the University of Chicago on microfilm in 1982 (McDavid et al. 1982).

These field records appear to have considerable value for addressing at least four types of research questions.

1. What were the phonological, grammatical, and lexical features of the speech of older Gullah speakers more than half a century ago, and what was the level of creole features in their speech at that time?

2. To what extent do the field records reveal local variation within the Gullah-speaking area or patterned differences between speakers according to age or gender? The records open the possibility of studying variation between individual speakers and groups of speakers of Gullah from the 1930s and moving beyond generalizations. Although Turner comments occasionally in his writing about the apparent concentration of forms from a given African language in one coastal area (as in Turner 1941, 73), in *Africanisms in the Gullah Dialect* he does not distinguish between the speech of his informants, and to date no other study has covered a sufficiently broad area of the Sea Island coast to allow the examination of geographical variation within Gullah.

3. What do the records reveal about Turner's early work on Gullah and how he and his perspective on African survivals developed? His field records, and to a considerable extent the Gullah texts in his book, offer limited evidence for an African element in Gullah. How he shifted his thinking and the focus of his work and managed to detect and collect Africanisms must itself be a fascinating story, one into which an assessment of his earliest study helps us gain insight.

4. How distinctive was Gullah in the 1930s from other English creoles and from Low Country South Carolina and Georgia speech? How does it compare

with the speech of several dozen informants, mostly whites, from mainland areas who were interviewed several years later by Raven McDavid, using virtually the same questionnaire, for the Linguistic Atlas of the Middle and South Atlantic States project?

This paper will address the first and third concerns, and in a preliminary way the second and fourth ones as well, in an effort to reach a more precise characterization of Turner's linguistic atlas data and to assess the patterns they reveal.

As was mentioned above, Turner's field records are in the form of lists of phonetic transcriptions of around eight hundred individual items, most elicited directly by short-answer questions from the worksheets, and some, especially the grammatical ones, recorded from a conversational context. It is easy to see in a general way how data of this sort might prove useful for comparing linguistic features, particularly vowel phenomena, across varieties of English because of the range of environments in which each vowel occurs. On the other hand, significant questions have been raised about the reliability of especially the lexical and grammatical data in linguistic atlas records. In line with these questions and before addressing the research concerns I have identified, several general limitations about the data in these twenty-one field records must be acknowledged.

First, Turner's transcriptions are typically quite broad, and closer to phonemic than phonetic. They show less detail than most other linguistic atlas records, which usually note finer features of vowel fronting and height and vowel offglides. Bear in mind, however, that Turner was a novice fieldworker at the time. The broadness of the transcriptions might make it difficult to use Turner's field records to explore systematic phonetic differences between Gullah speakers and other South Atlantic coastal speakers, and I do not attempt this in the current paper.

Second, absent from Turner's field records are the African-derived phonetic features he presents in chapter 7 of *Africanisms*—the labiovelar plosives, nasalized stops, bilabial fricatives, palatal plosives, palatal nasal, and so on. Turner probably conducted these interviews before he became acquainted with African languages and thus was unfamiliar with such sounds. It was not until 1936 that Turner began his studies at the School of Oriental and African Languages in London. In other words, he was neither trained nor attuned to identify the sounds he heard in Gullah in 1932. Still, there is something of a puzzle here that will be examined later: How is it that no African-derived phonetic features were recorded for the individuals Turner lists as his primary informants and on whose speech his discussion of Africanisms is based?

In addition to the broadness of Turner's transcriptions and their discrepancy with his later descriptions, two general limitations of linguistic atlas–type data must be dealt with. First is the familiar question of validity: How natural is single-item, elicited data of the type collected by linguistic atlas investigations with a short-answer questionnaire? This would seem to be an especially crucial question for Turner's research, given the extreme caution of Gullah speakers in talking to strangers (Turner 1949, 11). Second, there is the problem of representativeness of the data in linguistic atlas field records: How reliable an indicator of an individual's usage is the record of one or two instances of a form, especially a grammatical form? Keeping these questions in mind, let us now proceed carefully to an examination and assessment of Turner's twenty-one records.

Grammatical Patterns in the Records

Although the linguistic atlas questionnaire concentrates on lexical and phonological items expected to discriminate speakers geographically and socially, it gives some attention to grammatical items as well. This is particularly the case for verbs, primarily for their principal parts, but there is sufficient data in the field records at hand to make tentative statements about several aspects of the copula and auxiliary verbs. We will examine in some detail two of these: the patterning of the copula verb for first-person singular subjects (in affirmative, negative, and interrogative contexts) and the presence and patterning of auxiliaries in the present perfect (in affirmative, negative, interrogative, and progressive contexts).

With respect to grammatical forms, however, how do we address the two limitations mentioned above? Given the well-known tendency of single-item questionnaires to elicit more careful, more standard, and sometimes hypercorrect forms, there is no easy way to test the naturalness of the field record data. One thing we can do is compare the field data with the Gullah texts in *Africanisms*. As I have indicated, these texts are mostly from the same speakers, and one would expect that relatively less formal attention would be paid to individual linguistic forms in such running texts. This comparison may show whether some style shifting has occurred and whether questionnaire responses are more standard than forms from a discourse context.

Perhaps three further caveats are necessary. First, both of the grammatical features examined are probably more variable than will be reported here. Second, the field records sometimes list only unmarked main verbs (e.g., *drive*) as perfective forms and thus do not explicitly indicate whether they constitute the complete verb phrase used in perfective context; in other words, we must trust that the fieldworker reported the complete perfective verb phrase rather than only the principal part of the verb used as a past participle. Third, the matter of how to identify a perfective context itself is a problem because Gullah normally uses verbs unmarked for tense and aspect. Also, time adverbials are not present to aid interpretation of the data examined in this paper, either in the field records or in Turner's Gullah texts. The dimensions of this will become clearer below, but this problem affects the decision whether or not a specific context is perfective and therefore whether such auxiliaries as *bin* and *done* are used in a perfective manner. Nevertheless, it should be possible to make a rough assessment of how acrolectal or mesolectal the field record data are by examining the choice of auxiliary verbs for these two cases.

First-Person Singular Forms

Tables 1 and 3 show the distribution of forms taken from the field records for first-person singular *be* and present perfect for each of the twenty-one Gullah speakers. The subtotals for Georgia and South Carolina enable us to compare usage between the Gullah speakers in the two states. Tables 2 and 4 show the distribution of forms from the Gullah texts from chapter 9 of Turner's *Africanisms*.

The data on first-person singular *be* (copula and auxiliary) in Table 1 are based on three worksheet items: 25.5 for affirmative use (I'm right, am I not), 25.3 for negative use (I am not going to hurt him), and 24.6 (Am I going to get some?) for the interrogative.[3] Most striking in Table 1 is the complete lack of copula or auxiliary *am,* an acrolectal form. In general, these findings reveal what we would expect to find for Gullah, including the absence of a form of *be* in the affirmative context before verbal adjectives (*I right*). Although *Im* occurs five times in the affirmative context, there is little reason to suppose that it is a contraction of *I* + *am* rather than an unanalyzed form functioning as a pronoun for these speakers. *Im* was used by two of the Wadmalaw Island speakers and two from Johns Island, the two islands closest to Charleston; the influence of urban speech may be at play here. All five users of *Im* were literate to some extent. The uniformity of the negative (*I ain gwine/goin (uh) hurt him/um*) and interrogative responses (*Is I goin/gwine?*) is also noteworthy.

Table 2 presents the use of copula and auxiliary verbs in first-person singular contexts from the Gullah texts.[4] The figures in Table 2 resemble those in Table 1 and are in line with what one would expect in Gullah, with the zero form normally preceding verbal adjectives and progressive forms and

Table 1. Forms of First-Person Singular *Be* in Turner's Field Records

	Affirmative			Negative *ain*	Interrogative *is*
	zero	*Im*	unrecorded		
South Carolina informants					
P. Capers	1			1	1
Scott	1			1	1
Polite	1			1	1
Sweetwine			1	1	1
Smith		1		1	1
Ross		1		1	1
Crosby			1	1	1
Brown	1			1	1
Milligan	1			1	1
Quall		1		1	1
Singleton		1		1	1
L. Capers	1			1	1
Total	6	4	2	12	12
Georgia informants					
McIntosh	1			1	—
Rogers	1			1	1
Washington	1			1	1
Brown	1			1	1
Walker	1			1	1
Hall	1			1	1
Murray		1		1	1
Quarterman	1			1	1
White	1			1	1
Total	8	1	0	9	8
Total	14	5	2	21	20

Source: McDavid et al. 1982.
Note: Based on one affirmative, one negative, and one interrogative item for each informant.

Table 2. First-Person Singular *Be* in Turner's Gullah Texts

	Affirmative			Negative	Interrogative	
	zero	*Im*	*duh*	*ain*	zero	*ain*
Diana Brown	10			6	1	1
Rosina Cohen	1		1			
Sancho Singleton	2	1				
Mary Smalls	2					
Samuel Polite	2					
Total	17	1	1	6	1	1

Source: Turner 1949.

the single occurrence of auxiliary *duh* coming before a verb (Rosina Cohen, p. 269: *I duh stay dere now*). The fact that two-thirds of the data come from one speaker—Diana Brown—prevents generalizations. Nonetheless, by comparison, the field record data appear no closer to acrolectal patterns, and no more influenced toward standard usage by questionnaire methodology, than the data from running texts, and it is therefore possible to feel somewhat more secure about the validity of the primary data from the field records. The same can be said, as we will see shortly, with regard to the data on the patterning of the present perfect.

Forms of Present Perfect

The figures on the present perfect in Table 3 are based on nine worksheet items: three uses in an affirmative context—11.6 (I have driven many a nail), 12.3 (I have heard it), and 27.4 (I have brought your coat); three uses in a negative context—12.4 (I haven't done that), 12.5 (I haven't seen him), and 40.6 (I ain't done nothing); two uses in an interrogative context—48.5 (How often have you eaten today?) and 49.2 (How much have you drunk?); and one progressive context—item 13.6 (I have been thinking about that).

In general, forms for the present perfect show a degree of uniformity across Georgia but considerable individual (and not local) variation in South Carolina. In the affirmative context, all the auxiliaries are more prevalent in data from the South Carolina speakers: *done* (as in *I done bring de coat* and *I done drive de nail*), *bin* (as in *I bin yeddy* ['hear'] *dis tink too long* and *I bin drive a heap of nail*), and the two standard forms *have* and *habm* (as in *I have heard*

Table 3. Present Perfect Forms in Turner's Field Records

	Affirmative					Negative				Interrogative			Progressive					
	zero	done	bin	have	already	ain	never	didn	habm	zero	bin	done	was	bin	binnuh	just	-in	Ø
South Carolina																		
P. Capers	1	1			1	1	1	1		2								1
Scott	1	2				3				2				1			1	
Polite	2		1			3				2				1			1	
Sweetwine	3					3				1				1			1	
Smith	1		1	1		2			1	1				1			1	
Ross	3					1			2	1				1			1	
Crosby	1	1	1			2		1		1				1			1	
Brown	3					2						1		1			1	
Milligan	3					3				2				1			1	
Quall		1		2					2	2				1			1	
Singleton	2				1	2		1		2			1					
L. Capers	2		1			3				1	1			1			1	
Total	22	5	4	3	2	25	1	3	5	17	1	1	1	10			10	1
Georgia																		
McIntosh	3					2	1			2				1			1	
Rogers	3					3				2				1			1	
Washington	3					1	2			2				1			1	
Brown	1		2			3				1	1				1			1
Walker	3					3				1					1			1
Hall	3					2				2					1			1
Murray	2					3				2						1		1
Quarterman	2					1				2				1			1	
White	2	1				3				1				1			1	
Total	22	1	2			21	3			15	1			5	3	1	5	4
Total	44	6	6	3	2	46	4	3	5	32	2	1	1	15	3	1	15	5

Source: McDavid et al. 1982. *Note*: Based on three affirmative, three negative, two interrogative, and one progressive item for each informant.

Table 4. Present Perfect Forms in Turner's Gullah Texts

	Affirmative					Negative	
	zero	*done*	*have*	*had*	*has*	*aint*	*haven't*
Diana Brown	5	9		1		3	
Hanna Jenkins		3					
Rosina Cohen					1	1	
Mary Smalls					1		
Prince Smith			1				
Samuel Polite	1					1	1
Total	6	12	1	1	2	5	1

Source: Turner 1949.

dat and *I habm do such ting*). I will not speculate here about the reason for this patterning. In addition, the negative and interrogative forms are more uniform than the affirmative and progressive ones. Standard auxiliaries are few, with three South Carolina speakers accounting for all eight occurrences of *have* and *habm* (half were from Susan Anne Quall, one of the four speakers who used *Im* in Table 1). Almost half (four of nine) of the Georgia speakers used the bare verb *tink* rather than *tinkin* after *bin/binnuh* in the progressive, while this was the case for only one South Carolina speaker.

Table 4 presents a tally of the present perfect forms from Turner's Gullah texts.[5] Unfortunately, the data from the Gullah texts are once again quite limited, with only twenty-eight tokens and more than half of these again coming from Diana Brown. What there is, however, appears somewhat more standard than the field record data, and two standard auxiliary forms (*had* and *has*) occur only in the Gullah texts.

Tables 5 and 6 compare the distribution of forms for first-person singular *be* and present perfect for Turner's seven younger (sixty years old and younger) and fourteen older (over sixty) Gullah speakers.[6] Although limited, the data in these tables reveal generational differences for these informants and permit several observations. Especially notable is the relatively more homogeneous usage by younger speakers, who show less variation for each of the four contexts, and the relatively more standard usage by younger speakers in some respects (e.g., use of *Im*). Both auxiliary *bin* and *done* seem to characterize older speakers. Interestingly, all six cases of adverbial usage to express the perfect (with *already, never,* and *just*) are from younger speakers.

Table 5. Age Differences in First-Person Singular *Be* in Turner's Field Records

	Affirmative			Negative *ain*	Interrogative *is*
	zero	*Im*	unrecorded		
Younger speakers	4	3	0	7	7
Older speakers	10	2	2	14	13

Source: McDavid et al. 1982.
Note: Based on one affirmative, one negative, and one interrogative item for each informant.

Table 6. Age Differences for Present Perfect Forms in Turner's Field Records

	Affirmative					Negative			
	zero	*done*	*bin*	*have*	*already*	*ain*	*never*	*didn*	*habm*
Younger speakers	17	1	0	0	2	14	3	2	2
Older speakers	27	5	6	3	0	32	1	1	3

	Interrogative			Progressive					
	zero	*bin*	*done*	*was*	*bin*	*binnuh*	*just*	*-in*	Ø
Younger speakers	12	0	0	0	4	1	1	4	2
Older speakers	20	2	1	1	10	2	0	11	3

Source: McDavid et al. 1982.
Note: Based on three affirmative, three negative, two interrogative, and one progressive item for each informant.

Lexical Patterns in the Records

I will focus on the incidence of African-derived words and rely on Raven McDavid's (1952) essay in my comparison of Turner's Gullah usage patterns with vocabulary patterns in the South Atlantic area surveyed for the Linguistic Atlas of the Middle and South Atlantic States by McDavid and Guy Lowman. In comparison with what Turner lists in *Africanisms* (pp. 190–208 of chapter 3,

"West African Words in Gullah") there is a paucity of African-derived vocabulary in the records and an even greater absence of characteristically Caribbean terms. Still, McDavid discusses twenty-six lexical items in his essay, almost all of which occur in Turner's records, some of them only among Turner's linguistic atlas records. A number of African-derived terms such as *goober, cooter, cush, tote,* and *buckra* have more general currency in the South Atlantic area, but I will comment on only four items that show a difference between Gullah and nearby mainland speech or between Turner's Georgia and South Carolina records. A detailed examination of the field records would doubtless reveal other patterns of interest.

1. *Day clean* 'dawn' was elicited three times by Turner, once on Johns Island and twice on Wadmalaw, but not on the mainland in other records.
2. *Det rain* 'downpour' was elicited twice by Turner, but not on the mainland in other records.
3. *Swing-swong* 'swing' was elicited by Turner once in Georgia and ten times in South Carolina, but not by LAMSAS.
4. *Pinto* 'coffin' was elicited by Turner eleven times in South Carolina but not in Georgia.

In the course of summing up the distinctive regional patterns of fifteen different African-derived forms, McDavid says that "*day-clean, pinto,* and *swing-swong,* plus possibly *pinder,* may be useful in setting off South Carolina Gullah from Georgia Gullah, both in their present characteristics and in their African origins" (1952, 14).

These conclusions with regard to two grammatical features and a handful of lexical items only begin to tap the data in Turner's records and give us a more precise view of the patterns that Turner's early Gullah research reveals. Elsewhere in the field records are other forms of interest for further research; for example, the following:

1. Scattered examples of infinitival *fuh*
2. Lack of gender marking in third-person singular personal pronouns
3. At least partial lack of a grammatical mass-count distinction (with informants using "How *much* time . . ." and "How *much* glass . . ." for field record items 48.5 (How often have you eaten today?) and 49.2 (How much have you drunk?)
4. Variation in the form of main verbs in perfective and other verb phrases (e.g., for item 12.4 [I haven't done that], variation between *ain done, ain do,* and *didn done*)

5. Variation between *bin* and *binnuh* in the type of verb form that follows,
   with the preliminary evidence from Georgia field records indicating *binnuh*
   is followed by an unmarked verb two of the three times it occurs[7]

The Rest of the Story

As interesting and suggestive as Turner's field record data may be, however,
we must be careful not to make too much of them. The two dozen African-
derived forms documented from 1932–33 are a far cry from what Turner
presents in *Africanisms,* and even from what he had identified only five years
later. By the end of 1938 Turner had found "no less than 6,000 [African-
derived] words" that survived among Gullah speakers (Mencken 1945, 199).[8]
The Gullah speakers referred to were apparently the same twenty-one informants Turner had recorded hardly five years before. What should we make of
this discrepancy?

One might suppose that two different field-workers analyzed the speech of
two different sets of informants, but there is another way to view this situation.
The disparities between the linguistic atlas field records and *Africanisms,* rather
than raising questions about the authenticity of the African element in Gullah,
should be seen as testimony of the degree to which Lorenzo Dow Turner was
able to develop his thinking about the extent of the African element and his
skills to investigate this element. Of course, the design of the linguistic atlas
questionnaire was part of the problem; as McDavid points out, "only a small
number of Turner's putative Africanisms were covered by the items in the
Atlas questionnaire" (1952, 3). But Turner's greatest handicap was the mindset
of his profession that presumed that all Gullah forms derived from European
languages and accepted an African derivation only if no possible European
alternative could be cited. The contrast between the field record data and the
material in *Africanisms* throws into very sharp relief the quantum leaps Turner
was able to make in his thinking and research during the 1930s.

Although his early work revealed scant African influence, Turner ended up
finding significant influences in every area of the language. The mid-1930s
must have been a breathtaking time for him, as he gradually overcame the
deep-set suspicions of his informants and his ears opened to a thitherto hidden
world among the Gullah speakers who had become his confidants, and as he
gradually began to explore the African languages that he later chided his fellow
students of Gullah for ignoring so completely. Turner's achievement in break-
ing through the barriers of professional prejudice and undertaking a one-man
comparison of several dozen African languages with his Gullah data, despite

the few resources he had at hand, is matched only, perhaps, by the similar efforts of Melville Herskovits in the field of cultural anthropology. The full story of Turner's evolution must be quite a story indeed.

The present paper has examined grammatical features in two contexts from the field records of Lorenzo Dow Turner. It has described aspects of their patterning, suggested that grammatically the Gullah in these field records is on a mesolectal level, and provided support for the contention that these data collected with a linguistic atlas questionnaire are valid and reliable and deserve further study. I have also commented on several of the lexical Africanisms collected by Turner in these twenty-one records. The few Africanisms recorded in the linguistic atlas records provide only a hint of the African component that Turner was later to uncover. The main story lies in the next chapter of Turner's career, in the middle and late 1930s. Turner's early work was only a prelude to his astonishing and revolutionary contributions to research on a fascinating creole language.

Appendix: Lorenzo Dow Turner's Informants (from Turner 1949)

South Carolina

1. Paris Capers, Frogmore, St. Helena Island, Beaufort County; 60, M, three to four years' schooling, reads Bible and newspaper
2. Anne Scott, Frogmore, St. Helena Island, Beaufort County; 85, F, no schooling, illiterate
3. Sam Polite, Frogmore, St. Helena Island, Beaufort County; 89, M, no schooling, illiterate
4. Sackie Sweetwine, Martin's Point, Wadmalaw Island, Charleston County; 87, F, no schooling, illiterate
5. Prince Smith, Rockville, Wadmalaw Island, Charleston County; 88, M, no schooling, taught himself to read Bible
6. Sarah Ross, Rockville, Wadmalaw Island, Charleston County; 50, F, four years' schooling, reads Bible only
7. Anne Crosby, James Clark Shell House, Edisto Island, Charleston County; 87, F, no schooling, illiterate
8. Diana Brown, Seabrook, Edisto Island, Charleston County; 88, F, no schooling, illiterate
9. Hester Milligan, Seaside, Edisto Island, Charleston County; 49, F, no schooling, illiterate

10. Susan Anne Quall, Sand Hill, Johns Island, Charleston County; 78, F, four years' schooling, reads Bible and almanac with difficulty

11. Sancho Singleton, Johns Island, Charleston County; 50, M, two years' schooling, reads Bible and almanac with difficulty

12. Lucy Bailey Capers, Stater White Place, Johns Island, Charleston County; 97, F, no schooling, illiterate

Georgia

13. Bristow McIntosh, Townsend, Harris Neck, McIntosh County; 80, M, several years' schooling, reads Bible

14. James Napoleon Rogers, Townsend, Harris Neck, McIntosh County; 76, M, no schooling, illiterate

15. Mrs. Scotia Washington, Townsend, Brewers Neck, McIntosh County; 60, F, irregular schooling through fifth grade, reads Bible only

16. Katie Ben Brown, Raccoon Bluff, Sapelo Island, McIntosh County; 60, F, reached fourth or fifth grade, used to read Bible

17. Balaam Walker, Raccoon Bluff, Sapelo Island, McIntosh County; 59, M, two or three years' schooling, reads Bible with difficulty

18. Shadrach Hall, Raccoon Bluff, Sapelo Island, McIntosh County; 85, M, no schooling, illiterate

19. Belle Murray, Glynn Harrington, St. Simons Island, Glynn County; 59, F, three years' school, reads Bible and Sunday school books

20. Wallace Quarterman, Frederika, St. Simons Island, Glynn County; 90, M, no schooling, taught himself to read Bible

21. Dave White, South End, St. Simons Island, Glynn County; 76, M, no schooling, illiterate

Notes

1. In his preface to *Africanisms* (1949, xiv) Turner expresses his appreciation for help in the early days of his research not only to Hans Kurath, director and editor of LANE and LAUSC, but to other members of the LANE staff as well— Miles L. Hanley, associate director; Bernard Bloch, assistant editor; and Guy S. Lowman, Jr., principal field investigator. Lowman, a skilled field-worker and brilliant phonetician, accompanied Turner during some of the latter's early fieldwork on Gullah, although Turner later said that Lowman's presence inhibited his informants (1949, 12).

2. Wallace Quarterman, of Frederika, St. Simons Island, Glynn County, was born in Liberty County, two counties northward along the coast, and moved to St. Simons at an early age.

3. The forms of the questionnaire items given here are taken from A. L. Davis et al. (1973).

4. The data on which this table is based are listed below. The numbers on the left are the page numbers from which the data were taken from Turner's *Africanisms*.

Affirmatives:

261   (Diana Brown): *I gwine curse him; I gwine tell him; I gwine tell him*

263   (Diana Brown): *I Ø satisfied [with] what God done for me; I Ø satisfied; I Ø satisfied; I Ø satisfied; I Ø satisfied; I Ø goin again; I Ø satisfied*

269   (Rosina Cohen): *I duh stay dere now* (?)

275   (Rosina Cohen): *I Ø so glad to have a baby*

279   (Sancho Singleton): *I Ø willing to tell you; I feel like I Ø goin to die; Yes, I'm a hag*

279   (Mary Smalls): *I Ø goin to tell the story; I Ø sure goin to scare you again*

285   (Samuel Polite): *when I Ø goin plant de corn*

Negatives:

261   (Diana Brown): *I ain goin go pick; I ain no gone to be cursed; I ain no fuh go fuh flower; how I Ø goin leave my home . . . ?; ain I goin cook um fresh?*

263   (Diana Brown): *I ain gone worry*

265   (Diana Brown): *I ain fraid about a dark night*

Interrogative:

261   (Diana Brown): *how Ø I goin leave my home . . . ?; ain I goin cook um fresh?*

5. The data on which this table is based are listed below. The numbers on the left are the page numbers from Turner's *Africanisms*.

Affirmatives:

263   (Diana Brown): *I satisfied [with] what God Ø done for me; I satisfied [with] what God Ø done for me; [With] what God Ø done for me I satisfied; I know I satisfied with what him Ø done for me; when I done praise me god, tell me praise . . . ; they say they had culled Irish potato; my time done come through; I done been through that*

265   (Diana Brown): *Diana done been through so much thing in slavery*

267   (Diana Brown): *because I done been through it; because I Ø never see such thing since I born; I done tell them young one now; I done tell them*

271   (Diana Brown): *you see Diana done knock from side to side; when you done see me knock about on Edisto*

273   (Hanna Jenkins): *and I have pass through many danger; . . . have pass through many danger; And all the sin what I have done in this world*

279   (Mary Smalls): *the Lord has given me faith to stand*

283   (Prince Smith): *That was the way they had them fix*

287   (Samuel Polite): *when I done cover that corn; I ain't had no education*

Negatives:

263   (Diana Brown): *Thank God they ain't got me hand*

265   (Diana Brown): *They ain't—none of them—been there talk [in a] long time; you ain't never got but five and one cent in trade*

275   (Rosina Cohen): *I ain't seen my baby this month*

287   (Samuel Polite): *I ain't had no education*

289   (Samuel Polite): *I haven't got any education*

6. Turner's seven younger informants were Paris Capers, Sarah Ross, Hester Milligan, and Sancho Singleton in South Carolina; and Mrs. Scotia Washington, Balaam Walker, and Belle Murray in Georgia. Turner classifies Katie Ben Brown of Sapelo Island, Georgia, as an older informant, although he lists her age as "about sixty."

7. This distinction between the type of element typically following *bin* and *binnuh* is consistent with preliminary analyses of the literary dialogue used by Ambrose Gonzales in his Gullah stories, as analyzed by Katherine Mille (1990).

8. H. L. Mencken (1945, 199fn.) cites this figure from the "outlines of lectures [Turner] gave before the American Dialect Society at Columbia University in Dec., 1938, the Linguistic Club at Yale a few weeks earlier, and the University of Wisconsin in July, 1943."

Recollections of African Language Patterns in an American Speech Variety: An Assessment of Mende Influences in Lorenzo Dow Turner's Gullah Data

Joko Sengova

The languages of Sierra Leone have featured prominently in discussions of African "substrate" influence on the African-American speech variety Gullah (Hair 1965; Hancock 1969; Littlefield 1981; Wood 1974a; Opala 1986). According to a review of Lorenzo Dow Turner's *Africanisms in the Gullah Dialect* (1949) by P. E. H. Hair (1965), two of these languages, Mende and Vai, together account for 25 percent of the African personal names and 20 percent of the four thousand lexical items in Turner's Gullah data. Translated into rough statistics, this means that Mende and Vai contributed approximately 600 personal names, 60 words used in ordinary conversation, and 90 expressions found in folklore and prayers—a total of about 750 retentions. Frederic Cassidy (1980), on the other hand, thinks that such statistics, especially those in Hancock 1969, are much exaggerated because of an error in calculation. Most passages collected by Turner are in Mende, which is spoken almost solely in Sierra Leone and Liberia, while Vai and the Futa-Jallon dialect of Fulbe, recorded in the Gullah counting system (one to nineteen), are spoken predominantly in Liberia and Guinea, Sierra Leone's two closest neighbors.[1] Scholars, especially Ian Hancock (1971), have successfully pointed to astonishing similarities between Gullah and Sierra Leonean Krio. These similarities have led some (e.g., Roy 1985) to conjecture that Sierra Leonean Krio was transplanted to Africa from the New World.

Although this paper deals specifically with Mende influence in one particular New World anglophone creole—Gullah—it has implications for assessing language substrata in Atlantic creoles in general. First, I discuss the issue of determining the nature and classification of substrata. Is an element (1) a "transparent" linguistic element of the donor language or (2) an "opaque" form that requires painstaking comparative analysis of receptor elements and donor language data? Second, it will become obvious that linguistic competence in the

175

substrate language(s) is necessary for an investigator to undertake an analysis and determine the linguistic status of the substrata. Third, I present a comparative and practical approach whereby substratal elements are empirically and systematically assessed vis-à-vis their modern synchronic approximations or parallels. Such a framework ensures the careful examination of all elements while retaining only those that match forms of the source or donor language.

The Mende assessment reveals two categories of substrata: (1) items reflecting direct retention in both form and content and therefore requiring no reconstruction; and (2) Mende elements that were reinterpreted and leveled to suit structures and patterns of Gullah and that in some instances contrast sharply with modern Mende. The processes in the second category create opaque elements, whereas direct retentions are transparent elements.

What does all this mean with relation to the survival or existence of Gullah? I suggest that the time frame of Turner's data collection (the 1930s) is more or less synchronic with the present and that the Gullah speech patterns of the 1930s may still be present today. This thesis appears to be reinforced by evidence from many field studies (e.g., Hancock 1969, 1971; Jones-Jackson 1987; Joyner 1984; Mufwene 1986b, 1986c).

By far the most transparent Africanisms of Mende origin appear in songs and stories recorded by Turner among Gullah-speaking informants in South Carolina and Georgia during the early 1930s and published in *Africanisms*. This paper critically assesses the Mende data in three stories. My assessment suggests that certain Mende items can be retrieved and reconstructed to fit into syntactic gaps in these stories. Putative structures reflecting native "competence" rules of Mende are consequently provided with a view to postulating ways the forms might have been expressed by native speakers.

My discussion thus involves determining the status of Mende items in Turner's data in relation to current spoken Mende. Some items occur in syntactic patterns that are asymmetrical to grammatical strings of Mende and yet are related in formal "opaque" terms.[2] Others show absolute correspondence with Mende lexis and structure, including some salient grammatical features of modern spoken Mende and variations thereupon.

A satisfactory, objective analysis of the Mende data must include the recognition of lexicogrammatical transparencies and opacities, as well as certain linguistic anomalies that require dismissal from the texts where these occur. Such an analysis will then be pertinent to the study of African languages having substrate influence on Atlantic creoles.

Procedural Notes

The three songs and three stories from Turner (1949, 256–59) are reproduced in a form as close to the original orthographic style as possible. For structural comparison, they are juxtaposed with my reconstructed texts in appropriate parts of the paper. My style of orthography follows current practice for Mende (e.g., as in Innes 1967).

A number of diacritic conventions, illustrative devices, and abbreviations are used in this paper. Tone, an important prosodic feature of Mende, is marked as follows: ´ = high tone; ` = low tone; ˇ = rising tone; ^ = falling tone. These are exemplified in the Mende words *wá* 'come', *nà* 'there', *lòó* stand', and *síkà* 'hesitate.' Arrows are used to indicate certain changes in word morphology and sentence pattern without necessarily implying any theoretical equivalence between the two. For example:

[DET.]   *kpato* + *i* → *kpatoi* 'cutlass'
[C. MUT. + CONTRAC.]   *kula* + *ngili* → *kulayi' i* lit. 'wear clothes,' also 'deflower'
[CONTRAC.]   *tá lɔ́ lòó nì* → *tá' á lò' ì* 'he is standing up'
            he be stand ASP.

The square bracket notation is used to highlight abbreviations of grammatical processes such as determination, consonant mutation, and contraction when there is a need to provide brief explanations of such phenomena. Brace notation encloses morphological items or morphemes such as the definite/determiner suffix {-i}. The tilde, as in Turner, marks syllabic nasalization.[3]

Africanisms

Turner (1949) refers to but does not define the term *Africanism*. Most creolists and Gullah scholars use it with reference to African substrate influence. Creolists commonly refer to Africanisms by such labels as "retentions," "survivals," and "substrata," or simply as items of African linguistic cum cultural origin. The terms *item(s)* and *substrata* prevail in this discussion much more so than *retentions* or *survivals,* which constitute Africanisms of synchronic status.[4]

Turner (1949, 31) deals with three categories of Africanisms: (1) personal names, (2) other words used in conversation, and (3) words heard only in songs, stories, and prayers. My concern is with the third category—specifically, with three songs and three stories. One song, by Amelia Dawley of Harris Neck, Georgia, is entirely in Mende; the other two, sung, respectively,

by Lavinia Capers Quarterman and Emma Hall of Darien, Georgia, are designated "Mende-Gullah" songs by Turner, and their content reveals this to be
the case. The stories include three trickster tales of popular animal characters
commonly found in African folklore.

Turner uses *Africanisms* with reference to a West African region ranging
from Senegal in the north to Angola in the south, below the middle of the continent,[5] and all names, words, and expressions traceable to an ethnic African
language within this region are considered Africanisms.

Turner's geographical region for African substrate languages influencing
Gullah, however, leaves unanswered the question of the exact origin(s) of the
words *Gullah* and *Geechee,* two hot spots in the debate on the origin of pidgins
and creoles. Does the word *Gullah* in its American English spelling (including
its superimposed pronunciation) derive from Gola, an ethnic group of the Sierra
Leone–Liberia area, or does it come from Ngola, an Angolan ethnic group
of Bantu typology?[6] Are there, perhaps, genetic relationships yet unproven
between the Gola and the Ngola?[7] While Turner provides information on the
probable African sources of *Gullah,* he does not prefer one over the other.

On the origin of *Geechee,* Turner similarly identifies possible African
sources: for example, the entry under *gifi* (1949, 90), which points to Sierra
Leone and Liberia; and an interesting Kimbundu entry (1949, 127), *makifi* 'the
name of a heathen tribe in Angolan folklore.' A number of American scholars
believe that the term derives from the name of one of Georgia's tidal waters—
the Ogeechee River. The debate continues over which language(s) gave the
American Gullah and Geechee people their names and what exactly those
names were originally, and I will take up this issue again in a later section.[8]

Opaque versus Transparent Africanisms

Scholars investigating African substrate influences in Gullah have focused primarily on items with synchronic status in specific African languages. Usually
the items are identified by language informants and corroborated by as many
other speakers as possible. In such cases, the linguist need not have linguistic competence in the particular language under investigation. Practical field
experience and theoretical skills are sufficient to enable the linguist to match
the words and expressions of one language with one or more others. Forms
so analyzed constitute transparent Africanisms and are more easily discernible
than forms requiring more painstaking analysis.[9]

Transparencies, then, as the term is used here with reference to African language substrata, are those items easily susceptible to surface identification and

analysis. Items requiring deeper linguistic analysis than their surface mani-
festations suggest constitute *opacities*. Most forms that Turner analyzes are
transparent Africanisms. Those he failed to perceive, due probably to limitations of nonnative competence in the numerous languages that he so vigorously
researched, constitute opaque Africanisms. For example, in the Mende entries
in all three of his categories, Turner provides variant forms of morphemes
matching the distinction between words in citation and their morphologically
derived forms marked for determination. The following examples represent
Mende items in Turner's entries under the category "Personal Names." The
spellings reflect, as well as possible, Turner's phonetic rendition of the words
in his book.

1. *ndzowo* 'sweet potato'; *ndzowɛi* 'the sweet potato'
2. *kɒwa* 'great war'; *kɒwai* 'the great war'
3. *kpegbe* 'frog'; *kpegbei* 'the frog'
4. *kamba* 'grave'; *kambɛi* 'the grave'

The first word in each pair of examples represents a lexical item as it would
appear in citation as well as in certain grammatical environments.[10] The second word, marked in each case by the final suffix determiner {-i}, roughly adds
the notion of definiteness, as shown in the English glosses. Apart from displaying separate entries indicating the grammatical contrast, Turner does not
mention the notion of determination with respect to these examples. But it is
quite possible that he was aware of the phenomenon for Mende.

   A case of opacity with reference to Mende grammatical phenomena concerns
the mutation of certain consonants to others with which they bear phonological
relationships in mutation grids. The shifts illustrated in Figure 1 are commonly
referred to as "consonant mutation" and comprise consonants in the phonemic
inventory of Mende that participate in these phonological shifts (Innes 1962,
63; Meussen 1965; Sengova 1981). While Turner found examples of this phenomenon in the two principal dialects of Mende (Kɔɔ and Kpaa), he hardly
mentions it. It seems quite plausible that internalizing this system of phonological rules is an important key to constructing morphologically well-formed
words in Mende. In other words, a learner who has not properly internalized
the shifts would fail to produce forms matching the "correct" morphophonemic
shapes of words in sentences.[11]

   Below are examples of Gullah loanwords found in Turner's texts that display
Mende consonantal mutations.

5. *bimɛ (pimɛ)* 'run' [12]
6. *gɔli (kɔli)* 'leopard, greedy person'

$$p \rightarrow w \qquad\qquad ng \rightarrow w$$
$$nj \rightarrow y \qquad\qquad ng \rightarrow y^{*}$$
$$t \;\rightarrow 1 \qquad\qquad nd \rightarrow 1$$
$$mb \rightarrow b$$
$$f \;\rightarrow v$$
$$s \;\rightarrow \check{j}$$
$$k \;\rightarrow g$$
$$kp \rightarrow gb^{**}$$

Figure 1. Consonant Mutation Grid in Kɔɔ Mende

*Mende operates a seven-vowel system like several Niger-Congo languages, and to some degree the vowels seem to determine consonant shifts involving the glides /w/ and /y/. The following rules apply: (i) ng → w/__ ɔ, u, o; (ii) ng → y/__ s i, e, ɛ, a. In other words, /ng/ becomes /w/ before rounded vowels and /y/ before unrounded vowels (i.e., elsewhere).

**The nasals /m/, /n/, /ŋ/, and /ny/ and the obstruents /d/ and /h/ do not participate in these mutations.

7. *lahi* (*ndahĩ*) 'advise, caution'
8. *gbegbe* (*kpegbe*) 'frog'

Sierra Leonean Languages

The most conservative count usually lists thirteen ethnic groups, each with a distinct language, in the West African state of Sierra Leone. Table 1 lists the seventeen distinct languages, including all the African "minority" languages with an autochthonous speaking population, within the Sierra Leonean geo-political system. Mende is one of the principal languages, with close to a million native speakers. If the minority languages of the Southern and Eastern regions (whose speakers are often fluent in Mende as well) were included, the number would rise over the million mark. Although no stated official language policy exists with regard to the use of the African indigenous languages in Sierra Leone today, Mende, Temne, Limba, and Krio constitute the major "national" languages of this small nation-state (Sengova 1987).

The Mende-Gullah Connection

Mende is a Southwestern Mande language in the same group as Lɔkɔ (also spoken in Sierra Leone), Lorma, Kpelle, and Gbandi (spoken in neighboring

Table 1. Regional Distribution of Sierra Leonean Languages

Northern	Southern	Eastern	Western
Fula	Gola	Kissi	Krio
Kɔrankɔ	Krim	Kɔnɔ	Kru
Limba	Mɛnde	Mɛnde	
Lɔkɔ	Shabro/Bulɔm		
Madingo	Vai		
Susu			
Temne			
Yalunka			

Note: The column heads Northern, Southern, Eastern, and Western represent the four regional political divisions inherited from the colonial government. Despite their designation as regions, they continue to be called provinces (even in official circles), except the "Western area" (the capital Freetown and its environs), which, ironically, still maintains its own separate geographic name.

Liberia and Guinea; Welmers 1973; Dwyer 1972). It is not certain where the Mende people originated, but some historians speculate that they were migrant invaders who first entered Sierra Leone around the mid-sixteenth century after the disintegration and collapse of the once-powerful African states of Ghana, Mali, and Songhai. It is not known which of these kingdoms gave birth to the Mende, though scholars believe the Mende first entered Sierra Leone by way of Liberia through a series of so-called Mane invasions.[13]

By the second half of the eighteenth century, when the Atlantic slave trade to the Americas peaked, the Mende had become fairly settled and were part of the newly established British colony of Sierra Leone. During this period hundreds of thousands of West Africans, including many from Sierra Leone who possessed unsurpassed technological skills in rice agriculture, were shipped directly to South Carolina and Georgia, where rice cultivation flourished. Scholars have begun to recognize the Sierra Leone element in the development of Gullah, as well as some features of similarity in cultural, social, and religious practices (Creel 1988). Mende appears to have been the largest Sierra Leonean contributor of words and expressions to Turner's Gullah field data.[14]

Mende Influences

The present influence of the Mende over other groups in southern and eastern Sierra Leone (the Gola, Krim, Shabro, Vai, Kissi, and Kɔnɔ) may have actually started in the 1700s and probably reached its peak in the middle 1800s. When population censuses are conducted in Sierra Leone, the large numbers of speakers of Mende usually obtained include some or all of these "affiliated" groups. In the region in question, the minority groups not only succumb to Mende political influence and power but also become assimilated into Mende language and culture.[15]

Therefore it is probable that there were groups of Gola, Kissi, Mende, Krim, Vai, Shabro, and Kɔnɔ whose principal language was Mende among the ancestors of the present-day Gullah speakers brought to the United States in the eighteenth century. This would have substantially affected the development of Gullah on isolated Sea Island plantations of South Carolina and Georgia. This view would be even more credible if evidence pointing to further influence and ethnolinguistic dominance by certain African groups in predominantly African servile communities could be unearthed.[16] I should add that slaves were normally shipped directly to coastal South Carolina and Georgia from the slave entrepôt of Bunce Island, in the Sierra Leone estuary. This traffic was often determined by an intriguing economic partnership between two giant "rice and slaves" merchants: Richard Oswald, of a London-based firm, and Henry Laurens, a wealthy South Carolinian (Opala 1986). This scenario lends some validity to the view that the names *Gullah* and *Geechee* derive from a Sierra Leone/Liberia/Guinea provenance rather than from Angola or the Ogeechee River of Georgia.[17]

Mende Language Elements in Gullah Songs and Stories

The Gullah texts analyzed by Turner (songs, stories, and prayers) are said to "constitute only a small percentage of the materials" he collected among the Gullah (1949, 254). There may well be substantial but unknown texts reflecting similar African substrata that Turner did not publish.[18] Below I analyze the Mende elements in three songs (1949, 256) and Mende expressions from three Gullah stories (1949, 257–59).[19]

Songs

Song and dance are associated with the performance of African folklore in general. They are often accompanied by the clapping of hands or other kinesic movement, by musical instruments, or by combinations of these. Turner notes in his introduction to the Gullah texts that "such recreational forms among the Gullahs as singing (frequently accompanied by dancing and hand-clapping) and story-telling often reveal significant African survivals" (1949, 254). Whereas the two songs by Quarterman and Hall appear to fit this description, Amelia Dawley's song, below (Turner 1949, 256), is a repetitive funeral chant rendered entirely in Mende:[20]

   i. *a wɔkɔ mʋ mɔnɛ; kambɛɪ ya lɛ;   li, lɛ: ɪ   tɔmbɛ.*
    'In the evening we suffer; the grave not yet; heart, be cool perfectly.'
   ii. *a wɔkɔ mʋ mɔnɛ; kambɛɪ ya lɛ;   li, lɛ: ɪ   ka.*
    'In the evening we suffer; the grave not yet; heart, be cool continually.'
  iii. *ha sa wuli ŋgo, sihā; kpaŋga   lɪ   lɛ:;*
    'Death quickly the tree destroys, steals [it]; the remains disappear slowly;'
  iv. *ha sa wuli ŋgo; ndɛlɪ, ndi, ka.*
    'Death quickly the tree destroys; be at rest, heart, continually.'
   v. *ha sa wuli ŋgo, sihā; kpanga   lɪ   lɛ:;*
    'Death quickly the tree destroys, steals [it]; the remains slowly disappear;'
  vi. *ha sa wuli ŋgo; ndɛlɪ, ndi, ka.*
    'Death quickly the tree destroys; be at rest, heart, continually.'
  vii. *a wɔkɔ mʋ mɔnɛ; kambɛɪ ya lɛ;   li, lɛ: ɪ   tɔmbɛ.*
    'In the evening we suffer; the grave not yet; heart, be cool perfectly.'
 viii. *a wɔkɔ mʋ mɔnɛ; kambɛɪ ya lɛ;   li, lɛ: ɪ   ka.*
    'In the evening we suffer; the grave not yet; heart, be cool continually.'
  ix. *ha sa wuli ŋgo, sihā; kuhā nda   yia;*
    'Death quickly the tree destroys, steals [it]; from afar a voice speaks;'
   x. *ha sa wuli ŋgo; ndɛlɪ, ndi, ka.*
    'Death quickly the tree destroys; be at rest, heart, continually.'

In the following, Dawley's song is reconstructed in contemporary Mende:

   i. *À kpɔkɔ́ mú mɔ́né;   kámbéí líí ìì yà lè à lèì' ì gbí.*
   ii. *À kpɔkɔ́ mú mɔ́né;   kámbéí líí ìì yà lè à lèì' ì gbí.*
  iii. *Hàá à ngúlíí wɔ́'ɔ sá, í síhā̌, yě kpángáá à lí lè' è.*
  iv. *Hàá à ngúlíí wɔ́'ɔ sá, ndììlé lìí ká.*
   v. *Hàá à ngúlíí wɔ́'ɔ sá, í síhā̌, yě kpángáá à lí lè' è.*
  vi. *Hàá à ngúlíí wɔ́'ɔ sá, ndììlé lìí ká.*
  vii. *À kpɔkɔ́ mú mɔ́né;   kámbéí líí ìì yà lè à lèì' ì gbí.*
 viii. *À kpɔkɔ́ mú mɔ́né;   kámbéí líí ìì yà lɛ à lèì' ì gbí.*
  ix. *Hàá à ngúlíí wɔ́'ɔ sá, í síhā̌, kúhàmà, ngó'ó à yíà' à.*
   x. *Hàá à ngúlíí wɔ́'ɔ sá, ndììlé lìí ká.*

THE DAWLEY SONG

In Dawley's song, each word qualifies as a lexical item of Mende, yet reading a coherent meaning from each item at first glance presents some difficulty for a native speaker of Mende. The structure of the song as reconstructed in contemporary Mende reveals a stock of cohesive words in acceptable form based on well-formed morphosyntactic rules. This allows for easy interpretation. Thus, while Dawley's funeral song presents transparent and easily recognizable Mende words, their lexico-grammatical status in context sometimes makes their interpretation and meaning unclear. When the text is reconstructed so that words appear in appropriate grammatical shapes and syntactic order, the song achieves a high degree of clarity and comprehensibility, and it is acceptable to modern-day native speakers of Mende.

The punctuation in Turner's version of Dawley's song is problematic in that elements naturally belonging together are split by odd uses of commas and semicolons, thereby rendering certain portions of the text incoherent.[21] This could be interpreted as an attempt by Dawley to string together at random a set of words; or perhaps she was recollecting forms that she once knew. Turner's own remark (1949, 254) about linguistic "amnesia" on the part of two of his informants, Amelia Dawley and James Rogers, appears reminiscent of Gullah speakers of the 1930s and possibly today. While entire words and phrases were available to the subjects by rote for all their lives, knowledge and command of their African language versions, including acceptable grammatical rendition, were entirely lost.

WORD-PHRASE RECONSTRUCTION

The items in examples 9–17 below are forms from Turner's Gullah text in column A, and their reconstructions in contemporary Mende in column B.

A	B
9. *a wɒkɒ* 'in the evening'	*à kpɔkɔ́* 'evening'
10. *ndi/li* 'heart'	*ndíí/líí* 'heart'
11. *ha* 'death'	*hàá* 'death'
12. *wuli ŋgo* 'tree destroy'	*ngúlíí wɔ́* 'tree fell' (i.e., 'fell the tree')
13. *kpaŋga* 'the remains'	*kpángáá* 'small bush'[22]
14. *sihā* 'steals (it)'	*síhá̄* 'lend, borrow'
15. *kuhā nda* 'from afar'	*kúhàmà* 'far away, distant'
16. *lɛ:* 'slowly'	*lɛɛ:* 'slow, slowly'
17. *ndɛlɪ, ndi* 'be at rest'	*ndììlélìí* 'heart soak/wet' (i.e., 'peace, satisfaction, contentment')

Three interesting features of Mende grammar are reflected in the reconstructed words and phrases above: initial consonant mutation, determination,
and contraction. Consonant mutation is illustrated in examples 10, 12, and 17,
albeit in slightly different ways. In 10B, the full forms of the words as they
would appear, for instance, in current Mende orthography are given. The tone
markings are useful for differentiating contrastive minimal sets. A set relating
to the forms in 10B is analyzed below.

18. a. *ndíí/líí* 'heart'
    b. *ndìí/lìí* 'departure'
    c. *ndíí/lîì* 'fly' (i.e., insect)

Mutation is seen in the word for 'tree' (12B), whereas the text phrase in 12A is
ill formed in its initial consonant /w/, as well as in Turner's translation of the
word *ŋgo*. In idiomatic Mende, the reconstructed phrase is acceptable, whereas
Turner's version is not. The word *wɔ* derives from *pɔ*, meaning 'fell/cut down.'
Consonant mutation can also be seen in example 17, where the phrase must be
reordered to show how mutation rules apply. Thus, in 17B we have the phrase
ndììlélìì 'satisfaction, etc.' (cf. Figure 1). In the full forms of certain nominals
in column B, we can see the definite forms marked by the determiner suffix
{-í}: *ndíí* 'the heart' (10), *ngúlíí* 'the tree' (12), and *lélìí* 'wet/soaked' (17).

Consonantal elisions are typical in rapidly spoken Mende. An example is
16B: *lè'è* (cf. *lèlè*), although Turner saw this as syllabic vowel length (16A).
Viewed the latter way, the word could be confused with a similar item in the
text, *lè*, normally with low tone, meaning 'yet.' The final two reconstructions
above, 14B and 15B, represent minor lexical modifications, with the former
bearing on meaning and the latter on the choice of appropriate locative marker.

The following section deals with syntactic intricacies of the Dawley song
that require piecing together a number of patterns fitting the English sense of
the text. The syntactic reconstruction of certain clauses involves reordering
elements and in some cases inserting or replacing entire phrases in the text.
Where a totally new clause results, there is often no alarming disparity between
it and the original, which is evidence, it seems, that Mende influences abound
in these particular data.

SYNTAX

Turner's "literal or free translations" (1949, 254) turn out to be useful point-
ers for reconstructing the Mende texts. Once he gives clues to the meanings,
however loose, of items, it becomes much easier to reconstruct or insert miss-

ing grammatical constructions that suit the sentence patterns. In this way clear interpretive meaning is achieved.[23]

19. a.   Turner: *kɔmbɛɪ ya lɛ; li, lɛ :ɪ tɔmbɛ.*[24]
    b.   Mende: *kámbéí líí ì ì yà lɛ à lɛ̀ 'ì' ì gbí.*[25]
          Grave heart it NEG. ASP. yet ASSOC. cool ASP. all
          'The grave is still not yet satisfied.'
20. a.   Turner: *ndɛli, ndi, ka*[26]
    b.   Mende: *Ndììlélíì lɔ́ nà ká*
          Heart cool be there plenty
          'There is plenty of peace/satisfaction.'

In these two sentences, constituents have been reordered and structures have been expanded by the insertion of "new" elements, all of which appear to be intrinsic parts of the constructions to which they are added. To most native Mende speakers, 19b is a highly predictable utterance from the sense intended in Turner's sentence, whereas 20b is a much more complete utterance than its reduced counterpart (Mende reconstruction, lines iv, vi, and x). An even more complete utterance is the following:

21.   Mende: *Ndììlélìí tá ì yè lɔ́ lɔ̀ɔ nà káká*
       Heart it PAST be really there plenty plenty
       'There was indeed [no doubt] plenty of satisfaction.'

In reconstructing the following, from Dawley's song, line iii, Turner's original expression is reordered in its entirety. This clause is the most repetitive refrain of the Dawley song.

22. a. Turner: *ha sa wuli ŋgo*
    b. Mende: *Hàá à ngúlíí wɔ́ɔ̀ sá*
        Death it tree fell ASP. abruptly
        'Death strikes suddenly without prior notice.'

In Mende it is obligatory in certain sentences to recapitulate subject noun phrases with anaphoric referential pronouns; in others it is optional. Clause 22b requires the recapitulated subject pronoun *a* 'it,' the appropriate form in the pronominal paradigm.[27]

The final clause of the Dawley song has been reconstructed to match both the structure of a complete sentence and its original meaning in the text. Sentences of this type compare roughly in temporal semantic reference to the simple future construction in English, as well as to the so-called simple present. Sentence 23b is positive, and 24 is its negative counterpart.

23. a. Turner: *kuha nda yia*
    b. Mende: *Kúhámà ngó'ó à yíà'à*
       Far away voice it speak ASP.
       'Far away a voice speaks/shall speak.'
24.   Mende: *kúhámà ngó'ó èè yíà*
       Far away voice it NEG. speak.
       'Far away a voice does/shall not speak.'

Other Songs

The two songs by Lavinia Capers Quarterman and Emma Hall, respectively, mix Mende and English words and expressions. These are more realistic samples of what the Gullah language truly represents: it is at the same time a variety of spoken American English and an Atlantic creole with African-language substrata.

THE QUARTERMAN SONG

Turner collected the following brief song from Lavinia Capers Quarterman of Darien, Georgia, who accompanied it with dancing and hand clapping:

25. a. Turner: *le mbeɪ, ɟal, le mbeɪ; wa, ɟal, wa.*
       'Pass this way, girl, pass this way; come, girl, come.'
    b. Mende: *lè'è mbéí!   Ngéè   lè'è mbéí!*
       Pass here   I NEG. pass here'
       'Pass this way! I won't pass this way!
26.   Mende: *Gbéí kè bá hɔ'ɔ nyá má?*
       Why then you bump me on
       'Why then do you bump into me?'

The only English word in Lavinia's song is *ɟal* 'girl'; the rest is Mende. This song reminds me of my own boyhood in Sierra Leone, when we used to sing this chant (26) in hiding because of the subject matter. It is couched in "hidden" language in which the performer comments on the movement of a scrotal hernia as it is borne by a disparaged bearer. Although the chant has no unique melody to it, it nonetheless captures in rhythm the silent argument between the hernia and its bearer, who must humorously carry his burden.[28]

THE HALL SONG

Turner collected a longer song at Darien sung by Emma Hall and transcribed it
in five lines:

> *a wɒkɒ bɪ lɪ a, ba wa lɒ*
> 'In the evening when you go, you will come'
> *ɒl rɒʋŋ dɪ kʌntrɪ.*
> 'All round the country.'
> *tɪ bɪ bawo.*
> 'You will be healed.'
> *ɪts ə wɛrɪ fɒɪn ledɪ*
> 'It's a very fine lady'
> *bɪ bawo.*
> '[who] will heal you.'

This song is mixed; whereas the first, third, and fifth lines are Mende, the
second and fourth are clearly dialectal (creole) English resembling Krio. The
Krio equivalents of the second (27a) and fourth (27b) lines make this similarity
with Gullah even more obvious:

27. a. *ɔ́l ɔ̀bɔ́t dì kɔ́ntrì*
       'all about/around the country'
    b. *nà fáín-fáín lèdí*
       'it's a very fine lady'

Except for one clause—*bī lɪ a* 'when you go'—the first, third, and fifth lines
are expressions commonly heard in modern Mende. If we introduced some
items to reconstruct an actual Mende song in the present context, we would
have the four-line verse below, with the following specific changes made: first,
the embedding in item 28a of a Mende clause matching the sense of the second
line of Hall's song; second, attaching the clause *bi bawo' to' ba wa lɔ* as 28b to
achieve syntactic and semantic cohesion; third, introducing a Mende nonverbal
sentence in 28c to replace Hall's fourth line; and finally, inserting a subject
pronoun *a* 'she' as introducer of 28d.

28. a. *À kpɔ̀kɔ́, bí yá' á bí ndɔ' éí kpé' έ gá' á*
       in evening you go ASP. you country all surround
       'in the evening, after you depart and tour the entire country.'
    b. *bá wá lɔ̀ tí bí báwó:*
       you come ASP. they you heal
       'you shall return to be healed'

c. *nyà' ápò nyàndè nyàndè vú' í mìà*
   woman pretty pretty really be
   'it's a very pretty lady'
d. *À bí báwó*
   she you heal
   'that will heal you'

Stories

The Mende expressions extracted from Turner's three Gullah stories are strikingly similar to those found in the three songs just discussed. This supports the view that the items Turner recorded fit the description of formulaic expressions used by speakers in appropriate communicative contexts, which amounts to a mere recollection of forms once a part of the native competence of an older generation of Gullah speakers.

In reconstructing the items in the stories below, we will come across morphological adjustments similar to those made in the songs: sentence and word order rearrangements, sound substitutions typical of consonant mutation, and filling gaps where words or whole expressions are thought to be missing.

"The Leopard and the Young Lady"

The Mende expressions in this trickster tale, *dɪ lɛpɘd an dɪʃaŋ lɛdɪ* (Turner 1949, 257–58), are contained in a four-line dialogue between the leopard and an old man named Sambo.[29] Leopard addresses Sambo in the first two lines of the text, while the old man replies in the third and fourth lines. Again, the expressions, though clearly Mende, fail to communicate a coherent meaning in context. Compare the text (29) and my reconstruction (30) below.

29. Turner: *woŋga! woŋga! woŋga! lɒ*
    'Kinsfolk! Kinsfolk! Kinsfolk! Look!'
    nda hoʋ mbeɪ. na ta   sondʋ ndi lɛ.
    'Wait here. That crime, it afflicts the heart.'
    komɛ! sɔ   mbɛ.   na tia sondʋ ndi lɛ,
    'Gather around! Take it from me. If the crime afflicts the heart,'
    ndi lawo.
    'open the heart' (i.e., tell the truth about the whole affair)
30. Mende: *Nyá bòndá' à! Nyá bòndá' à! Nyá bòndá' à! À nà lɔ́!*
    'My people! My people! My people! You there, behold' (i.e., look!)

À nyá màáwú' ó lè péí. Sòndú hìndèí ná tá,
You me wait yet before. Curse thing that it.
'Hold on one moment. That cursed affair'
à wá' à à ndììnyániì.
It come ASSOC. heart spoil
'brings affliction to the heart.'
À gòmé wú jí jɔ̀' ɔ́ à ngé.   Sòndú hìndèí ná tá
You meet you this get ASSOC. me. Curse thing that it
'Assemble and take this from me. If that cursed affair'
ì wà' á' à à ndììnyáni,
It come ASSOC. heart spoil
'brings affliction to the heart,'
À wù lííhù láwó tɔnyéí và
Your you heart in open truth for.
'[then] open up your hearts to the truth.'

I have performed radical reconstruction with respect to this text and must therefore treat in detail the items and expressions subjected to such rigorous scrutiny. The first change I have made is in the first line in the word *woŋga,* which appears to be the Gullah informant's recollection of the Mende word *bonda'a* 'kinsfolk'; /b/ and /nd/ have disappeared, and in their place have been adopted the Gullah approximations /w/ and /ng/. Recall that initial /kp-/ is similarly produced as /w/ in the words *kpɔkɔ, wɒkɒ.* The expression *nyá bòndáà* 'my people' is commonly heard as an appeal to one's kinsfolk, as is clearly the case in the text. In other contexts with no emotive purpose in mind, a speaker may simply say *bòndèí sìà* 'kinsfolk' as in an afternoon or midday greeting. Further, in the first line, I match Turner's translation with the sentence: *A na lɔ* 'look.' Three Mende variants of this form in a situation where a speaker is calling attention to an audience are the following:

31. a. *À jí lɔ́ lè!*
       you this see yet
       'look/behold!'
    b. *À tɔ lè hùé!*
       you see yet please
       'please look!'
    c. *À kpé' è lè   hùé!*
       you look yet please
       'please look this way!'

In the second line of the text I deal with three separate expressions: first, *nda hov mbeɪ,* glossed as 'wait here' by Turner. This expression is often used in Mende by a lead singer or performer of a song or story as a pausal cue for some significant digression, such as a specific message to an audience. For example,

32. *À ngò' é láhòú mbéí lè.*

you song mouth-hold here yet

'Please stop the singing for a moment.'

(Note the initial consonant mutation in *lahou,* as opposed to the text expression.) It seems unlikely, however, in the context of the leopard's address in Turner's Gullah story, that this expression could have been made. A more likely Mende form is that in 30: *A nya maawu'o lɛ pɛi,* or an alternate such as the following:

33. *Á nyá hàké tò mbéí*

you me excuse here

'[Please] excuse me for one moment.'

The medial phrase of the second line, *na ta,* referring to 'that crime' in Turner's sense, appears to be incomplete. The initial phrase, *sondu hind i,* provides the proper reference to a 'crime, cursed affair,' or 'behavior.' By itself, *na ta* literally means 'that it.' We could also have any of the following as alternates in Mende:

34. a. *Sòndúí ná tá*

   Curse that it

   'That cursed affair/behavior'

   b. *Ỳé hìndá nyàmùí ná tá*

   One thing bad that it

   'That misdemeanor'

   c. *Ỳé kpàvìnjá híndèí ná tá*

   One wrong-doing thing that it

   'That wrong doing'

A concept or word roughly equivalent to the English word *crime* does not exist in Mende. Any of the three expressions *sòndúí, hìndá nyàmùí,* or *kpàvìnjá* can convey the sense of the English word.

This obviously means making some further adjustments in the last expression: *sondu ndi lɛ,* as well as matching it with a Mende form in the sense of Turner's translation. The final clause of 30 that I wish to consider, *à wá' à*

à ndììnyánìí, seems to offer this solution. It is syntactically appropriate for
pegging to the introductory phrase above rather than the reduced, unordered
expression of the text. Placing this specifically within the perspective of the
text, the "jigsaw" may be put back together as follows (i.e., before the reconstruction of 30):

35. **sondu——na ta——ndi lɛ.*[30]

The difference between this line and Turner's third line is that the forms are
adjusted to match the conditional or hypothetical meaning into which Turner's
line translates.

To match the text translation, the expression *kome! sɔ mbɛ,* which Turner
translates as two sentences, would have to be *À gòmé wú jí jɔ' ɔ à ngé,* 'Assemble and take this from me.' The two expressions have been collapsed into
a single structure formally, reflecting changes in the initial consonants /k/ and
/s/, in the words *komɛ* and *sɔ,* to /g/ and /ǰ/. I have filled in gaps to match
the translation of the second expression. It should also be noted that the word
mbɛ used in the text means 'for me,' a variant of the phrase *nyá wé* (literally
'me for'), whereas *à ngé* means 'from/by/with me.'

An appropriate and common alternate of the introductory sentence in 29 is
the following:

36. *À yándɔ   wú jí húmè' í à ngé.*
    You gather you this hear from ASSOC. me
    'Gather around and hear this from me.'

The final line in Turner's text consists of the two words *ndi lawo,* apparently
a contracted form of the sentence in 30. I offer in 37 a much longer variant
which is even more appropriate in contexts such as this one, where a general
appeal to tell the truth is made emotionally at a gathering of Mende folk, as the
folklore seems to suggest.

37. *À kpùà lííhũ wú tɔ nyéí lé kɔ' ɔ lóʼè hìndéí jí mà.*
    You pull heart-in you truth say foot stand thing this on
    'Make up your minds and speak the truth concerning this whole affair.'

"The Tortoise and the Deer"

This story, commonly titled *hàkú tàá ndɔpá,* "Tortoise and Deer," is still
told today among the Mende and other Sierra Leonean ethnic groups. It reflects
the calm but calculated stealth and wisdom of a small animal such as the forest
tortoise, qualities often identified among the Mende. In this story the tortoise

demonstrates a universally held belief: The race is not always won by the swift; sometimes the slow win!

The remarks of both the deer and the tortoise as portrayed by Turner would, however, fail to make sense to the average native Mende speaker. At best, the two lines strike this writer as a "recalled" chant rendered at fast pace. Compare the text (38) and, following that, what sense I make out of it (39):

38. Turner: *Sasi,   bɛ: ku gbla   nda.*
    'Boaster, you cannot be near the door.'
    to   ŋgo   aku   gbla   nda.
    'Send word that he [the tortoise] can be near the door.' [31]
39. Mende: *Sàsímɔ́í, béé   gú bà á yè pé' ɛ́ jí gbèlángá.*
    Arrogant one you NEG. able you NEG. be house this near
    'Arrogant one, there's no chance you could be [here] at the finishing point [this minute].'
    Ngó'ó lòó bé hàkú à gú lɔ́ í yè pé' ɛ́ jí gbèlángá.
    Message send you say tortoise he able ASP. he be house this near-at
    'Go ahead and tell everyone that [I] Tortoise can indeed be [here] at the finishing point [this minute].'

The word *sasi* more correctly means 'to be squeamish, impudent, arrogant'; I choose the last sense. I have also "beefed up" the text with words and expressions that I felt were lost in the reduced speech of the Gullah informants. Basically, then, the following portions of the text correspond to my reconstruction in 39 above.

40. *sasi = sàsímɔ́í*   The suffix *-mɔ́í* for determination is required to designate the personality being addressed.
    to ngo = ngó'ó lòó   'send word/message' (but note reordering and consonant mutation on *tòó*).

The larger constructions match fairly well, except that in the first line the following distinction should be noted:

41. *bɛ: ku = béé gú* 'you cannot'   NEGATIVE
    a   ku = à gú lɔ́ 'he can'   POSITIVE

Compare now

42. Mende: *béé gú   bà á yè   pé' ɛ́ jí gbèlángá*
    You NEG. able you NEG. be house this near-at

versus

43. Mende: *à gú lɔ́ í yè   pé'ɛ́ jí gbèlángá*
    He able ASP. he be house this near-at

"The Wolf, the Rabbit, and the Whale's Egg"

The third story, which also concerns animals, has the title *dɪ wʊf, dɪ rabɪt, an dɪ wel eg*.[32] I approach this tale in a slightly different manner from much of the preceding.

The Mende words in their syntactic form make absolute sense, although they do not necessarily correspond to the translation. Conseqently, the English translation supersedes the inherent meaning conveyed by the words in context. This suggests that more meaning than exists has been read into the text and that the translation may be the result of a paraphrased elicitation in which the informant in conversation with the linguist "fills in gaps" originally left out, thus making reference to phenomena otherwise not mentioned in the text.

Mention is made, for instance, of "the door" when no such Mende word exists in the text. I present two versions of the original in addition to the text itself: first, a translation of the words as they might present themselves to the "native" ear; second, my usual reconstruction of the text matching Turner's translation.

44.   Turner: *o: nda wo! o: nda wo!*[33]
       'Please, open the door! Please, open the door!'
       hov nda tɪtɪtɪ![34]
       'Hold the door very tightly!'
45. a. 'Please open it! Please open it!'
    b. 'Hold onto it very tightly!'
46. a. Mende: *Pé'ɛ́ láwó, hèé!   Pé'ɛ́ láwó, hèé!*
       'Door open please! Door open please!'
    b. *Hòù pé'ɛ́ là à kpàyá vú'í!*[35]
       Hold door   at ASSOC. strength actually.
       'Hold onto the door very tightly!'

Two Mende constructions should be noted with regard to the initial consonant mutation in 46a above:

47. *pé'ɛ́ + ndáwó → pé'ɛ́ láwó* 'open the door'
    pé'ɛ́ + ndà   → pé'ɛ́ là 'at the door'

Thus the following constructions are deviant:

48.   **pé'ɛ́ ndáwó; pé'ɛ́ ndà*[36]

To assess Turner's linguistic material based purely on the data in his seminal work is to undertake only a fragment of the study of Africanisms in Gullah. Since an examination of Turner's work must start somewhere, however, this appears to be a valid base from which to launch a detailed study of his entire linguistic research, particularly as it relates to African substrate influence in varieties of English worldwide.

In this paper I have used a detailed descriptive analysis to assess Mende language influences and patterns in Lorenzo Dow Turner's Gullah data. The specific targets of this assessment are three songs and three stories. Apart from Mende influences found in Turner's category "Personal Names," no other data so richly display the Mende element in Turner's material. An examination of all of Turner's field data would likely reveal further influences and patterns from Mende. The present assessment is the first ever attempted by a native speaker of Mende, and its substantive dimensions must now be placed within a summary perspective.

This paper supports the view that Africanisms identifiable in languages such as Mende are present in Turner's Gullah data. Whether these still survive today, assuming Gullah itself does, is another matter.[37] Recent findings on the status of Gullah designate it a creole language, with the implication that it contains patterns akin possibly to several languages, though the degree of influence of the superstrate and substrate languages may vary.[38] This creole, then, may still be obtainable, given favorable circumstances and the proper procedures. An optimistic view assumes that Gullah does still exist, though its use may not be as obviously prevalent as other varieties of American English.[39]

Critical analysis of the Mende items in Turner's data allows a delineation of linguistic elements recalled as part of a typical language "loss" situation—in this case the loss of Mende. Several examples in the sample texts reflect items of exclusive Mende origin, although, not surprisingly, they do not in every case match elements of actual spoken Mende. The items seem to qualify as mere recollections of actual competence structures lost as a result of cultural transplantation and language loss through generations of slavery. This would explain the many "gaps" and synchronically deviant items that I have analyzed.

The analysis of Mende items provides a framework for detailing words, sounds, phrases, and sentences, and consequently for evaluating meaning in the texts. This approach permits the reordering of sentence structures to suit competence patterns of Mende. It also permits the restructuring of words and expressions based on morphophonemic rules of Mende and allows for the proper semantic interpretation of the text. All of this points to a cautious conclusion that the data contain African substrata. But they should be viewed as forms not necessarily and always conforming strictly to putative structures and patterns of any given language. Where items flawlessly matching African languages are found, they must be so assessed. Where deeper analysis is required of certain text items beyond mere transparency or coincidence, these must be so acknowledged. Where so-called retentions fail to fit, however, into the structure or pattern of the language under investigation, these must be recognized as such and rejected.

In summary, while Mende items exist in Turner's Gullah data, they frequently reflect lost forms, words, and expressions sometimes retained as formulaic patterns, but not necessarily matching current spoken Mende. I grant some degree of authenticity to the Mende items, however, because they are susceptible to linguistic reconstructions that match the semantic content of the texts. In the reconstructions offered throughout this paper, certain features of Mende grammar such as contraction, consonant mutation, and determination have emerged. Though some of the items are obviously transparent forms, in many cases, given the linguistic situation of Gullah, we need to go beyond these artificialities to correctly plot the forms of the African substrate language.

Notes

Many thanks to Michael Montgomery of the University of South Carolina at Columbia and Thomas Stewart of South Carolina State College, Orangeburg, for encouraging me to develop preliminary thoughts and findings of my Gullah research. I am also grateful to Carol Scotton and the Linguistics Program at USC for hosting a colloquium at which I presented a version of this paper and to South Carolina State College for providing transportation.

1. A primarily economic and political alliance was established in the 1970s by Guinea, Liberia, and Sierra Leone; together they constitute the Mano River Union (MRU).

2. This distinction equals that involving simple language data versus complex data, the difference being that transparencies lend themselves to immediate surface analysis, whereas opacities require much deeper analysis. The distinction must not be mistaken for a formal theory of transformational grammar.

3. The following abbreviations are used in this paper: ASP. = aspect; ASSOC. = associative marker {a}; C. MUT. = consonant mutation; CONTRAC. = contraction; DEF. = definite/determiner suffix {-í}; DET. = determination; NEG. = negation marker; PRON. = pronominal; SG. = singular; STAB. = stabilizer; S. RECAP. = subject recapitulation (cf. Welmers 1973).

4. Although in theory I subscribe to the view that Gullah *may* still exist, I remain

uncertain as to its nature, including the presence or status of forms of African-language origin that it may still retain.

5. The area specified as comprising the Senegal area down to Angola does not constitute current West African regional or physical geography.

6. Compare the classifications of Guthrie (1953) and Greenberg (1963).

7. Scholars with a keener interest in the field of historical-comparative linguistics may wish to pay attention to issues of this type in the classification of African languages. There ought to be reasons, for instance, other than mere "coincidence" or accident, why there is a Kissi tribe in the Sierra Leone area as well as in southern Africa; similarly, Ngola, a Bantu language, may have historical ties with Gola, and so forth. The synchronic diversity of the African continent and its peoples could well be partly explained from the perspective of a more congenial homogeneity during ancient times.

8. See the section on Mende influences below; also, Stewart and Sengova, unpublished data.

9. In certain cases, the linguist is both informant and analyst if the data he or she investigates are part of his or her own language system. This is the case with the present author in this study.

10. For example, phrases containing the noun as initial constituent, roughly matching English genitival phrases (Innes 1967):

  i. *njòwó + ndáwá* → *njò'òlá'á*
     'potato' 'leaf'   'potato leaves' (vegetable/sauce)
  ii. *kámbá + sìà*   → *kámbájìà*
      'grave' 'walk'   'cemetery'

11. As I show throughout, some Mende items in Turner's texts represent "errors" of this type, where the wrong initial consonant appears in a word in addition to deviant word order in a phrase. For example, *le li, ndi,* —; which should actually be *ndìlléli(i)* 'satisfaction/peace/contentment.'

12. Turner's data show /p/ shifting to /b/ in certain words, as this example shows, reflecting the older Kpaa dialect system, which seems to have fizzled out into an archaism (cf. Figure 1). This shift showing lenition, however, also found in t → d, s → z, is quite common in other Southwestern Mande languages such as Lorma, Kpelle, and Gbandi spoken in Guinea and Liberia.

13. For example, A. Abraham (1969), Bah (1983), and Dwyer (1972).

14. Hair (1965), Hancock (1969, 1971), and Opala (1986).

15. Most native speakers of these "minority" languages have at least passive competence in Mende. Many nonnative speakers of Mende speak Mende or Krio as a second language, and it is not unusual to find polyglot speakers of at least four languages (e.g., Kissi, Mende, Kono, Shabro, Krio, English). As we would expect, intergroup marriages exist in the area under survey.

16. Conditions favoring homogeneity on the slave plantations might include the

need for stronger group solidarity, harmony, and kinship loyalties. Several slave chronicles refer to slaves running away from one plantation to another to seek family members and kinsfolk.

17. The sources of this speculation are as follows: *Gullah* derives from *Gola,* and *Geechee* derives from *Giizi;* by the same token, *Giizi/Geechee* probably gave the Georgia river its name (Sengova and Stewart, unpublished data).

18. Lorenzo Dow Turner's field notes are now available at Northwestern University's Africana library; taped recordings of these notes are in Indiana University's Archives of Traditional Music. These materials were obtained in 1987–88 through a Fulbright grant for rigorous study by the Sierra Leone–Gullah Research Committee.

19. See also Margaret Wade-Lewis's *Lorenzo Dow Turner: First African-American Linguist* (1988a).

20. Joseph Opala, anthropologist and cochair of the Sierra Leone–Gullah Research Committee, and ethnomusicologist Cynthia Schmidt located Mende female performers in 1990 who sang a chant similar to Amelia Dawley's song. The performers live in Pujehun, southern Sierra Leone; taped recordings of that song are now being studied.

21. On the other hand, it is quite legitimate to speculate a printer's or publisher's error with regard to this problem.

22. Turner glosses this word as 'the remains,' but Innes (1969) has it meaning 'piece of bush adjoining a farm which is accidentally burnt when the farm is burnt.' Together, these amount to 'small bush.'

23. The bare text sentence structure will precede the numbered examples in each case in these sets of examples. The reader is again referred to the two versions of Dawley's song to compare the forms under scrutiny.

24. My Mende field consultants and I found the use of *tɔmbɛ* unsuitable in the context of the Dawley song (ll. i and vii). We therefore substituted a more appropriate word, *gbi* 'at all,' lit. 'all.' We further substituted this word for *ka* 'plenty' in lines ii and viii, where it is similarly inappropriate, but retained it in lines iv and vi, where it is suitable (cf. the Mende reconstruction).

25. See Welmers (1973) for a detailed description of the morpheme {a} used as an "associative" marker in Southwestern Mande languages such as Mende and Kpelle.

26. It is interesting that the expression *ndɛ lɪ, ndi, ka,* though not acceptable in Mende, closely resembles the corresponding Krio expression *kolat b ku.* Compare the three forms for Gullah, Krio, and contemporary Mende.

Gullah: *ndɛlɪ,   ndi   ka*
       cool   heart   a lot
  Krio: *kòlát dé bɔkú*
       cold   heart   be plenty
       'There's plenty of satisfaction'

Mende: *ndììlé lìí lɔ́ nà ká*
      cold heart be there plenty
      'There is/was plenty of satisfaction'

The spaces left between certain words in the text (e.g., Dawley's song, ll. v and vi) seem to suggest omissions of words; if this is the case, my insertions in item 21 would be justified.

27. See Sengova (1981), chapters 3 and 4, for a detailed presentation of the Mende pronominal system and its operation in syntactic structure.

28. As the chant goes, the owner first instructs his burden to move in a comfortable direction as he walks, but the latter refuses, of course: "Why, then, must you keep bumping into me making me uncomfortable?" the carrier complains in the second line. It is still not clear to me, however, whether this chant represents an original invention or a modification of a more traditional Mende chant.

29. The name *Sambo* appears in Turner's list of Gullah personal names under three languages: Hausa, Mende, and Vai (1949, 155). The Mende entry has to do with 'shame' and 'disgrace'; the name exists in some family circles I know in Sierra Leone's Bonthe Shabro district, where it has been associated with an unknown myth.

30. There seems to be an error with Turner's use of *ndi lɛ* 'satisfaction' rather than *ndi le* 'affliction of the heart' (i.e., 'anger'). Since Turner's intended meaning is the latter, the form with vowel /e/ rather than /ɛ/ on *le* should have been used. Compare a current orthographic representation of the forms with tone marks to differentiate them as near minimal pairs:

  i. *ndíí* + *téwé* → *ndììlé'è*
     heart cut   'anger, losing one's temper'
 ii. *ndíí* + *ndélíí* → *ndììlé'ìí*
     heart soak   'peace, satisfaction, etc.'
              C. MUT., CONTRAC.

31. The expression *a ku* in the second line appears to be a misrepresentation of the animal's name, *haku* 'tortoise.' This error bears an interesting similarity to the pronunciation of *h-* words by native speakers of Krio, in whose phonemic inventory there exists no /h/.

32. The expression *dɪ wel eg* closely resembles Krio, where it could similarly be *di wel eg* or *di wel in eg*.

33. Though written as if there were separate words (*nda wo*), the word *ndawo* 'open' is derived from the combination of two words by consonant mutation and contraction as follows:

   ndá + *ngóló* → *ndáwó*
   mouth break   'open'

   C. MUT.; CONTRAC.

34. Compare the two verbs *ndáhòú* 'cease doing, hold on' (i.e., for a while) and *hòúndà* 'hold, stifle at neck.' Both verbs are derived from a combination of the lexeme *hou* 'hold' plus a noun used as a locative marker, in the first place as prefix and in the second as suffix. Many Mende verbs display this morphology.

35. I feel that the phrase *à kpàyá vú' í* 'very tightly' is more appropriate within the context of an instruction than the ideophone *tɪtɪtɪ*, which could well be describing other situations such as extreme darkenss caused by rain clouds.

36. Note, however, that there exists a form *pè' éndà* 'cover' with rising tones on the verb *pè' é* 'cover,' which should not be mistaken for the above. This obviously is a case for marking tone in Mende, where words may easily be misconstrued out of context if tonal pitch behavior is not specified.

37. Some scholars subscribe to the view that Gullah exists as an authentic creole language (e.g., M. Alleyne 1980; Cassidy 1980; Cunningham 1970, 1992; Hall 1966; Hancock 1971, 1975; Jones-Jackson 1987; Joyner 1984; Mufwene 1986b, 1986c; Mufwene and Gilman 1987; and Rickford 1980). Others think Gullah either no longer exists or is in the last stages of decreolization (Bickerton 1975; Dillard 1972; W. Stewart 1969a; Traugott 1976).

38. If Gullah were decreolizing, one would expect an evolution toward the supralexifier source—"standard" American English similar to that plotted for other varieties of Vernacular Black English (Traugott 1976). Compare this with the situation of Krio in Sierra Leone, where English (supposedly British) is the "official" language and Krio was for a long time stigmatized, its use for all formal purposes discouraged. Presently, however, there is approximately 80 percent adoption of Krio as the lingua franca by the Sierra Leonean population, whose multilingualism needs linguistic healing through a common "neutral" medium of communication. Rather than decreolize, therefore, Sierra Leone Krio, the West African cousin of Gullah, has adopted a trend of accommodating to the closest African languages of contact, Temne and Mende, which also happen to be the most widely used languages in the community.

39. During a short time on Saint Helena Island and in Beaufort, South Carolina, in the fall of 1987, a number of community people constantly assured a colleague and me that Gullah was still spoken on parts of the Georgia and Carolina Sea Islands. More recently, I have been privileged to listen attentively to African Americans in Orangeburg and Charleston, South Carolina, speaking a variety of Black English with astonishing similarities to Krio, and perhaps subtly to Mende. The data are being recorded and studied.

Bibliography

Abraham, Arthur. 1969. Some suggestions on the origins of the Mende chiefdoms. *Sierra Leone Studies* 25:30–36.

Abraham, R. C. 1958. *A dictionary of modern Yoruba*. London: University of London Press.

Albury, Paul. 1975. *The story of the Bahamas*. London: Macmillan Caribbean.

Alleyne, Mervyn C. 1971. Acculturation and the cultural matrix of creolization. In *Pidginization and creolization of languages,* ed. Dell Hymes, 169–86. Cambridge: Cambridge University Press.

————. 1980. *Comparative Afro-American: an historical-comparative study of English-based Afro-American dialects of the New World*. Ann Arbor: Karoma.

————. n.d. Continuity and change in Caribbean languages. MS.

Alleyne, Warren, and Henry Fraser. 1988. *The Barbados-Carolina connection*. London: Macmillan Caribbean.

Allsopp, Richard. 1983. Linguistic economies in middle-level Caribbean English attributable to African sources. Paper presented at the Second World Congress on Communication and Development in Africa and the African Diaspora, Bridgetown, July 24–28.

Asante, Molefi. 1970. *Rhetoric of black revolution*. Boston: Allyn and Bacon.

Awoyale, Yiwola. 1983. On the development of the verb infinitive phrase in Yoruba. *Studies in African Linguistics* 14:71–102.

Bah, Alpha M. 1983. Fulbe migration and settlement among the Kissi of Koindu. Ph.D. dissertation, Howard University.

Bailey, Beryl Loftman. 1962. Language studies in the independent university. *Caribbean Quarterly* 8:38–42.

————. 1966. *Jamaican Creole syntax: a transformational approach*. Cambridge: Cambridge University Press.

Bailey, Guy, Natalie Maynor, and Patricia Cukor-Avila, eds. 1991. *The emergence of Black English: texts and commentary*. Philadelphia: Benjamins.

Bailey, Guy, and Garry Ross. 1988. The shape of the superstrate. *English Worldwide* 9:193–212.

Baird, Keith E., and O. Chuks-Orji, eds. 1972. *Names from Africa: their origin, meaning and pronunciation*. Chicago: Johnson Publishing.

Baker, Philip. 1990. Off target? *Journal of Pidgin and Creole Languages* 5:107–19.

Baker, Philip, and Chris Corne. 1986. Universals, substrata and the Indian Ocean creoles. In *Substrata versus universals in creole genesis,* ed. Pieter Muysken and Norval Smith, 163–83. Philadelphia: Benjamins.

201

Bamgbose, Ayo. 1971. The verb-infinitive phrase in Yoruba. *Journal of West African Languages* 8:37–52.

Bartram, William. 1928. *Travels of William Bartram.* Ed. Mark Van Doren. Reprint. New York: Dover, 1955.

Bastide, Roger. 1978. *The African religions of Brazil.* Baltimore: Johns Hopkins University Press.

Baugh, John. 1980. A re-examination of the Black English copula. In *Locating language in time and space,* ed. William Labov, 83–106. New York: Academic Press.

———. 1983. *Black street speech.* Austin: University of Texas Press.

———. 1985. Creoles and West African languages: a case of mistaken identity. Paper presented at the Workshop of Universals versus Substrata in Creole Genesis, University of Amsterdam, April 10–12.

Beier, A. L. 1985. *Masterless men: the vagrancy problem in England, 1560–1640.* London: Methuen.

Bickerton, Derek. 1973. On the nature of a creole continuum. *Language* 49:640–69.

———. 1975. *Dynamics of a creole system.* Cambridge: Cambridge University Press.

———. 1977. Putting back the clock in creole studies. *Language* 53:353–61.

———. 1979a. Beginnings. In *The genesis of language,* ed. Kenneth C. Hill, 1–22. Ann Arbor: Karoma.

———. 1979b. The status of *bin* in the Atlantic creoles. In *Readings in creole studies,* ed. I. F. Hancock et al., 309–14. Ghent: E. Story–Scientia.

———. 1980a. Creolization, linguistic universals, natural semantax and the brain. In *Issues in English creoles: papers from the 1975 Hawaii Conference,* ed. R. Day, 1–18. Heidelberg: Groos.

———. 1980b. Decreolization and the creole continuum. In *Theoretical orientations in creole studies,* ed. Albert Valdman and Arnold Highfield, 109–28. New York: Academic Press.

———. 1981. *Roots of language.* Ann Arbor: Karoma.

———. 1984. The language bioprogram hypothesis. *Behavioral and Brain Sciences* 7:173–221.

Birdwhistell, Ray L. 1970. *Kinesics and context: essays on body motion communication.* Philadelphia: University of Pennsylvania Press.

Bivins, John, Jr., and Paul Welshimer. 1981. *Moravian decorative arts in North Carolina.* Ed. Frances Griffin. Winston-Salem, N.C.: Old Salem.

Bliss, Alan. 1979. *Spoken English in Ireland, 1600–1740.* Dublin: Dolmen Press.

Bookout, Timmy Joe. n.d. Review of the literature. MS, Atlanta, Ga.

Boretzky, Norbert. 1993. The concept of rule, rule borrowing, and substrate influence in creole languages. In *Africanisms in Afro-American language varieties,* ed. Salikoko S. Mufwene, 74–92. Athens: University of Georgia Press.

Botume, Elizabeth H. 1893. *First days amongst the contrabands.* Boston: Lee and Sheperd.

Brook, G. L. 1963. *English dialects.* London: Deutsch.

Brunt, R. J., Werner Enninger, and Karl-Heinz Wandt. 1983. The English of the Old Order Amish of Delaware: phonological, morpho-syntactical and lexical variation of English in the language contact situation of a "trilingual" speech community. Paper presented at the American Dialect Society meeting, University of Delaware, June.

Campbell, Emory. 1984. "Cultural Activities in the Sea Islands." *Highlander Reports,* Newsletter of the Highland Folk Center, New Market, Tenn., November.

Carter, Harold. 1976. *The prayer tradition of black people.* Valley Forge, Pa.: Judson Press.

Cassidy, Frederic G. 1961a. *Jamaica talk: three hundred years of the English language in Jamaica.* London: Macmillan. 2d ed., 1971.

———. 1961b. Toward the recovery of early English-African pidgin. In *Symposium on Multilingualism,* 267–77. Brazzaville, Tex.: Committee for Technical Cooperation in Africa.

———. 1980. The place of Gullah. *American Speech* 55:3–16.

———. 1983. Sources of the African element in Gullah. In *Studies in Caribbean language,* ed. Lawrence Carrington, 75–81. St. Augustine, Trinidad: Society for Caribbean Linguistics.

———. 1986a. Barbadian Creole: possibility and probability. *American Speech* 61:195–205.

———. 1986b. Some similarities between Gullah and Caribbean creoles. In *Language variety in the South: perspectives in black and white,* ed. Michael Montgomery and Guy Bailey, 30–37. University: University of Alabama Press.

Cassidy, Frederic G., and R. B. Le Page, eds. 1980. *Dictionary of Jamaican English.* 2d ed. Cambridge: Cambridge University Press.

Chambers, J. K., and Peter Trudgill. 1980. *Dialectology.* New York: Cambridge University Press.

Chase, Judith Wragg. 1971. *Afro-American art and craft.* New York: Van Nostrand.

Chaudenson, Robert. 1986. And they had to speak any way . . . : acquisition and creolization of French. In *The Fergusonian impact,* ed. Joshua A. Fishman et al., 1:69–82. Berlin: Mouton de Gruyter.

———. 1988. *Créoles et enseignment du français.* Paris: L'Harmattan.

———. 1990. Du mauvais usage du comparativisme: le cas des études créoles. *Travaux du Cercle Linguistique d'Aix-en-Provence* 8:123–58.

———. 1992. *Des îles, des hommes, des langues: langues creoles—cultures creoles.* Paris: L'Harmattan.

Cheshire, Jenny, ed. 1991. *English around the world: sociolinguistic perspectives.* Cambridge: Cambridge University Press.

Christian, Donna, Walt Wolfram, and Nanjo Dube. 1988. *Variation and change in*

*geographically isolated communities: Appalachian English and Ozark English.
Publication of the American Dialect Society* 74. Tuscaloosa: University of Alabama Press.

Clifton, James M., ed. 1978. *Life and labor on Argyle Island: letters and documents
of a Savannah River rice plantation, 1833–1867.* Savannah: Beehive Press.

Clowse, Converse D. 1971. *Economic beginnings in colonial South Carolina.*
Columbia: University of South Carolina Press.

Comrie, Bernard. 1976. *Aspect: an introduction to the study of verbal aspect and
related problems.* Cambridge: Cambridge University Press.

Creel, Margaret Washington. 1988. *"A peculiar people": slave religion and
community-culture among the Gullahs.* New York: New York University Press.

Cunningham, Irma A. 1970. *A syntactic analysis of Sea Islands Creole (Gullah).*
Ann Arbor: University Microfilms.

————. 1988. Some innovative linguistic and procedural notions, relative to Sea
Island Creole, in general: some aspects of the Sea Island Creole verbal aux-
iliary in particular. In *Methods in dialectology,* ed. Alan R. Thomas, 46–54.
Clevedon, Eng.: Multilingual Matters.

————. 1992. *A syntactic analysis of Sea Island Creole. Publication of the American Dialect Society* 75. Tuscaloosa: University of Alabama Press.

Curtin, Philip D. 1969. *The Atlantic slave trade: a census.* Madison: University of
Wisconsin Press.

Dabbs, Edith M. 1970. *Face of an island: Leigh Richmond Miner's photographs of
St. Helena Island.* Columbia, S.C.: R. L. Bryan.

Dalphinis, Morgan. 1985. *Caribbean and African languages.* London: Karia Press.

Davies, Kenneth G. 1957. *The Royal African Company.* London: Longmans-Green.

Davis, Alva L., Raven I. McDavid, Jr., and Virginia G. McDavid, eds. 1973. *A
compilation of the work sheets of the Linguistic Atlas of the United States and
Canada and associated projects.* Chicago: University of Chicago Press.

Davis, Gerald L. 1976. Afro-American coil basketry in Charleston County, South
Carolina. In *American folklife,* ed. Don Yoder, 151–84. Austin: University of
Texas Press.

Davis, Lawrence M. 1971. Dialect research: mythology and reality. In *Black-white
speech relationships,* ed. Walt Wolfram and Nona H. Clarke, 90–98. Arlington,
Va.: Center for Applied Linguistics.

Day, Gregory K. 1978. Afro-Carolinian art, towards the history of a southern
expressive tradition. *Contemporary Art/Southeast* 1.5:10–21.

Day, Gregory K., and Kay Young Day [Kate Porter Young]. 1971. *Preliminary field
report.* Washington, D.C.: Smithsonian Institution.

Day, Kay Young [Kate Porter Young]. 1983. My family is me: women's kin net-
works and social power in a black Sea Island community. Ph.D. dissertation,
Rutgers University.

DeCamp, David. 1971a. Introduction: the study of pidgin and creole languages. In

Pidginization and creolization of languages, ed. Dell Hymes, 13–39. Cambridge: Cambridge University Press.

———. 1971b. Toward a generative analysis of a post-creole speech continuum. In *Pidginization and creolization of languages,* ed. Dell Hymes, 349–70. Cambridge: Cambridge University Press.

———. 1973. Foreword to *Africanisms in the Gullah dialect,* by Lorenzo Dow Turner, v–xi. Ann Arbor: University of Michigan Press.

DeCamp, David, and Ian Hancock, eds. 1974. *Pidgins and creoles: current trends and prospects.* Washington, D.C.: Georgetown University Press.

D'Eloia, Sarah G. 1973. Issues in the analysis of Negro Nonstandard English: a review of J. L. Dillard's *Black English: its history and usage in the United States. Journal of English Linguistics* 7:87–106.

Derby, Doris Adelaide. 1980. Black women basket makers: a study of domestic economy in Charleston County, South Carolina. Ph.D. dissertation, University of Illinois.

Dial, Adolph L., and David K. Eliades. 1975. *The only land I know: a history of the Lumbee Indians.* San Francisco: Indian Historian Press.

Dillard, J. L. 1972. *Black English: its history and usage in the United States.* New York: Random House.

———, ed. 1975. *Perspectives on Black English.* The Hague: Mouton.

———. 1985. *Toward a social history of American English.* Berlin: Mouton.

Doar, David. 1936. *Rice and rice planting in the South Carolina Low Country.* Charleston, S.C.: Charleston Museum.

Donnan, Elizabeth. 1927–28. The slave trade into colonial South Carolina. *American Historical Review* 33:804–28.

———. 1935. *Documents illustrative of the history of the slave trade to America.* 4 vols. Washington, D.C.: Carnegie Institution.

Duggan, Betty J., and Brett H. Riggs. 1991. *Studies in Cherokee basketry. Occasional Paper no. 9.* Knoxville, Tenn.: Frank H. McClung Museum, University of Tennessee.

Dunn, Richard S. 1970. The English sugar islands and the founding of South Carolina. *South Carolina Historical Magazine* 72:81–93.

Dwyer, David. 1972. Linguistic comments on the Mane invasion. Paper presented to the Institute of African Studies, Fourah Bay College, Freetown, Sierra Leone.

Eaton, Allen H. 1937. *Handicrafts of the southern highlands.* Reprint. New York: Dover, 1973.

Eliason, Norman E. 1956. *Tarheel talk: an historical study of the English language in North Carolina to 1860.* Chapel Hill: University of North Carolina Press.

Escure, Genevieve. 1983. The acquisition of creole by urban and rural black Caribs in Belize. *York Papers in Linguistics* 2.

Fasold, Ralph. 1972. *Tense marking in Black English: a linguistic and social analysis.* Arlington, Va.: Center for Applied Linguistics.

Federal Writers' Program. 1940. *South Carolina folk-tales: stories of animals and supernatural beings compiled by workers of the Writers' Program of the Work Projects Administration.* Bulletin of the University of South Carolina, Columbia.

Feest, Christian F. 1980. *Native arts of North America.* New York: Oxford University Press.

Fenn, Elizabeth A., and Peter H. Wood. 1983. *Natives and newcomers: the way we lived in North Carolina before 1770.* Chapel Hill: University of North Carolina Press.

Fischer, David Hackett. 1989. *Albion's seed: four British folk ways in America.* New York: Oxford University Press.

Gilman, Charles. 1981. Pidgin languages: from selection or simplification. Paper presented at the Tenth Annual Linguistic Symposium, Milwaukee, University of Wisconsin.

———. 1986. African areal characteristics: Sprachbund not substrate? *Journal of Pidgin and Creole Languages* 1:33–50.

Gonzales, Ambrose E. 1922. *The black border: Gullah stories of the Carolina coast.* Columbia, S.C.: State Company.

———. 1924. *With Aesop along the black border.* Columbia, S.C.: State Company.

Goodman, Morris. 1985. Review of *Roots of language,* by Derek Bickerton. *International Journal of American Linguistics* 51:109–37.

———. 1993. African substratum: some cautionary words. In *Africanisms in Afro-American language varieties,* ed. Salikoko S. Mufwene, 64–73. Athens: University of Georgia Press.

Greenberg, Joseph. 1963. *The languages of Africa.* Bloomington: Indiana University.

Greene, Jack P. 1987. Colonial South Carolina and the Caribbean connection. *South Carolina Historical Magazine* 88:192–210.

Griffin, Frances, ed. 1981. Moravian decorative arts in North Carolina, by John Bivins, Jr., and Paul Welshimer. Winston-Salem, N.C.: Old Salem, Inc.

Guthrie, Malcolm. 1953. *Bantu languages of western equatorial Africa.* London: International African Institute.

Hair, P. E. H. 1965. Sierra Leone items in the Gullah dialect of American English. *Sierra Leone Language Review* 4:79–84.

Hall, Robert A., Jr. 1953. *Haitian Creole: grammar, texts, vocabulary.* Philadelphia: American Folklore Society.

———. 1966. *Pidgin and creole languages.* Ithaca: Cornell University Press.

Hamel, Paul B., and Mary U. Chiltoskey. 1982. *Cherokee plants and their uses.* Asheville, N.C.: Hickory.

Hancock, Ian F. 1969. The English-derived Atlantic creoles: a provisional comparison. *African Language Review* 8:7–72.

———. 1971. A study of the sources and development of the lexicon of Sierra

Leone Krio. Ph.D. dissertation, University of London School of Oriental and African Studies.

———. 1975. *Creole features in the Afro-Seminole speech of Brackettville, Texas.* Society for Caribbean Linguistics Occasional Paper 3.

———. 1980a. Gullah and Barbadian: origins and relations. *American Speech* 55:7–35.

———. 1980b. Texas Gullah: the creole English of the Brackettville Afro-Seminoles. In *Perspectives on American English,* ed. J. L. Dillard, 305–33. The Hague: Mouton.

———. 1986a. The cryptolectal speech of the American roads: Traveler cant and American Angloromani. *American Speech* 61:206–20.

———. 1986b. The domestic hypothesis, diffusion and componentiality: an account of Atlantic anglophone creole origins. In *Substrata versus universals in creole genesis,* ed. Peter Muysken and Norval Smith, 71–102. Philadelphia: Benjamins.

———. 1987. A preliminary classification of the anglophone Atlantic creoles, with syntactic data from 33 representative dialects. In *Pidgin and creole languages: essays in memory of John E. Reinecke,* ed. Glenn G. Gilbert, 264–333. Honolulu: University of Hawaii Press.

———. 1988. Componentiality and the origin of Gullah. In *Sea and land: cultural and biological adaptations in the southern coastal plain,* ed. James L. Peacock and James C. Sabella, 13–24. Athens: University of Georgia Press.

Hancock, Ian F., and Peter Gingiss. 1975. A Manding-based lingua franca as the Atlantic creole substrate. Paper presented at the Sixth Annual Conference on African Linguistics, Columbus, Ohio, April 12–14.

Hanley, Miles L. 1931. Progress of the linguistic atlas and plans for the future work of the Dialect Society. *Dialect Notes* 6.91–98.

Harris, John. 1984. English in the north of Ireland. In *Language in the British Isles,* ed. Peter Trudgill, 115–34. Cambridge: Cambridge University Press.

———. 1985. Expanding the superstrate: habitual aspect markers in Atlantic Englishes. *Sheffield Working Papers in Language and Linguistics* 2:72–97. Also published in *English World-wide* 7:171–99.

———. 1991. Ireland. In *English around the world: sociolinguistic perspectives,* ed. Jenny Cheshire, 37–50. Cambridge: Cambridge University Press.

Hayes, Alfred. 1965. Paralinguistics and kinesics: pedagogical perspectives. In *Approaches to semiotics,* ed. Thomas Sebeok, Alfred Hayes, and Mary C. Bateson, 145–72. The Hague: Mouton.

Hazaël-Massieux, Guy. 1982. Ambiguities genetiques et bipolarite dans le fonctionnement du creole de Guadeloupe. *Etudes Creoles* 4.47–62.

———. 1984. Geneses des creoles. *Notre Librairie* 73:19–27.

Heine, Bernd. 1976. *A typology of African languages (based on the order of meaningful elements).* Berlin: Dietrich Reimer.

Herault, Georges. 1981. Les langues Kwa. In *Les langues dans le monde ancien et moderne,* ed. Gabriel Manessy and Albert Valdman, 139–45. Paris: Centre National de Recherche Scientifique.

Herskovits, Melville J. 1941. *The myth of the Negro past.* New York: Harper and Brothers.

Higginson, Thomas Wentworth. 1870. *Army life in a black regiment.* Reprint. East Lansing: Michigan State University Press, 1960.

Hinson, Glenn. 1979. An interview with Leon Berry, maker of baskets. *North Carolina Folklore Journal* 27.2.

Holloway, Joseph, ed. 1990. *Africanisms in American culture.* Bloomington: Indiana University Press.

Holm, John. 1976. Variability of the copula in Black English and its creole kin. MS. Revised version published in *American Speech* 59 (1984):291–309.

———. 1978. The creole English of Nicaragua's Miskito Coast. Ph.D. dissertation, University College, London.

———, ed. 1983a. *Central American English.* Heidelberg: Groos.

———. 1983b. On the relationship of Gullah and Bahamian. *American Speech* 58:303–18.

———. 1984. Variability of the copula in Black English and its creole kin. *American Speech* 59:291–309.

———. 1991. The Atlantic creoles and the language of the ex-slave recordings. In *The emergence of Black English: texts and commentary,* ed. Guy Bailey, Natalie Maynor, and Patricia Cukor-Avila, 231–48. Philadelphia: Benjamins.

Holm, John, and Alison Watt Shilling, eds. 1982. *Dictionary of Bahamian English.* Cold Spring, N.Y.: Lexik House.

Holt, Grace Syms. 1972. *Stylin' outta the black pulpit.* In *Rappin' and stylin' out,* ed. Thomas Kochman, 189–204. Urbana: University of Illinois Press.

Hopkins, Tometro. 1992. Issues in the study of Afro-Creoles: Afro-Cuban and Gullah. Ph.D. dissertation, Indiana University.

House, Albert Virgil, ed. 1954. *Planter management and capitalism in ante-bellum Georgia, the journal of Hugh Fraser Grant, ricegrower.* New York: Columbia University Press.

Hymes, Dell, ed. 1971. *The pidginization and creolization of languages.* Cambridge: Cambridge University Press.

———. 1974. *Foundations in sociolinguistics: an ethnographic approach.* Philadelphia: University of Pennsylvania Press.

Innes, Gordon. 1962. *A Mende grammar.* London: Macmillan.

Innes, Malcolm. 1967. Mende. *African Language Review* 6:120–27.

———. 1969. *Mende-English dictionary.* Cambridge: Cambridge University Press.

Jacoway, Elizabeth. 1980. *Yankee missionaries in the South: the Penn School experiment.* Baton Rouge: Louisiana State University Press.

Jahn, Janheinz. 1961. *Mantu: the new African culture.* London: Faber and Faber.

Jenewari, Charles E. W. 1989. Ijoid. In *The Niger-Congo languages: a classification and description of Africa's largest language family,* ed. John Bendor-Samuel, 105–18. Lanham, Md.: University of America Press.

Jennings, Francis. 1975. *The invasion of America.* New York: Norton.

Johnson, Guy B. 1930. *Folk culture on St. Helena Island, South Carolina.* Chapel Hill: University of North Carolina Press.

———. 1980. The Gullah dialect revisited: a note on linguistic acculturation. *Journal of Black Studies* 10:417–24.

Johnson, Joseph A. 1961. *The soul of the black preacher.* Philadelphia: Pilgrim Press.

Jones, Charles C. 1888. *Negro myths from the Georgia coast.* Boston: Houghton Mifflin.

Jones-Jackson, Patricia A. 1978. The status of Gullah: an investigation of convergent processes. Ph.D. dissertation, University of Michigan, Ann Arbor.

———. 1982. The oral tradition of prayer in Gullah. *Journal of Religious Thought* 39:21–33.

———. 1987. *When roots die: endangered traditions on the Sea Islands.* Athens: University of Georgia Press.

Joyner, Charles. 1984. *Down by the riverside: a South Carolina slave community.* Urbana: University of Illinois Press.

Kloe, Donald R. 1974. Buddy Quow, an anonymous poem in Gullah-Jamaican dialect written circa 1800. *Southern Folklore Quarterly* 38:81–90.

Kouwenberg, Silvia. 1991. Berbice Dutch Creole: grammar, text, and vocabulary. Ph.D. dissertation, University of Amsterdam.

Krapp, George Philip. 1924. The English of the Negro. *American Mercury* 2:190–95.

Kurath, Hans. 1928. The origin of the dialectal differences in spoken American English. *Modern Philology* 25:385–95.

Labov, William. 1969. Contraction, deletion and inherent variability of the English copula. *Language* 45:715–62.

———. 1970. Language characteristic of specific groups: blacks. In *Reading for the disadvantaged: problems of linguistically different learners,* ed. Thomas D. Horn, 139–57. New York: Harcourt, Brace and World.

———. 1971. The notion of "system" in creole languages. In *Pidginization and creolization of languages,* ed. Dell Hymes, 447–72. Cambridge: Cambridge University Press.

———. 1972. *Language in the inner city.* Philadelphia: University of Pennsylvania Press.

———, ed. 1980. *Locating language in time and space.* New York: Academic Press.

———. 1982. Objectivity and commitment in linguistic science: the case of the Black English trial in Ann Arbor. *Language in Society* 11:165–201.

Lamb, Frank W. 1962. *Indian baskets of North America*. Riverside, Calif.: Riverside Museum Press.

Larson, Mildred L. 1978. *The functions of reported speech in discourse*. Dallas: Summer Institute of Linguistics.

Lasansky, Jeannette. 1979. *Willow, oak, and rye: basket traditions in Pennsylvania*. University Park: Pennsylvania State University Press.

Lefebvre, Claire. 1986. Relexification in creole genesis revisited: the case of Haitian Creole. In *Substrata versus universals in creole genesis,* ed. Pieter Muysken and Norval Smith, 279–300. Philadelphia: Benjamins.

Leftwich, Rodney L. 1970. *Arts and crafts of the Cherokee*. Glorietta, N.M.: Rio Grande Press.

Le Page, R. B. 1960. *A historical introduction to Jamaican Creole. Creole Language Studies* 1. London: Macmillan.

Levinsohn, Stephen H., ed. 1981. *Discourse studies in Djuka and Saramaccan*. Suriname: Summer Institute of Linguistics.

Lichtveld, Lou. 1954. Enerlei creools? *Nieuwe West-Indische Gide* 35:59–71.

Littlefield, Daniel C. 1981. *Rice and slaves: ethnicity and the slave trade in colonial South Carolina*. Baton Rouge: Louisiana State University Press.

———. 1987. Continuity and change in slave culture: South Carolina and the West Indies. *Southern Studies* 27:202–16.

Longacre, Robert E. 1983. *The grammar of discourse*. New York: Plenum.

Lyons, John. 1977. *Semantics*. Vol. 2. Cambridge: Cambridge University Press.

McBride, Bunny. 1990. *Our lives in our hands: Micmac Indian basketmakers*. Gardiner, Maine: Tilbury House.

McDavid, Raven I., Jr. 1952. Africanisms in the eastern United States. Paper presented at the Modern Language Association meeting, Boston.

McDavid, Raven I., Jr., William A. Kretzschmar, Jr., and Gail J. Hankins, eds. 1982. Gullah. *The Linguistic Atlas of the Middle and South Atlantic States and affiliated projects: basic materials*. Microfilm MSS on Cultural Anthropology 71.378. Joseph Regenstein Library, University of Chicago.

McDavid, Raven I., Jr., and Virginia Glenn McDavid. 1951. The relationship of the speech of the American Negroes to the speech of whites. *American Speech* 26:3–17.

McNeill, David. 1985. So you think gestures are nonverbal? *Psychological Review* 92:350–71.

Manessy, Gabriel. 1985. Remarques sur la pluralisation du nom en creole et dans les langues africaines. *Etudes Creoles* 8:129–43.

Matthews, William. 1939. South western dialect in the early modern period. *Neophilologus* 24:193–209.

Mbiti, John S. 1970. *African religions and philosophy*. New York: Anchor Books.

Melmed, Paul Jay. 1970. Black English phonology: the question of reading interference. Ph.D. dissertation, University of California.

Mencken, H. L. 1945. *The American language: an inquiry into the development of English in the United States.* Supplement 1. New York: Knopf.

Merrens, Harry Roy. 1964. *Colonial North Carolina in the 18th century: a study in historical geography.* Chapel Hill: University of North Carolina Press.

Meussen, A. E. 1965. A note on permutation in Kpele-Mende. *African Language Studies* 6:112–16.

Mille, Katherine W. 1990. A historical analysis of tense-mood-aspect in Gullah creole: a case of stable variation. Ph.D. dissertation, University of South Carolina.

Mintz, Sidney W., and Richard Price. 1976. *An anthropological approach to the Afro-American past: a Caribbean perspective.* Philadelphia: Institute for the Study of Human Issues.

Mitchell, Henry. 1970. *Black preaching.* Philadelphia: Lippincott.

Montgomery, Michael. 1989. The roots of Appalachian English. *English World-wide* 10:227–78.

———. 1991. The linguistic value of the ex-slave recordings. In *The emergence of Black English: texts and commentary,* ed. Guy Bailey, Natalie Maynor, and Patricia Cukor-Avila, 173–89. Philadelphia: Benjamins.

———. 1993. Africanisms in the American South. In *Africanisms in Afro-American language varieties,* ed. Salikoko Mufwene, 439–57. Athens: University of Georgia Press.

Mufwene, Salikoko S. 1983a. Observations on time reference in Jamaican and Guyanese creoles. In *Studies in Caribbean language,* ed. Lawrence D. Carrington, 155–77. St. Augustine, Trinidad: Society for Caribbean Linguistics.

———. 1983b. Review of *Comparative Afro-American,* by Mervyn Alleyne. *Carib* 3:98–113.

———. 1983c. *Some observations on the verb in Black English Vernacular.* African and Afro-American Studies and Research Center, Papers Series 2, University of Texas at Austin.

———. 1984. Observations on time reference in Jamaican and Guyanese creoles. *English World-wide* 4:199–219.

———. 1985. The linguistic significance of African proper names in Gullah. *New West Indian Guide* 59:146–66.

———. 1986a. Notes on durative constructions in Jamaican and Guyanese Creole. In *Varieties of English around the world,* ed. Manfred Görlach and John A. Holm, 167–81. Philadelphia: Benjamins.

———. 1986b. Restrictive relativization in Gullah. *Journal of Pidgin and Creole Languages* 1:1–31.

———. 1986c. The universalist and substrate hypotheses complement one another. In *Substrata versus universals in creole genesis,* ed. Peter Muysken and Norval Smith, 129–62. Philadelphia: Benjamins.

———. 1987. Review of *Language variety in the South: perspectives in black and white*, ed. Michael Montgomery and Guy Bailey. *Journal of Pidgin and Creole Languages* 2:93–110.

―――. 1988a. Formal evidence of pidginization/creolization in Kituba. *Journal of African Languages and Linguistics* 10:33–51.

―――. 1988b. Why study pidgins and creoles? *Journal of Pidgin and Creole Languages* 3:265–76.

―――. 1989. Equivocal structures in some Gullah complex sentences. *American Speech* 64:304–26.

―――. 1990a. Creoles and Universal Grammar. In *Issues in creole linguistics*, ed. Pieter Seuren and Salikoko Mufwene, 783–807. *Linguistics* 28.

―――. 1990b. Transfer and the substrate hypothesis in creolistics. *Studies in Second Language Acquisition* 12:1–23.

―――. 1991a. Is Gullah decreolizing? A comparison of a speech sample of the 1930's with a speech sample of the 1980's. In *The emergence of Black English*, ed. Guy Bailey, Natalie Maynor, and Patricia Cukor-Avila, 213–30. Philadelphia: Benjamins.

―――. 1991b. On the infinitive in Gullah. In *Verb phrase patterns in Black English and creole*, ed. Walter F. Edwards and Donald Winford, 209–22. Detroit: Wayne State University Press.

―――. 1991c. Pidgins, creoles, typology, and markedness. In *Development and structures of creole languages: essays in honor of Derek Bickerton*, ed. Francis Byrne and Thom Huebner, 123–43. Philadelphia: Benjamins.

―――. 1991d. Review of John Holm's *Pidgins and creoles*, vols. 1 & 2. *Language* 67:380–87.

―――. 1991e. Some reasons why Gullah is not dying yet. *English World-wide* 12:215–43.

―――. 1992a. Africanisms in Gullah: a re-examination of the issues. In *Old English and new: Studies in language and linguistics in honor of Frederic G. Cassidy*, ed. Joan Hall, Nick Doane, and Dick Ringler, 156–82. New York: Garland.

―――. 1992b. Ideology and facts on African American English. *Pragmatics*.

―――. 1992c. Why grammars are not monolithic. In *The joy of grammar: a festschrift in honor of James D. McCawley*, ed. Diane Brentari, Gary N. Larson, and Lynn A. MacLeod, 225–50. Philadelphia: Benjamins.

―――. 1993a. African substratum: possibility and evidence. In *Africanisms in Afro-American language varieties*, ed. Salikoko Mufwene, 192–208. Athens: University of Georgia Press.

―――, ed. 1993b. *Africanisms in Afro-American language varieties*. Athens: University of Georgia Press.

―――. 1993c. Are there possessive pronouns in Atlantic creoles? In *Atlantic meets Pacific: linguistic, social, and contact-related dimensions of pidgin and creole languages*, ed. Francis Byrne and John Holm, 133–43. Philadelphia: Benjamins.

Mufwene, Salikoko, and Marta B. Dijkhoff. 1989. On the so-called "infinitive" in Atlantic creoles. *Lingua* 77:297–330.

Mufwene, Salikoko, and Charles Gilman. 1987. How African is Gullah and why? *American Speech* 62:120–39.

Muhlhausler, Peter. 1984. Roots of language? A review article on a book by Derek Bickerton. *Folia Linguistica* 18:263–77.

Murtagh, William J. 1967. *Moravian architecture and town planning*. Chapel Hill: University of North Carolina Press.

Muysken, Pieter. 1981. Creole tense/mood/aspect systems: the unmarked case? In *Generative studies on creole language*, ed. P. Muysken, 181–99. Dordrecht: Foris.

———. 1983. Review of *Roots of language*, by Derek Bickerton. *Language* 59:884–901.

Nichols, Patricia C. 1976. Linguistic change in Gullah: sex, age, and mobility. Ph.D. dissertation, Stanford University.

Niles, Norma. 1980. Provincial English dialects and Barbadian English. Ph.D. dissertation, University of Michigan.

Opala, Joseph A. 1986. *The Gullah: rice, slavery, and the Sierra Leone–American connection*. Freetown, Sierra Leone: United States Information Service.

Orton, Harold, M. F. Wakelin, and W. J. Halliday, eds. 1967–68. *Survey of English dialects*. Volume 4, *The southern counties*. Leeds, Eng.: E. J. Arnold & Son.

Oxford English Dictionary. Compact edition. 1971. Oxford: Oxford University Press.

Parsons, Elsie Clews. 1918. *Folk-tales of Andros Island, Bahamas*. Memoirs of the American Folklore Society 13, New York.

———. 1923. *Folk-lore of the Sea Islands, South Carolina*. Memoirs of the American Folklore Society 16, Cambridge, Mass.

Partridge, Eric. 1959. *Name this child; a handy guide for puzzled parents*. London: Hamish Hamilton.

Peek, Philip. 1978. Afro-American material culture and the Afro-American craftsman. *Southern Folklore Quarterly* 42:109–32.

Penn National, Industrial, and Agricultural School. 1910–51. Annual reports. South Caroliniana Library, University of South Carolina, Columbia.

Peyre, Thomas Walter. Journal, 1834–1851(?). South Carolina Historical Society, Charleston.

Phillips, Ulrich B. 1918. *American Negro slavery*. Reprint. Baton Rouge: Louisiana State University Press, 1969.

Pinson, Joseph N., Jr., and Wade T. Batson. 1971. The status of *Muhlenbergia filipes* Curtis (Poaceae). *Journal of the Elisha Mitchell Scientific Society* 87.4: 188–91.

Pipes, William H. 1951. *Say amen brother*. New York: William Frederick Press.

Potter, James. Journal for Argyle Plantation, 1828–1831. Georgia Historical Society, Savannah, Georgia.

Pringle, Elizabeth W. Allston. 1940. *Chronicles of Chicora Wood*. Boston: Christopher.

———— [Patience Pennington]. 1961. *A woman rice planter*. 1913. Reprint. Cambridge, Mass.: Belknap Press, 1961.

Quirk, Randolph, Sidney Greenbaum, Geoffrey Leach, and Jan Svartvik. 1985. *A comprehensive grammar of the English language*. London: Longman.

Reinecke, John E. 1937. Trade jargons and marginal languages. Ph.D. dissertation, Yale University.

Religious heritage of the black world, preserved Africanisms in the New World. Atlanta: Interdenominational Theological Center.

Rhett, Robert Goodwyn. 1940. *Charleston; an epic of Carolina*. Richmond: Garrett and Massie.

Rickford, John R. 1974. The insights of the mesolect. In *Pidgins and creoles: current trends and prospects,* ed. David DeCamp and Ian F. Hancock, 92–117. Washington, D.C.: Georgetown University Press.

————. 1977. The question of prior creolization of Black English. In *Pidgin and creole linguistics*, ed. Albert Valdman, 190–221. Bloomington: Indiana University Press.

————. 1980. How does *doz* disappear? In *Issues in English creoles*, ed. Richard Day, 77–96. Heidelberg: Julius Groos.

————. 1986. Social contact and linguistic diffusion. *Language* 62:245–89.

————. 1992. The creole residue in Barbados. In *Old English and new: studies in language and linguistics in honor of Frederic G. Cassidy,* ed. Joan H. Hall, Nick Doane, and Dick Ringler, 183–201. New York: Garland.

Roberts, Peter. 1980. The adequacy of certain theories in accounting for important grammatical relationships in creole languages. In *Issues in English creoles,* ed. Richard Day, 19–38. Heidelberg: Julius Groos.

————. 1988. *West Indians and their language*. Cambridge: Cambridge University Press.

Rogers, George C., Jr. 1970. *The history of Georgetown County, South Carolina*. Columbia: University of South Carolina Press.

Rogers, Norman. 1979. *Wessex dialect*. Bradford-on-Avon: Moonraker Press.

Rosengarten, Dale. 1985. Field notes and interviews, Low Country basket project. McKissick Museum, Columbia, S.C.

————. 1987. *Row upon row: sea grass baskets of the South Carolina lowcountry*. 2d ed. Columbia, S.C.: McKissick Museum.

Ross, Mabel H., and Barbara K. Walker. 1979. *"On another day . . ." tales told among the Nkundo of Zaire*. Hamden, Conn.: Archon Books.

Rossbach, Ed. 1973. *Baskets as textile art*. New York: Van Nostrand.

Roy, John D. 1977. The origin of English creole: evidence from the lexical structure. Master's thesis, Columbia University.

————. 1985. Evidence for the origin of English creole. Paper presented at the

Ninth Annual Language and Culture in South Carolina Symposium, Columbia, April 26–27.

Sass, Herbert Ravenel. 1936. *A Carolina rice plantation of the fifties.* New York: William Morrow.

Sauvageot, Serge. 1981. Le Wolof. In *Les langues dans le monde ancien et modern,* ed. Gabriel Manessy and Albert Valdman, 33–52. Paris: Centre Nationale de Recherche Scientifique.

Schiffer, Nancy. 1984. *Baskets.* Exton, Penn.: Schiffer.

Schneider, Edgar Werner. 1981. *Morphologische und syntaktische variablen im amerikanischen Early Black English.* Frankfurt am Main: Peter Lang.

———. 1982. On the history of Black English in the USA: some new evidence. *English World-wide* 3:18–46.

———. 1983. The diachronic development of the Black English perfective auxiliary phrase. *Journal of English Linguistics* 16:55–64.

———. 1989. *American early Black English: morphological and syntactic variables.* Tuscaloosa: University of Alabama Press.

———. 1990. The cline of creoleness in English-oriented creoles and semi-creoles of the Caribbean. *English World-wide* 11:79–113.

———. 1993. Africanisms in the grammar of Afro-American English: weighing the evidence. In *Africanisms in Afro-American language varieties,* ed. Salikoko Mufwene, 209–21. Athens: University of Georgia Press.

Sebeok, Thomas, ed. 1960. *Style in language.* New York: Technology Press and Wiley.

Sengova, Joko. 1981. A classification of tense, aspect, and time specification in the verb system of Mende. Ph.D. dissertation, University of Wisconsin.

———. 1987. The national languages of Sierra Leone: a decade of policy experimentation. *Africa* 57:519–30.

Seuren, Pieter. 1986. Adjectives as adjectives in Sranan: a reply to Sebba. *Journal of Pidgin and Creole Languages* 1:123–34.

———. 1987. A note on *siki. Journal of Pidgin and Creole Languages* 2:57–66.

Sieber, Roy. 1980. *African furniture and household objects.* Bloomington: Indiana University Press.

Singler, J. V. 1984. Variation in tense-aspect-modality in Liberian English. Ph.D. dissertation, University of California at Los Angeles.

———. 1990a. Introduction: pidgins and creoles and tense-mood-aspect. In *Pidgin and creole tense-mood-aspect systems,* ed. J. V. Singler, vii–xvi. Philadelphia: Benjamins.

———. 1990b. On the use of sociohistorical criteria in the comparison of creoles. In *Issues in creole linguistics,* ed. Pieter Seuren and Salikoko Mufwene, 645–59. *Linguistics* 28.

———, ed. 1990c. *Pidgin and creole tense-mood-aspect systems.* Philadelphia: Benjamins.

Smith, Alice R. H. n.d. Selected watercolors from *A Carolina rice plantation of the 1850s*. Reproduced, annotated, and edited by George C. Rogers. Columbia: South Caroliniana Library.

Smith, D. E. H. 1950. *A Charlestonian's Recollections: 1843–1913*. Charleston, S.C.: Carolina Art Association.

Smith, Julia Floyd. 1973. *Slavery and plantation growth in antebellum Florida, 1821–1860*. Gainesville: University of Florida Press.

———. 1985. *Slavery and rice culture in low country Georgia, 1750–1800*. Knoxville: University of Tennessee Press.

Smith, Riley B. 1973. Interrelatedness of certain deviant grammatical structures in Negro nonstandard dialects. In *Black language reader,* ed. Robert H. Bentley and Samuel D. Crawford, 90–96. Glenview, Ill.: Scott, Foresman.

South Carolina State Board of Agriculture. 1883. *South Carolina: resources and population, institutions and industries*. Charleston, S.C.: Walker, Evans and Cogswell.

Sparkman, James R. n.d. Memorandum book. South Caroliniana Library, University of South Carolina, Columbia.

Stanton, Gary, and Tom Cowan. 1988. *Stout hearts: traditional oak basket makers of the South Carolina upcountry*. Columbia, S.C.: McKissick Museum.

Stephenson, Sue H. 1977. *Basketry of the Appalachian Mountains*. New York: Van Nostrand Reinhold.

Stewart, Sadie. 1919. Seven folk-tales from the Sea-Islands, South Carolina. *Journal of American Folk-Lore* 32:394–96.

Stewart, Tom, and Joko Sengova. n.d. On the origins of "Gullah" and "Geechee." MS.

Stewart, William A. 1962. Creole languages in the Caribbean. In *Study of the role of second languages in Asia, Africa and Latin America,* ed. F. A. Rice, 34–53. Washington, D.C.: Center for Applied Linguistics.

———. 1967. Sociolinguistic factors in the history of American Negro dialects. *Florida FL Reporter* 5.11, 22, 24, 26, 30. Reprinted in *Perspectives on Black English,* ed. J. L. Dillard, 222–32. The Hague: Mouton, 1975.

———. 1968. Continuity and change in American Negro dialects. *Florida FL Reporter* 6.3–4:14–16, 18. Reprinted in *Perspectives in Black English,* ed. J. L. Dillard, 233–47. The Hague: Mouton, 1975.

———. 1969a. Historical and structural basis for the recognition of Negro dialect. In *Report of the Twentieth Round Table Meeting on Linguistics and Language Studies,* ed. James E. Alatis, 239–47. Washington, D.C.: Georgetown University Press.

———. 1969b. On the use of Negro dialect in the teaching of reading. In *Teaching black children to read,* ed. Joan C. Baratz and Roger W. Shuy, 156–219. Washington, D.C.: Center for Applied Linguistics.

———. 1972. Acculturative processes in the language of the American Negro. In

Language in its social setting, ed. William W. Gage, 1–46. Washington, D.C.: Anthropological Society of Washington.

Stoney, Samuel Gaillard, and Gertrude Mathews Shelby. 1930. *Black genesis.* New York: Macmillan.

Swadesh, Morris M. 1951. Review of *Africanisms in the Gullah Dialect,* by Lorenzo Dow Turner. *Word* 7:82–84.

Swanton, John R. 1946. *The Indians of the southeastern United States.* Reprint. Washington, D.C.: Smithsonian Institution Press, 1984.

Sylvain, Suzanne. 1936. *Le Creole Haitien: morphologie et syntaxe.* Wetteren, Belgium: Imprimerie De Meester.

Szwed, John F., and Roger D. Abrahams, eds. 1978. *Afro-American folk culture: an annotated bibliography of material from North, Central, and South America, and the West Indies.* 2 vols. Philadelphia: Institute for the Study of Human Issues.

Tarone, Elaine. 1972. Aspects of intonation in vernacular white and Black English. Ph.D. dissertation, University of Washington.

Tedlock, Dennis. 1975. On the translation of style in oral narrative. In *Toward new perspectives in folklore,* ed. Americo Parades and Richard Bauman. Austin: University of Texas Press.

Teleki, Gloria Roth. 1975. *Baskets of rural America.* New York: Dutton.

———. 1979. *Collecting traditional American basketry.* New York: Dutton.

Thomas, John P. 1930. The Barbadians in early South Carolina. *South Carolina Historical Magazine* 31:75–92.

Thomason, Sarah G. 1983. Chinook Jargon in areal and historical context. *Language* 59:820–70.

Thompson, R. W. 1961. A note on some possible affinities between creole dialects of the Old World and those of the New. In *Proceedings of the 1959 Conference on Creole Language Studies,* ed. Robert B. Le Page, 107–13. London: Macmillan.

Tindall, George Brown. 1952. *South Carolina Negroes, 1877–1900.* Columbia: University of South Carolina Press.

Todd, Loreto. 1974. *Pidgins and creoles.* London: Routledge and Kegan Paul.

Traugott, Elizabeth. 1976. Pidgins, creoles, and the origins of vernacular Black English. In *Black English: a seminar,* ed. Deborah Harrison and Tom Trabasso, 57–93. Hillsdale, N.J.: Erlbaum.

Trevaylor, Nicky [Thomas Newall]. 1935. *Echoes from carn, cove and cromlech.* St. Ives: J. Lanham.

Trowell, Margaret, and K. P. Wachsmann. 1953. *Tribal crafts of Uganda.* London: Oxford University Press.

Trudgill, Peter, ed. 1984. *Language in the British Isles.* Cambridge: Cambridge University Press.

———. 1986. *Dialects in contact.* Oxford: Blackwell.

Turner, Lorenzo Dow. 1941. Linguistic research and African survivals. *American Council of Learned Societies Bulletin* 32:68–89.

————. 1949. *Africanisms in the Gullah dialect.* Chicago: University of Chicago Press. Reprinted in 1974 with an introduction by David DeCamp by the University of Michigan Press, Ann Arbor.

Twining, Mary A. 1970. Field notes, interviews, and accession records. William Mathers Anthropology Museum, Bloomington, Ind.

————. 1977. An examination of African retentions in the folk culture of the South Carolina and Georgia Sea Islands. 2 vols. Ph.D. dissertation, Indiana University.

————. 1978. Harvesting and heritage: a comparison of Afro-American and African basketry. *Southern Folklore Quarterly* 42:159–74.

————. 1980. Sea Island basketry: reaffirmations of West Africa. In *The first national African-American crafts conference: selected writings,* ed. David C. Driskell, 35–39. Memphis: Shelby State Community College.

Twining, Mary A., and Keith E. Baird, eds. 1991. *Sea Island roots: African presence in the Carolinas and Georgia.* Trenton, N.J.: Africa World Press.

Vlach, John. 1978. *The Afro-American tradition in decorative arts.* Cleveland: Cleveland Museum of Art.

————. 1980. Arrival and survival: the maintenance of an Afro-American tradition of folk art and craft. In *Perspectives on American folk art,* ed. Ian M. G. Quimbyu and Scott T. Swank, 177–217. New York: Norton.

Voorhoeve, Jan. 1973. Historical and linguistic evidence in favor of the relexification theory in the formation of creoles. *Language in Society* 2:133–45.

Wade-Lewis, Margaret. 1986. Focus on creolists no. 15: Lorenzo Dow Turner. *Carrier Pidgin* 14.2:1–3.

————. 1988a. The African substratum in American English. Ph.D. dissertation, New York University.

————. 1988b. *Lorenzo Dow Turner: first African-American linguist.* Institute of African and African-American Affairs, Occasional Paper 2. Philadelphia: Temple University Press.

Wakelin, Martyn. 1984. Cornish English. In *Language in the British Isles,* ed. Peter Trudgill, 195–98. Cambridge: Cambridge University Press.

Washabaugh, William. 1977. Constraining variation in decreolization. *Language* 53:329–52.

Welmers, William E. 1973. *African language structures.* Berkeley: University of California Press.

Wendall, Margaret M. 1982. *Bootstrap literature: preliterate societies do it themselves.* Newark, Del.: International Reading Association.

Whinnom, Keith. 1971. Linguistic hybridization and the "special case" of pidgins and creoles. In *Pidginization and creolization of language,* ed. Dell Hymes, 91–116. Cambridge: Cambridge University Press.

——— . 1981. Non-primary types of language. *Logos Semanticos* 5:227–41.

White, Jon Manchip. 1979. *Everyday life of the North American Indian*. London: Batsford.

Wilson, Charles Reagan. 1988. Caribbean influence. In *Encyclopedia of southern culture*, ed. Charles R. Wilson and William Ferris, 405–7. Chapel Hill: University of North Carolina Press.

Winford, Don. 1984. Aspect of the syntax of *fi* complements in Caribbean English Creole. Paper presented at the Society for Caribbean Linguistics conference, Jamaica.

——— . 1992. Another look at the copula in Black English and Caribbean creoles. *American Speech* 67:21–60.

Wolfram, Walt. 1969. *A sociolinguistic description of Detroit Negro speech*. Arlington, Va.: Center for Applied Linguistics.

——— . 1980. *A*-Prefixing in Appalachian English. In *Locating language in time and space*, ed. William Labov, 107–42. New York: Academic Press.

Wolfram, Walt, and Donna Christian. 1976. *Appalachian speech*. Arlington, Va.: Center for Applied Linguistics.

Wolfram, Walt, and Nona Clarke, eds. 1971. *Black-white speech relationships*. Arlington, Va.: Center for Applied Linguistics.

Wolfram, Walt, and Ralph Fasold. 1974. *The study of social dialects in the United States*. Englewood Cliffs, N.J.: Prentice-Hall.

Wood, Peter H. 1974a. *Black majority: Negroes in colonial South Carolina from 1670 through the Stono rebellion*. New York: Knopf.

——— . 1974b. It was a Negro taught them: a new look at labor in early South Carolina. *Journal of Asian and African Studies* 9:159–79.

Work Projects Administration. Georgia Writers Project, Savannah unit. 1940. *Drums and shadows: survival studies among the Georgia coastal Negroes*. Reprint. Athens: University of Georgia Press, 1986.

Works Progress Administration. 1941. *South Carolina folk tales*. Compiled by workers of the Writers' Program of the Work Projects Administration in the state of South Carolina. Columbia: University of South Carolina Press.

Wright, Elizabeth. 1914. *Rustic speech and folk-lore*. London: Milford.

Wright, Joseph, ed. 1898–1905. *The English dialect dictionary*. 6 vols. Oxford: Oxford University Press.

Contributors

Keith E. Baird is the interim chair of the African and African American Studies Program and a professor of history at Clark Atlanta University. With Mary Twining he edited *Sea Island Roots: African Presence in the Carolinas and Georgia,* and with Ogonna Chuks-Orji he authored *Names from Africa.* His research interests are African world studies, Africa in antiquity, and creole languages.

Frederic G. Cassidy is an emeritus professor of English at the University of Wisconsin. A widely known expert on Jamaican Creole, he edited *Jamaica Talk* and the *Dictionary of Jamaican English* with R. B. LePage. He is currently editor in chief of the *Dictionary of American Regional English.*

Ian F. Hancock is a professor of linguistics at the University of Texas at Austin. He has studied Sierra Leone Krio and Texas Gullah and is one of the originators of the complementarity hypothesis. He has published widely on the history of English settlements on the West African coast and the development of Guinea Coast Creole English and is also well known for his work on Romani.

Tometro Hopkins is an assistant professor in the Linguistics Program at Florida International University. Her research interests are the description and sociolinguistic analysis of Gullah, Black English in the United States and abroad, and Afro-Cuban speech in South Florida. She is currently working on a descriptive study of the Gullah language.

Patricia Jones-Jackson was an associate professor of English at Howard University at the time of her death in 1986.

Michael Montgomery is a professor of English and linguistics at the University of South Carolina at Columbia. He has published widely on both historical and contemporary aspects of southern American English and Appalachian English. He was a consulting editor for Language for the *Encyclopedia of Southern Culture.*

Salikoko S. Mufwene is a professor of linguistics at the University of Chicago. He has published essays on the genesis and structures of pidgins and creoles, especially Gullah, African-American English, Jamaican Creole, and Kikongo-Kituba, as well as on the subject of decreolization. He edited *Africanisms in Afro-American Language Varieties* (1993) and is an associate editor of the *Journal of Pidgin and Creole Languages.*

Peter A. Roberts teaches in the Unit of Use of English and Linguistics at the Uni-

221

versity of the West Indies, Cave Hill Campus, Barbados. He is the author of *West Indians and Their Language* (1988).

Dale Rosengarten, guest curator for McKissick Museum's Low Country Basket Project, is author of the exhibition catalog *Row upon Row: The Grass Baskets of the South Carolina Low Country.* She is a graduate of Harvard University and lives in McClellanville, South Carolina, with her husband and two sons. She is currently pursuing a doctorate at Harvard in the history of American civilization.

Joko Sengova is an assistant professor in the Department of English and Communication at the College of Charleston, where he also teaches in the Languages and Sociology and Anthropology departments. He is a research associate at the Avery Institute for African-American History and Culture. His principal research interests are African languages and cultures, Gullah, and non-Western literatures translation. He has published essays on the languages of Sierra Leone and a monograph on Mende.

Mary A. Twining is an associate professor of English at Clark Atlanta University. With Keith Baird she edited *Sea Island Roots: African Presence in the Carolinas and Georgia.* Her research interests are the Sea Islands of the southeastern United States, African and African-American folklore, and the life and lore of women.

Author Index

Language Index

Acrolect, 60, 77, 80, 93
African-American English, 7, 11, 39–47, 50–59
Afrish, 27
Afro-American English, 6, 87, 89, 92–94, 100
Afro-Creole languages, 62, 75
Akan, 48–49, 97
American Black English, 15, 89–92, 102
American English, 55, 195
Anglophone creoles, 95, 97–98
Appalachian English, 40, 43
Ashanti, 48

Bajan. *See* Barbadian English creole
Bambara, 25, 30–31, 33, 48
Bamgbose, 47
Bantu, 20, 47–50, 178, 197
Barbadian English, 9
Barbadian English creole, 6, 21, 77, 89, 105
Basilect, 54, 60, 66, 72, 77, 93, 123
Bay Islands Creole, 98
Bini, 25, 31
Black English, 39, 77, 87, 90, 95–96, 99, 100
Black street speech, 96
Bobangi, 25
British English, 46, 52, 99

Cameroonian, 76
Caribbean English Creole(s), 10, 39–59 passim, 87, 89–92, 104
Cornish English, 104

Djerma, 25
Djuka, 5, 97

Eastern Kwa, 50
Efik, 24–25, 29, 51
English creole. *See* Anglophone creoles; Barbadian English Creole; Caribbean English Creole(s); Guinea Coast Creole English; Guyanese Creole English; Hawaiian Creole English; Kittitian English Creole; Nicaraguan English Creole; West African anglophone creole
English language, 6, 30, 91, 94, 97, 197; African-American, 7, 11, 39–47, 50–59; Afro-American, 6, 87, 89, 92–94, 100; American, 55, 195; American Black, 15, 89–92, 102; Appalachian, 40, 43; Barbadian, 9; Black, 39, 77, 87, 90, 95–96, 99, 100; British, 46, 52, 99; British dialects of, 45, 159; colonial, 55; Cornish, 104; dialects of, 57, 58; Irish, 46, 58 (*see also* Hiberno-English); metropolitan, 97, 100, 104; nonstandard, 42–44, 52, 55–56, 58; North American, 158; pidgin, 9, 21–22 (*see also* West African Pidgin English); southwestern British dialects of, 12, 100–104, 106; standard, 6, 42, 55, 88, 90–92, 94, 102, 123–24
Ewe, 5, 24–25, 28, 30, 36, 38, 47, 48, 100

Subject Index

A (auxiliary verb), 51, 53, 77,
82–85, 104
Adair, James, 136
Adjective complement, 84
Adjectives, 52, 59
Adverbials, 163
Africa, 8–9, 13, 31
African-American church, 115, 120
Africanisms, 2–4, 12, 15, 27, 49, 98,
160–61, 170–71, 176–79, 195
Afrogenesis of creole languages, 62
Agglutinating language, 47
Ain't, 83, 86
All Saints Parish (S.C.), 11, 14
Amen corner, 118, 121
American Council of Learned
Societies, 159
American Revolution, 13–14, 137, 148
American South, 6–8
Amish, 42, 43, 144
Anglo-Saxon peoples, 139
Angola, 5, 9, 17–18, 20, 25–26, 59,
148, 178, 182
Anterior aspect, 62, 78
Antigua, 106
Antilles, 102
Appalachian mountains, 42, 139, 141
Archaic period, 134
Archives of the Indies (Spain), 16
Argyle Plantation (S.C.), 149
Artemis, 30
Ash tree, 141
Asia, 133, 150
Aspect, verbal, 27, 42, 61–86, 91–94,

100, 103–4, 163. *See also* Habitual
aspect; Perfective aspect
Aspiration, 102
Auxiliary verb, 7, 60–86 passim,
87–94 passim, 162–68

Baggett, Clarence, 141
Bahamas, 13, 15
Baptists, 116–18
Barbados, 5–6, 8–10, 17–18, 20–22,
38, 96, 100, 146
Bartram, William, 137
Basket makers: African-American,
141–42, 146–51, 157; Appalachian,
157; European, 133, 139–46; Native
American, 133–39, 141, 146, 150,
154, 157
Basket making, 3, 12; coiling, 134;
Pennsylvania, 141; twining, 134
Basket name, 23, 25, 36–37
Baskets: berry, 140; bread-raising, 140,
144; bulrush, 152–54; "burden,"
150; bushel, 141; cane, 138;
Carolina, 140; carrying, 140; cheese,
140; coiled, 143, 150; coiled grass,
138, 148, 154; coiled sea grass, 133,
146; coiled straw, 133, 144; corn,
141; cotton, 141; curd, 140; egg,
138, 140–41; fanner, 146–50; field,
148; fish, 137; flower, 140; gizzard,
138; "head tote," 150; hen, 140;
market, 141, 143; melon, 140;
melon-shaped, 141; peck, 141; rice
fanner, 148; ring, 137; river cane,

Baskets (*continued*)
  133; rye straw, 144; sewing, 143,
  149; show, 154; splint, 133, 137,
  140, 141, 150; split oak, 133;
  storage, 140, 150; straw, 140; white
  oak melon, 138; wickerware, 133,
  140; work, 154
Be, 42, 64, 66–67, 72–74, 83, 89–92,
  100, 162–63, 167
Beckles, I. M., 16
Been. See *Bin/been*
Bee skeps, 143
Bell, Meritha, 138
Benin, 18, 20, 26, 33
Berry, Leon, 141–42
Bes, 92
Bethlehem, Pa., 144
Bible, 118, 122
Bin/been, 53, 57, 59, 77–82, 85, 98,
  123, 163, 165–67, 170
Bina/binnuh, 123, 170, 174
Bioprogram, 58
Bloodroot, 136
Bohemia-Moravia, 144
Boston, Mass., 153
Bowles, William Augustus, 16
Brazil, 117
Brazilian Macumba, 116
Br'er Rabbit, 34
Brewer's Neck (Ga.), 159
Bristol, England, 100
Britain, 101, 104
British Isles, 40, 42, 45–46, 139
British traders, 48
"Buddy Quow," 16
Bunce Island, Sierra Leone, 182
Bureau of Indian Affairs, 138
Butternut, 136

Cadence, 121
Calabar, 20

Call and response, 116, 117
Cameroon, 26
Cane, 134, 136
Cape Fear Valley (N.C.), 138
Caribbean, 2, 8, 9–14, 16–17, 19–20,
  22, 31, 34, 38, 40, 43, 100
Carolina colony, 10, 20
Catawba Indians, 136, 146
Catholics, 116
Celtic peoples, 139
Central America, 117
Charleston, S.C., 5, 8–10, 16–10,
  20–22, 27, 38, 142, 153–54, 163
Charleston County, S.C., 148
Charleston house, 9–10
Cherokee Indians, 133–38, 141,
  146, 156
Cherokee Removal, 137
Children's game, 106
Chitimacha Indians, 136
Choctaw Indians, 136
Cicero, 115
Civil War, 1–2, 11, 15, 149, 160
Columbian Quincentenary, 1
Columbus, Christopher, 134
Combahee River, S.C., 149
Complementizer, 54
Componentiality, 11–12, 90–106
Congo, 5, 9, 18, 26, 148
Congo-Angola region, 4
Consonant mutation, 177, 179–80,
  185, 196, 199
Continuative/continuous aspect,
  62–64, 66, 69–70, 75, 78, 91
Continuative marker, 51, 61–62,
  71–72, 76
Continuity of culture and language, 4,
  38–41, 43–44, 46, 52, 55–57;
  African, 51
Contraction, 177, 185, 196, 199
Convergence of languages, 42–43